Integrating Rules and Connectionism for Robust Commonsense Reasoning

Sixth-Generation Computer Technology Series

Branko Souček, Editor
University of Zagreb

Integrating Rules and Connectionism for Robust Commonsense Reasoning

RON SUN
Department of Computer Science
The University of Alabama
Tuscaloosa, Alabama

A Wiley-Interscience Publication

JOHN WILEY & SONS, INC.

New York – Chichester – Brisbane – Toronto – Singapore

Library of Congress Cataloging in Publication Data:
Sun, Ron, 1960–
   Integrating rules and connectionism for robust commonsense reasoning/ Ron
Sun.
     p. cm. — (Sixth-generation computer technology series)
   Includes index.
   ISBN 0-471-59324-9 (alk. paper)
   1. Case-based reasoning. 2. Cognition. 3. Neural computers.
  I. Title. II. Series.
  Q338.8.S85 1994
  006.3—dc20   93-19460

CONTENTS

ILLUSTRATIONS

FOREWORD

When Ron Sun first proposed his ideas for achieving commonsense reasoning, I was skeptical. This must have been around 1988 at Brandeis University, where he was my Ph.D. advisee. Ron envisioned a hybrid system—CONSYDERR—with a rule-based portion and a connectionist portion, joined by links, solving the same problems in parallel, and influencing each other during different phases of an overall system schedule. Despite my general belief in the fundamental correctness of Minsky's society of mind ideas concerning cognitive architecture in people, it was easy to be more critical of Ron's specific architecture than of Minsky's compendium of design ideas and observations. Why just two levels? Why these particular two levels?

Three years later, while I still retained some level of skepticism, Ron showed that his system could handle every example I threw at him. This gave me sufficient confidence in his dissertation. Subsequently, he was selected for the David Marr Award at the Cognitive Science Conference in 1991, which further confirmed the importance of this work. More recently, I have encountered some ideas and problems that cause me to think that Ron is on to something even bigger. I have come to see that his work is closely related to some deep issues in the evolutionary "design" of the brain and in software engineering. Let me explain.

Evolution in the brain has taken place by accretion of new layers on top of relatively unchanged old structures, rather than by mutation of these old structures. Thus the brain stem and midbrain are relatively unchanged from those of other primates; our big differences are in the growth of the cortex on top of (or around) these older layers. Why should evolution work this way? Presumably, once various functions are worked out, it is maladaptive to modify them in almost any fashion. However, it apparently is beneficial to add new structures (e.g., the cortex) around the old ones (e.g., the midbrain) that may trap conditions that would not be understood by (or that might be misunderstood by) the older structures. Such structures can clearly be captured in a two-level model.

What does this have to do with software engineering? With the discoveries of neuroscientists now flooding the scientific literature as well as the daily papers, I believe there will be great opportunities for designing computer systems that operate on principles quite different from those used in today's general purpose computers. However, one cannot imagine scrapping our software legacy of operating systems, compilers, and applications—trusted software that operates in many cases continuously with 99.9% uptime. Many systems that are in constant use were written 20 or more years ago. Many of the people who wrote them have retired, and no one can understand 20-year-old code in any case. It is rumored that many mainframe applications will cease to function on January 1, 2000. On that date, ancient COBOL programs will subtract 99 from 00 (i.e., the two-digit encoding for the years 2000 and 1999), generating an error for each such operation. Another special kind of problem arises because these applications were written when memory was very precious, and so used many tricks—such as combining several operations in one instruction—which make the old code virtually undecipherable. Yet we will certainly want to exploit novel architectures, e.g., massively parallel, neurally inspired systems. But it's hard to imagine how we could ever translate legacy software to run on such systems.

What can we do to break this impasse? One possibility is to build hybrid systems, with traditional general-purpose computers surrounded by systems/devices of new design, with sophisticated communication channels between them. These surrounding machines can pass requirements through to old devices when appropriate, but at the same time can trap novel or modified operations that cannot be dealt with by the old chips. This is highly reminiscent of Ron's design for CONSYDERR! It shows the universality of two-level structuring.

With enough examples from radically different realms, I see that important principles are coming out of this work. I therefore recommend Ron's book with great enthusiasm.

DAVID L. WALTZ

Princeton, New Jersey

PREFACE

One of the more difficult problems for artificial intelligence research is the problem of modeling commonsense reasoning. The use of traditional models to capture the flexible and robust nature of commonsense reasoning presents great difficulties. In this book I attempt to tackle this problem by adopting innovative approaches. In a nutshell, I am concerned with understanding and modeling commonsense reasoning with a combination of rules and similarities, under a connectionist rubric. I survey the areas of reasoning, connectionist models, inheritance, causality, rule-based systems, and similarity-based reasoning, and introduce a new framework and a novel connectionist architecture for modeling commonsense reasoning that synthesizes some of these areas. Along with this framework, I describe a set of interrelated new ideas regarding modeling commonsense reasoning that are very relevant to current artificial intelligence and cognitive science research and the ongoing methodological debate.

To make these issues clearer, I will describe very briefly the main thrust of this work. First, some reasoning data and examples are analyzed to gain an insight into the matter. This analysis establishes a framework for modeling such data based on the notions of rules and similarities, and then, through detailed thought experiments and derivations, the framework is translated into a connectionist architecture. The architecture is capable of carrying out both rule-based reasoning and similarity-based reasoning naturally, for similarity-based reasoning is inherent in connectionist models and rule-based reasoning is integrated into connectionist networks through encoding rules in these networks.

Technical details aside, an important conclusion from the research described in this book is that the synergy resulting from the interaction of the two different types of representation and processing (such as rule-based reasoning and similarity-based reasoning) can and should be utilized. This synergy enables the handling of a large number of difficult issues in common-sense reasoning, within *one* integrated framework. The results presented in the book suggest that connectionist models incorporating rule-based reasoning can be effective and efficient models of reasoning.

Based on this architecture, a number of technical and theoretical issues are addressed in the book. For example, to understand rule encoding in connectionist architectures, a formal analysis of the rule encoding scheme is performed. Unlike previous work, the analysis shows that it handles a superset of some important logics. To further improve the rule-based reasoning capability of this connectionist architecture, variables are added, and a solution to the connectionist *variable binding* problem is proposed which has a number of advantages over existing solutions. I also explore the notion of *causality* in the connectionist model and show that commonsense causal knowledge can be well represented in connectionist frameworks in general and in this architecture in particular. Several other aspects of the architecture are also discussed in the book to demonstrate how connectionist models can supplement, enhance, and integrate symbolic rule-based reasoning in tackling commonsense reasoning.

This book is aimed at readers who are interested in the broad subject of modeling and understanding cognitive processes, especially commonsense reasoning, who are interested in overcoming the limitations of currently available computational machinery and striving for a new generation of commonsensical intelligent systems, and who are interested in a multidisci-plinary attack on AI problems based on the confluence of many different intellectual sources. Specifically, it should be useful for researchers and students in artificial intelligence, cognitive science, neural networks, and other related areas. It should also be suitable for interested laypersons who wish to be informed of the new research being carried out.

HISTORY OF THE WORK

This book is adapted from my Ph.D. dissertation, completed at Brandeis University. The research it describes was started during the summer of 1988 and carried out during my three years in the Michtom School of Computer Science at Brandeis University. Some of the ideas in this book, however, can be traced far back in time, to early 1984. During that period, while I was reading psychology and AI literatures, some ideas about human (and ma-chine) reasoning started to come to my mind, I did not get a chance to pursue these ideas any further until the summer of 1988 when I finally had the opportunity to do so. I think I made the right decision to go to Brandeis University. But it was never easy, I guess no matter where I was, to go through the process of forming a new idea, presenting it convincingly, and gaining support for it. The most important thing I have learned during my graduate school years is how to narrow down a goal, form a reasonable agenda, and accomplish the agenda. By the late summer of 1990, I had accomplished a reasonable number of items on my agenda and started the actual writing of the dissertation. The writing was completed in the summer of 1991.

After completing the dissertation, I started to write journal papers based on the work reported in the dissertation. I received a large number of requests for copies of my dissertation (given the size of the work, I could not possibly fulfill all these requests). Several people who read my papers and/or the dissertation suggested to me the idea of publishing it in book form. I signed the book contract with John Wiley & Sons, Inc., in the summer of 1992, eight years after I first had the idea and four years after I started actually doing the research.

The manuscript was thoroughly revised and augmented since then. The revision took another six months. The book is the final outcome of this long process.

ACKNOWLEDGMENTS

I wish to take this opportunity to acknowledge the following people. First of all, during my years at Brandeis University, many people have helped me in pursuing this research: I want to thank Dave Waltz for his constant guidance and for his careful reading of numerous rough drafts; I want to thank James Pustejovsky for spending many hours with me discussing the research and for his extremely helpful comments on the manuscript; I want to thank Tim Hickey for many very useful discussions that have helped me to clarify formal aspects of my work; Pattie Maes also provided valuable feedback. Jerry Samet introduced me to the philosophy of mind. Larry Bookman wrote detailed comments on my papers, and the frequent discussions with him were thought-provoking.

During the publication process that transformed the original dissertation into this book, I have received comments and feedback from a number of colleagues, to whom I owe my gratitude. Dan Levine provided thorough, thoughtful, and inspiring comments and detailed suggestions for revisions, as well as reference materials. Branko Souček provided positive and encouraging comments that led to the publication of the book. Steve Sloman commented extensively on my work, thus helping me to greatly clarify my thinking about the issues. Thanks also go to several anonymous reviewers for various suggestions.

I have benefited from interactions with many others (names are listed in random order): Jim Hendler, Lokendra Shastri, Tim Finin, Jude Shavlik, Ryszard Michalski, Gomer Thomas, George Mou, Rick Alterman, Allan

Collins, Helen Gigley, Shashi Shekhar, John Barnden, Michael Dyer, Dave Touretzky, Jordan Pollack, and Michael Arbib. Others have undoubtedly been omitted, due to my less than perfect memory.

I wish to thank the Wiley editors for their professional help.

I acknowledge the financial support that I received during the years I carried out the work that led to this book. My three-year stay at Brandeis was supported by fellowships, scholarships, and assistantships provided by the university and indirectly from various funding agencies. My work at the University of Alabama (during the revision of the manuscript) was supported by the university and its College of Engineering. The David Marr Award from the Cognitive Science Society is also gratefully acknowledged.

*Integrating Rules and Connectionism
for Robust Commonsense Reasoning*

CHAPTER 1 ———————————

Introduction

The complexity of philosophy is not in its matter, but in our tangled understanding.
    —L. Wittenstein, PHILOSOPHICAL REMARKS

1.1 OVERVIEW

The dream of building truly intelligent machines that are as capable as human beings and that can interact with people in a natural and meaningful way has had a long history, as demonstrated by the work of Leibniz, Boole, Turing, and many others (see, e.g., Turing 1950). It predates artificial intelligence, a field that investigates computational ways of capturing intelligence (formed in 1956 with the Dartmouth conference, as commonly recognized). Artificial intelligence (AI) builds on this age-old dream: it is in fact the first serious and massive effort at understanding and capturing intelligence computationally, and it has been inspired by the invention and the gradual popularization of digital computers; for the success of simple logics (carried out by hardware switching elements) in formulating arithmetic computations in digital computers led to the hope that they could also capture more "intelligent" processes, such as problem solving and planning, up to the level of complete human intelligence.

In nearly four decades following the inception of AI, it has had some successes in formulating many processes that were thought to require high-level "intelligence," such as chess, medical diagnosis, and symbolic mathematics (Nilsson 1980, Buchanan and Shoftliffe 1984). However, none of the successful AI systems have real "common sense," the ability of human beings to understand simple, common things and to get to the heart of a problem without enumerating all the rules and following them one by one.

The problem of common sense and commonsense reasoning has become one of the central issues in artificial intelligence: How can we capture commonsense reasoning *computationally*, both effectively and efficiently in terms of computational resources? The question can be broken down into a number of subquestions based on our current understanding of this issue and all the available scientific theories:

- How can we conceptually characterize commonsense reasoning in a simple and uniform way? What kinds of formalisms and models are suitable?
- How can real AI systems capture common sense and commonsense reasoning?
- What are the problems and difficulties with existing approaches?
- Can connectionist models, which are relatively new on the horizon, deal with commonsense reasoning?
- More important, can connectionist models do better than existing approaches in accounting for commonsense reasoning?

This work is intended to examine such questions. What this work shows is that connectionist models of reasoning can implement some traditional "symbolic" AI paradigms, but they are not mere "implementations" of their symbolic counterparts; rather, they can be better computational models of commonsense reasoning than the traditional ones. They can be better because they take into consideration the approximate, evidential, and flexible nature of commonsense reasoning, and they also account for the spontaneity and parallelism in commonsense reasoning, which are very important but often neglected.

This chapter provides an introduction that motivates the work described in subsequent chapters, as well as to provide a summary of what this book is all about. In the rest of this chapter, I first briefly review various approaches to commonsense reasoning, and then I introduce the problem of modeling common patterns in commonsense reasoning and explain the difficulties involved. Then I outline a solution to the problem. The rationales for this research are enumerated next, followed by some clarifications. Some guides for readers are provided at the end of the chapter.

1.2 COMMONSENSE REASONING

1.2.1 The Problem of Commonsense Reasoning

Reasoning is a fundamental aspect of human cognition. It is involved in all kinds of cognitive processes, ranging from language understanding to decision making. Therefore, it is of utmost importance to achieve a better understanding of reasoning. Among various types of reasoning, *commonsense reasoning* is the most fundamental, because it represents a basic and prevailing activity. Therefore, it is well justified for me to concentrate in this book on the study of commonsense reasoning, which is, by the way, an all-embracing concept by itself.

It is extremely difficult to define what commonsense reasoning is, just as it is hard to define what intelligence is, or what knowledge is. Roughly speaking, it is taken to mean informal kinds of reasoning in everyday life regarding mundane issues, where usually no exhaustive search is performed and speed is often more important than accuracy. In the real world, despite the lack of complete and precise knowledge, a commonsense reasoner can come up with a plausible conclusion regardless, based on the basic understanding of types of situations and taking into account background knowledge. Commonsense reasoning thus results in knowledge that often seems obvious, direct, and relevant, but such knowledge may also be incomplete, inexact, and metaphorical. Because of the ease with which commonsense reasoning is performed, one tends to fail to see the significance and the pervasiveness of such reasoning. However, commonsense reasoning is believed to be underlying all other kinds of reasoning activities, in that it provides a basis upon which other kinds of reasoning competence are established, and a background upon which other reasoning processes and outcomes are verified, validated, and strengthened. The work by McCarthy (1968) was the earliest to characterize some aspects of commonsense reasoning with respect to the goal of AI.

To be commonsensical, we need a vast array of commonsense knowledge and a reasoning capability that can derive plausible conclusions from existing knowledge. Therefore, to develop intelligent systems with common sense, we need (1) to identify relevant knowledge from various areas, such as space, time, quantities, goals, needs and plans (cf. Davis 1990), and (2) to establish a commonsense inference capability that can use existing knowledge to arrive at useful conclusions for various situations, efficiently and effectively. In the end, we need to implement all of the above in a computational architecture, in an efficient manner with performance at least roughly comparable to that of human beings. In this endeavor, it is important to establish the inference capability as a starting point.

1.2.2 Various Existing Approaches

Now let us take a cursory look at some common approaches to commonsense reasoning. This examination is intended simply to provide a background for subsequent developments. Detailed reviews and comparisons are given in Chapter 8.

Rule-Based Reasoning   There is a long history of believing that rules can be used to explain human thinking, including commonsense reasoning.

Human intelligence is believed, in Plato's work for example, to be from rational verbal inferences from facts; *syllogism*, *modus ponens*, and *modus tollens* (which are variants of rule-based reasoning) are the essential forms of reasoning, according to philosophers such as Aristotle. Kant in his famous *A Critique of Pure Reason* (see Kant 1953) develops this theme further and suggests that cognition is pure reason with innate frameworks and rules ("synthetic a priori") that determines ubiquitously correct forms of reasoning, working on the constructed world built through sensory, *lebenswelt* (life-world).

There is also a long tradition of psychological study of reasoning using rule-based (logical) approaches. Jean Piaget attempted to build models of human reasoning in which logic serves as the foundation. The cognitive development in children is described in terms of acquiring a system of mental logic gradually, and changes are interpreted as emergence of new logical competence (Girotto and Legrenzi 1990).

The advocates of this approach for AI include Herbert Simon, Allen Newell, and others. Their *physical symbol hypothesis* spawned enormous research effort in traditional "symbolic" AI, which typically uses discrete symbols as basic representational primitives and performs symbol manipulation in reasoning, and typically, reason in a sequential, deliberative manner. Generally, in rule-based reasoning, some generic syntactic forms that consist of *antecedents* and *consequents* (or conditions and conclusions) are used as basic representational means (cf. Klahr et al. 1989, and Newell and Simon 1972), and reasoning amounts to deriving from antecedents the resulting conclusion. Among the existing paradigms of AI, the rule-based paradigm is by far the most successful. It is telling that, among the areas of which "symbolic" AI achieved certain successes, the most notable is rule-based expert systems (see Buchanan and Shortliffe 1984).

Now let us examine a few approaches in the rule-based paradigm. Roughly speaking, traditional rule-based systems can be classified into two general categories: (1) systems based on formal logics and (2) production systems. *Formal logics* are simple, formally defined languages, capable of expressing rules in a rigorous way, including propositional and predicate logics (Chang and Lee 1973). *Propositional logic* deals with declarative sentences (propositions) that can be either true or false. Propositions can be combined, using logical connectives (e.g., $\vee$, $\wedge$, $\neg$), to form compound propositions. *Predicate logic* (first-order logic) is made up of predicates that contain arguments (and therefore there are also terms for arguments and quantifiers constraining arguments in this type of logic). It is more complex, because of the introduction of arguments and consequently their bindings to terms, but it is thus more expressive: it can represent n-ary relations, among other things. Usually, rules are encoded using the Horn clause formalism, in which conditions are the conjunction of atomic propositions and conclusions are single atomic propositions, and a logical implication connects them; for example, $A \wedge B \wedge C \rightarrow D$ is a Horn clause.

Production systems are no different from logics in terms of commonsense reasoning (Klahr et al. 1989, Posner 1989, Anderson 1983). Production systems usually consist of a production (rule) base (for storing all the rules) and a working memory (for storing intermediate results) and use a control structure to decide which rules are eligible to fire, how rules are picked for actual firing, and in which order they are supposed to fire.

However, this type of account is not free from problems. Technical problems aside, some people pointed out early on that there was something wrong with such a purely rationalistic research agenda. Hubert Dreyfus, a persistent opponent of "symbolic" AI, enunciated (cf. Dreyfus 1972):

> Intuitive expertise, acquired through concrete experience, is an endangered species. We must resist the temptation to exalt calculative reason as personified by the computer. Instead, we must recognize that facts, rules and logic alone cannot produce either common sense, the ability to go to the heart of a problem, or intuition, our capacity to do what works without necessarily knowing why.

In the area of planning, through studying human planning activities, Agre (1988) also recognized the importance of intuition and subconscious actions, or in his words, improvisatory planning and reactive routines. It seems that most of the time, one simply follows the established patterns of activities, without much deliberative thought and/or detailed reasoning. AI needs to address this type of processes.

Recent Extensions of Rule-Based Reasoning   In an effort to amend various deficiencies of rule-based reasoning (such as those pointed out above and others; see Chapters 2 and 3 for details), I will look into two recent extensions of rule-based reasoning as examples, for they are most relevant to what I will develop in this work.

Fuzzy logic (Zadeh 1965) is intended to capture the vagueness in linguistic expressions, such as "tall" or "warm," which have no clear-cut boundaries. The basic idea as follows: for each concept, there is a set of objects satisfying that concept to a certain degree, which form a subset called the *fuzzy subset*. This fuzzy (sub)set contains as its elements pairs consisting of an object and its grade of membership, which represents the degree (i.e., the confidence) with which it satisfies the concept associated with the set. Given this idea, it is easy to construct a logic with which one can reason about the fuzzy truth values of various concepts. One version of fuzzy logic (for *generalized modus ponens*) is as follows[1]: for an implication

$$\textit{if } X \textit{ is } B \textit{ then } Y \textit{ is } C$$

---

[1]It is adopted from Zadeh (1988).

given

$$X \text{ is } A$$

infer that *Y is D*, for some *D*, where *X* and *Y* are fuzzy variables, and *A*, *B*, *C*, and *D* are fuzzy sets. It it handled by turning the implication into an equivalent form:

$$\neg (X \text{ is } B) \vee (Y \text{ is } C)$$

So the generalized modus ponens inference becomes as follows: given

$$(X \text{ is } A) \wedge (\neg (X \text{ is } B) \vee (Y \text{ is } C))$$

decide *D* such that *Y* is *D*.

According to Zadeh (1988), numerical calculations can be used in place of logical operations: MIN is used for ∧ (i.e., logical AND) and + is used for ∨ (i.e., logical OR). For logical negation ¬ (i.e., logical NOT), $m_{\neg B}(x) = 1 - m_B(x)$, where *m* is the grade of membership for the respective fuzzy sets.

In contrast to fuzzy logic, *probabilistic approaches* toward reasoning treat beliefs as probabilistic events, and utilize probabilistic laws for belief combination. For updating a probability based on evidence received, the Bayesian rule can be used:

$$p(B|A) = \frac{p(A|B)p(B)}{p(A)}$$

where *A* is the known evidence, *B* is a possible outcome, $p(A)$ is the a priori probability of *A*, $p(B)$ is the a priori probability of *B*, $p(A|B)$ is the conditional probability of *A* given *B*, and $p(B|A)$ is the posteriori probability of *B* (i.e., the conclusion needed).

Bayesian reasoning can be implemented in a network fashion (Pearl 1988). However, the results so far seem to indicate that only very simple types of Bayesian reasoning can be handled efficiently by these kinds of networks. Probabilistic reasoning in general is very complex computationally, especially when compared with human commonsense reasoning. Note that human reasoning does not always conform to the assumptions and the laws of probability theory (Tversky and Kahneman 1983), probably in part because of the complexity of the formal models (Cherniak 1986).

Knowledge Engineering The CYC project by Lenat and associates (see Ghua and Lenat 1990) tackles the problem of commonsense reasoning by engineering a huge amount of knowledge into a system and hoping that an enormous amount of knowledge can help to circumvent the limitations of current AI systems in their lack of common sense. Their wish seems to be that *quantity* (the amount of knowledge) might be able to substitute for *quality* (the common sense). They state (Guha and Lenat 1990):

> We don't believe there is any shortcut to being intelligent, and yet-to-be-discovered Maxwell's equations of thought, and AI RISC architecture that will yield vast amount of problem-solving power. ... Rather, the bulk of the effort must be manual entry of assertion after assertion.

Following this philosophy, in CYC, they put in not only a vast amount of domain-specific facts but also a long list of other types of knowledge (which include, using the CYC terminology, basic ontologies, "prescientific" knowledge, problem-solving heuristics, and meta-level knowledge for problem solving). In the inference engine of CYC, they use a few formal theories of reasoning but add a large number of heuristic methods (e.g., those regarding goals, causality, and time). And for the sake of efficiency, they have developed many specialized inference procedures for various purposes.

Overall, CYC is a collection of modules, procedures, categories, processes, and objects; various radically different techniques are concocted together. One argument against such an approach is the lack of clarity, comprehensibility, and manageability. One lesson that many researchers have drawn from decades of AI research is that a simple approach with clearly definable principles should be favored. As someone puts it, maybe God can build a mind as a kludge; mere mortals need some simple principles in order to understand it. As a practical matter, the lack of uniformity also thwarts attempts at developing learning capabilities in commonsense reasoning systems.

Qualitative Reasoning   Some AI researchers believe that common sense starts with the understanding of basic physical objects and processes. They try to formalize such understanding in logical or other terms. For example, Hayes (1978, 1979) studied the *naive physics* of liquids and solid objects, and formalized their basic properties as logic axioms. De Kleer and Brown (1986) identified causal relations in physical devices by performing *qualitative simulations* of the physical processes involved, Iwasaki and Simon (1988) identified causality through analyzing established quantitative relations (e.g., differential equations) of the physical processes. Forbus (1985) developed a *qualitative process* theory in which a physical process is characterized as states, transitions, and their preconditions and influences.

Such qualitative reasoning theories may have some limited use in expert system, but it should be noted that they have neither solid foundations in physics, mechanics, or any other scientific theories, nor any proven connection to human cognitive processes of understanding such physical processes. They are actually approximations of scientific theories of physical processes, in a computational framework.

Case-Based Reasoning   Case-based systems reason by retrieving previous similar "cases" (such as problem-solving scenarios, past episodes, existing plans, or past successful diagnosis) and adapting them to the current situation. One example that supports the idea of case-based reasoning is as follows (Hammond 1989):

> When an architect starts a new design for a client, he does not go back to first principles and try out all possible combinations. Instead he recalls past plans and change them to fit his current needs.

Case-based inference is believed to be the most basic element of reasoning by its advocates, for example, by Riesbeck and Schank (1989), who characterize the complete process of case-based reasoning as the following sequence of steps:

- INPUT. Receive data.
- INDEX. Find relevant pointers.
- RETRIEVE. Find relevant cases based on indices.
- ADAPT. Modify the retrieved cases for the current situation.
- TEST, REPAIR, AND STORE. Try out the solution and store it into the case base after it is tuned into a correct form.

This entire process is construed to be sequential, and basically it iterates until a satisfactory solution is found.

It seems that in human reasoning in such situations as described above, there are also rules involved, for example, for reasoning from first principles when existing cases fail to produce a satisfactory solution, or when repeated use of the same case leads to the establishment of an abstract rule. Although case-based inference (or the use of analogous knowledge in general) is very important for commonsense reasoning, abstract knowledge encoded in rules is also needed (see Chapters 2 and 3 for more details).

1.2.3   Connectionism

Connectionism is a relatively new approach towards modeling intelligence and cognition. Connectionist models are usually composed of large number of interacting simple processing elements, each of which performs simple computation such as a weighted sum of its inputs or a sigmoid function of the weighted sum. The overall computational capability stems from the massive interaction of these simple elements. It has been proven that such networks can perform arbitrary mapping of inputs and outputs (for any measurable function; see Hornik et al. 1989). Connectionism aims for computational systems that can learn from experience and that are capable of generalization from data, by using continuous numerical functions and learning incrementally. Thus connectionist models provide the inherent advantages of uniform representation, simple and generic mechanisms, and mathematical analyzability, which make them more appealing than some AI systems that often, though not always, amount to ad hoc tricks. Fine-grained, massively parallel connectionist networks can account naturally for the parallelism in human memory and reasoning, including commonsense reasoning.

Although compared with "symbolic" AI, connectionism currently seems to be better in modeling only certain aspects of cognitive processes, most notably in low-level processes such as vision, pattern recognition, and sensory-motor control, connectionism is also an attractive alternative in modeling high-level cognitive processes; for it comes with the promise of being a robust, fault-tolerant, parallel-distributed cognitive architecture that uses simple processing elements but renders a lot processing power, that can learn from experience, and that is capable of generalization from data. Although in the past there has been little work in utilizing the connectionist paradigm directly for the study of commonsense reasoning, there have been some efforts related to reasoning and cognition. For example, an interesting approach is that of Grossberg and associates (see, e.g., Grossberg 1987). Grossberg came up with a number of network models to model classical conditioning and other phenomena, culminating in the *activation resonance theory* (ART). He developed mechanistic explanations for a range of classical conditioning data, and posited cognitive constructs such as drive representation, incentive, expectancy, and frustration to account for various situational, contextual, and motivational forces. It is interesting to note that this work was developed at approximately the same time as "symbolic" AI, but it went quite the opposite way.

One important issue in modeling high-level cognitive capabilities by connectionist networks is how to deal with rule-following behaviors and how to carry out rule-based reasoning. One point of view is that rulelike behavior is the result of a complex interaction of network components, and therefore there is no fundamental difference between rules and nonrules. Another viewpoint advocates implementing rules directly in connectionist network. Touretzky and Hinton (1985) were the first to implement rule-based reasoning in connectionist networks. They basically emulate the structure of a symbolic rule-based (production) system, with separate modules for working memory, rules, and facts. The resulting system is the equivalent of a simple sequential symbolic rule-based system. Barnden (1988) represents another early attack on the same problem. In his system, data reside in gridlike networks, coded with the help of adjacency relations and some highlighting techniques. Rules are hardwired with circuitry for detecting the presence of data that match a particular rule, and a conclusion module associated with each rule is used to add a new data structure representing the conclusion of the matching rule. Beside these, Sun (1989, 1991b), Ajjanagadde and Shastri

(1989), Lange and Dyer (1989), and many others also implement rules in connectionist models.

Thus it is quite clear that connectionist models are capable of implementing rule-based reasoning in a variety of ways as well as other types of high-level reasoning (Rumelhart et al. 1986). Then the following questions arise:

- Can connectionist models do better in terms of accounting for common-sense reasoning?
- Can commonsense reasoning data that are difficult to be accounted for by the traditional rule-based paradigm be explained by connectionist reasoning models?

The questions can also be asked the other way around:

- Can we develop some connectionist architecture that can *better* model commonsense reasoning and that can deal with some chronic problems plaguing "symbolic" reasoning systems (see Chapter 2), with the hope of enhancing our understanding of commonsense reasoning in general and connectionist reasoning in particular?

1.3 THE PROBLEM OF COMMON REASONING PATTERNS

In this section, as a preview, the problem of modeling common patterns in commonsense reasoning is identified and the difficulties involved are sketched out. A solution is then roughly outlined, which is the main thrust of this book.

1.3.1 The Existence of Patterns

I am neither concerned about the study of a particular domain, nor about idiosyncratic commonsense reasoning in a particular domain. I deal with commonsense reasoning in general, or more specifically, I deal with common, recurrent *patterns* in commonsense reasoning across domains.

Do there exist any domain-independent, recurrent common patterns in reasoning, especially in commonsense reasoning, after all? This is a controversial question. There is clearly no consensus regarding it.

Since the time of Aristotle, it has been widely recognized that reasoning seems to follow some syntactic patterns, the simplest of which are *syllogism*, *modus ponens*, and *modus tolens*, as mentioned earlier. These patterns have been studied extensively and later developed into modern mathematical logic through the work of Frege, Russell, and others. There is no doubt that these patterns are extremely limited in their expressive and reasoning power (they cannot even describe formal mathematical reasoning completely). It is precisely because of such limitations that some researchers oppose altogether the use of formal systems (including formal logics) in artificial intelligence research. I find that this point of view is less than fully justified: scientific progress is made by a long process of discovering new models and tuning (or discarding) old ones, and therefore the disillusionment is ill-founded. Formal models with simple, elegant constructs can provide deeper understanding than informal ones, because they allow more analyses to be performed and thus a clearer understanding can be achieved. The basic belief behind this work is that even though there has been to date no satisfactory formal model of patterns of commonsense reasoning available, there is no reason to give up searching for such patterns and models, therefore resorting some ad hoc method (or a combination of many of such methods) for dealing with the representation and use of commonsense knowledge. This is true especially in light of the new developments in connectionist models, which provide a new kind of simple and elegant formalism that may prove to be of great value in the study of commonsense reasoning patterns.

Allan Collins, a well-known psychologist, collected a large number of protocols of commonsense reasoning (see Collins 1978, Collins and Michalski 1989) in the area of elementary geography and the like. Noticing the inadequacy of traditional logics in explaining those reasoning patterns, he argues for the development of different formalisms or frameworks in studying common reasoning patterns found in various commonsense reasoning tasks. Although rejecting traditional logics, Collins and Michalski (1989) believe in the existence of common patterns (versus domain specific ad hoc mechanisms) that are widely applicable across domains. Collins and his colleagues have done a good job in terms of analyzing the data, identifying some common patterns, and establishing a unifying vocabulary for describing them (e.g., Collins 1978, Collins and Michalski 1989). What is still needed is a computational framework for commonsense reasoning that is uniform and computationally tractable and from which various inference patterns contained in the data can emerge into existence naturally. It is also important to account faithfully for the speed and spontaneity of human reasoning processes (e.g., by adopting massively parallel structures). This framework ought to be analytically simple, structurally unified, and mechanistically sound, given the discussion above.

1.3.2 How Can We Account for Common Patterns?

Let me preview below some major arguments and conclusions in this book. First, although having some helpful characteristics, existing connectionist models (or any computational models for that matter) so far cannot deal very well with the patterns identified in commonsense reasoning in a single framework (see Chapter 2 for the details of these patterns). The problem with most existing connectionist models (barring a few mentioned earlier) is that they tend to be too unstructured, too uniform, and sometimes not accurate enough (see Chapter 2). They learn the mapping from input data to output data by minimizing an overall error measure (i.e., *energy*), and thus can perform the mapping only approximately most of the time. Although some of these features can help to give rise to the generalization capability in connectionist models, they also give rise to the inaccuracy and critical errors.

The problem with existing rule-based approaches as discussed earlier is the *brittleness* problem of traditional "symbolic" systems in general, a problem that has been plaguing "symbolic" AI for a long time. Many common patterns are actually instances of the problem (see Chapter 2 for a detailed discussion). Roughly, I can equate the brittleness problem with the inability of a system to deal with reasoning involving partial information, uncertain or fuzzy information, lack of applicable rules, rule interaction, inference through bottom-up and top-down inheritance, and learning new rules, in a unified framework and in a computationally adequate way. And it is also difficult for traditional rule-based reasoning to achieve the corresponding massive parallelism that is apparent in human reasoning.

To account for common patterns in commonsense reasoning, we have to be able to deal with these difficult aspects of the brittleness problem. A detailed analysis of these aspects (in Chapter 2, with many examples) shows that while they look like a disparate set of problems, they can all be characterized as reasoning with rules supplemented by (feature) similarity-based reasoning, unified under a connectionist rubric.

1.3.3 Precision and Flexibility

One important issue that emerged from the preceding brief look at the problems with existing models is how we should handle the rigor and clarity in reasoning as evident in commonsense reasoning data on the one hand, and the approximate, evidential character of the same process on the other hand.

From a detailed analysis of the data (in Chapters 2 and 3), I conclude that we need clearly defined structures to enable effective inferences and we need precise ways of encoding knowledge (as possessed by a cognitive agent): the exact prerequisites for an action, the precise outcome of a given situation, and so on. This rules out some types of models (e.g., most existing simple connectionist models) as unsuitable, because of their imprecise nature.

The same data also show that there is much flexibility in commonsense reasoning. To model this, we also need corresponding flexibility in the reasoning process of a model. Specifically, we need a means of evidential combination, with graded information (fuzzy, uncertain, etc.), capable of accumulating confidence incrementally (see Chapter 2 for explanations). We should also be able to deal with analogous knowledge (as shown in the data; see Chapter 2).

To satisfy the requirements on both sides, I have to be very careful to strike a balance between them. This places a major constraint on the design of a model to account for commonsense reasoning patterns.

1.3.4 A New Approach

While the detailed specification and derivation of the new solution to the paradox of precision versus flexibility will be given in later chapters, some sketches are presented next to provide an overall picture.

Based on a detailed analysis, a framework consisting of rule- and similarity-based reasoning is proposed to account for some common reasoning patterns found in commonsense reasoning and to remedy the brittleness problem. Within this framework, a connectionist architecture for robust reasoning, CONSYDERR,[2] is developed. In this architecture, a dual-representation scheme is devised which utilizes both *localist representation* and *distributed representation* with features. Each representation is in a subnetwork (or a "level") by itself, forming a separate feedforward network, with connections established between corresponding nodes across levels. I explore the synergy resulting from the interaction between these two types of representation (and between the two levels of the network), which helps to address problems such as partial information, lack of applicable rules, property inheritance, and rule interaction. Because of this synergy, the architecture is capable of accounting for many difficult patterns in commonsense reasoning. This architecture shows that connectionist models of reasoning are not just "implementations" of their symbolic counterparts and they are actually better computational models of commonsense reasoning.

In each level of the CONSYDERR architecture, rules are encoded as links between nodes (representing concepts, propositions, or features), and the computation at each node is structured so that it can implement the evidential combination, within rules and across rules, correctly. This computation, as shown later, is able to capture commonsense causal reasoning and does not require anything more than the weighted-sum computation with multiple sites competing for activation (Feldman and Ballard 1982).

1.4 WHAT IS THE POINT?

Given all the above, one may still ask the question: What is the point of doing all that? To make things clear, in this section I articulate the answer to

---

[2] It stands for a "CONnectionist SYstem with Dual-representation for Evidential Robust Reasoning."

this question directly. However, justifications for this answer are developed in subsequent chapters.

First, CONSYDERR is an *integrated* architecture, simple but capable of dealing with a wide range of problems, such as evidential rule-based reasoning, similarity-based reasoning, top-down and bottom-up inheritance, and dealing with incompleteness and inconsistency of rules through interaction and generation. (The protocols and examples in Chapter 3 provide justifications for the role of each of these problems in commonsense reasoning.) Moreover, CONSYDERR is meant to be a *better* computational model for accounting for commonsense reasoning, by using evidential rule application plus similarity matching, which is motivated by the dissatisfaction with existing models, rule-based or connectionistic, in accounting for the robustness, flexibility, and evidentiality of commonsense reasoning. To say the least, a model for accounting for commonsense reasoning data as the one developed herein can provide useful insights into the relevant cognitive capabilities and the possible computational architectures for modeling them.

Second, this work is an attempt at addressing the brittleness problem of traditional "symbolic" AI, by combining rules with (similarity-based) connectionist models. It will be shown that the CONSYDERR architecture is a useful framework in which several aspects of this brittleness problem (as discussed in Chapter 2) can readily be handled.

Third, the capability of CONSYDERR in dealing in one unified framework with many difficult problems in reasoning can be credited to the dual-representation (localist and distributed) scheme used, and the synergy resulting from interaction between the two types of representation. It will be shown that interaction between the two levels of CONSYDERR with different types of representation helps to perform *intensional* (i.e., meaning-oriented and feature-based) reasoning along with usual *extensional* reasoning.

Fourth, an important aspect of this work is to explicate the relationship between rules and connectionist models, especially the weighted-sum model. This work shows, by formal derivations and many examples, that there is little, if any, difference between rules and weighted-sum connectionist models in terms of their static descriptive capabilities. In other words, they are somehow equivalent in their *static* behavior: each of them can express the kind of relations the other can (for details, see Chapter 5). The difference is in their *dynamic* behavior: while in traditional symbolic systems rules are isolated (or "modular"), disembodied, and context-free pieces of knowledge, in connectionist systems they are more integrated, more embodied in the overall process of reasoning, and they interact with each other dynamically (see Chapter 6). Those "rules" in connectionist systems are represented by, or embodied in, connections between nodes (as discussed in detail in Chapter 5). Another way to look at this is that while connectionist models are *syntactically* similar to rules (more so than commonly thought), they are different in terms of their semantic contents: one tends to be more abstract and isolated, and the other more grounded in lower-level processes.

Finally, I show, by theoretical construction, that connectionist models provide a framework for representing and reasoning about commonsense causal knowledge. As demonstrated in Chapter 5, weighted-sum connectionist models are equivalent to a logic that is in turn a generalization of a logic formalism for capturing causal reasoning (Shoham 1987). The basic idea is that different conditions of a rule exert different weights, or play different roles, in obtaining causal outcomes, which can be expressed as modality, as in Shoham (1987), or as weighted-sum computations for evidential combination, as in the present framework. Therefore, connectionist models are well suited for commonsense causal reasoning. Conversely, the power of simple weighted-sum connectionist models can be attributed largely to their capability for capturing causal reasoning.

To summarize, this work provides a better model of commonsense reasoning patterns; it combines rules and connectionism, so on one hand it can cope with the brittleness problem of rule-based reasoning, and on the other hand it enables connectionist networks to represent rules and to reason with them effectively; it also demonstrates the static/syntactic similarity and the dynamic/semantic difference between rules and connectionist models; and it shows that the synergy resulting from the interaction between two types of representation is the key to its capability.

1.5 SOME CLARIFICATIONS

In this section I discuss briefly a number of issues that need to be clarified before I proceed to the detailed study.

Rules are mentioned throughout this work and are used in different senses: for example, (1) it can be used to refer to *forms*, that is, structures for encoding knowledge of various sorts that consist of conditions and a conclusion so that whenever the conditions are met (in some way) the conclusion can be reached; (2) it can also be used to refer to *contents*, such as traffic rules, grammatical rules, or rules for arithmetics; and (3) it can also be used to refer to the perspectives and approaches traditionally associated with rule-based reasoning. These are distinct senses, and they are not interchangeable. In this work, the word "rule" is used in one sense or another, or sometimes in several senses combined. Most of the time, the meaning should be self-evident. Wherever there is a possibility of misunderstanding, the sense in which the word is used will be indicated.

Learning is an important issue and it is tied intrinsically to representation and reasoning. It has been argued (by, e.g., Hanson and Barr 1990) that the biggest advantage of connectionist models is that they provide a way to study representation and learning together. Although this particular viewpoint may be debatable, I fully recognize the importance of learning, and the intrinsic relationship and interaction between learning and representation. For example, we need to determine what kinds of representation are innate, what kinds are learned, and how they are learned. However, since representation itself comprises such a huge topic, it will be better to concentrate in this work on one aspect only and perform an in-depth study instead of providing superficial coverage of many different aspects. Therefore, I will not get into learning in any depth in this work.

Brittleness is one of the main issues dealt with in this work, and I show that integrating rules and connectionism provides some remedies. But by no means am I claiming that the brittleness problem is solved completely. As a matter of fact, it is far from that. We cannot solve all the problems at once; progress is made through consistent and gradual advances.

Domain independence is assumed in this work, based on the recurrent, domain-independent nature of commonsense reasoning patterns. I believe in the existence of domain-independent, generic mechanisms, and their use in various cognitive processes, at least to a certain extent. (Otherwise, how can one explain the same types of reasoning processes used for some totally different tasks?) However, it is not my intention to join in any meta-level debate regarding such issues, and I fully appreciate the importance of domain-specific (as opposed to domain-independent) investigations of commonsense reasoning.

Formal logics are criticized in various ways throughout this work. However, it should be made clear that I fully appreciate the usefulness of formal logics as normative analyses of cognition and as a way of generating mathematical insights into the matter. In other words, it has an important role in the formalization of intelligence and in the building of intelligent systems, although it needs to be extended and supplemented by other means.

Natural language processing, concept formation, and **categorization** are not addressed in this book. These are major issues in cognitive science and they are better dealt with in research more specifically geared toward them.

Grand unified theories of cognition are *not* what I am aiming for, and therefore this work should not be questioned along this line. For example, I did not answer questions such as: How can the system be connected to sensory-motor systems? How can it represent spatial relations? Or how does a system like that capture the ideas proposed by philosopher X, psychologist Y, or linguist Z? Admittedly, studies of such questions can be fertile grounds for future development of this work.

Marker passing and **spreading activation** have been proposed for quite a long time and they are similar in many ways to structured localist connectionist networks (cf. Charniak 1983). In my view, this fact does not render connectionist models, including the architecture developed herein, useless. Quite to the contrary, it adds support to the connectionist approach, because these approaches bring with them various cognitive and computational justifications, and they contribute ideas and techniques to the connectionist approach. What is important is not what label to put on a model, but what a model can do.

1.6 THE ORGANIZATION OF THE BOOK

To make the organization of this book clear, a summary of the chapters in the book is provided below.

- **Chapter 2** starts by introducing a set of reasoning examples, including Collins' protocols, and common patterns embodies in them. Then difficulties in accounting for these patterns by existing computational approaches are identified. This leads to the brittleness problem of traditional "symbolic" AI in general, which is analyzed in detail. Based on this analysis, a rough framework for solving the problem is suggested and applied to the data.
- **Chapter 3** develops a computational architecture for implementing the framework for accounting for common patterns in commonsense reasoning: first the need for multiple levels is identified, and then the appropriateness of connectionist implementation of each of these levels is argued for. Further explications and specifications are made through analyzing the characteristics of the problem to be solved and through deriving formally structural parameters in accordance with these characteristics.
- **Chapter 4** contains a set of experiments performed on the architecture, including detailed explanations of how each of the protocols and the examples can be generated, as well as formal evaluations of the architecture, systematic explorations of the architecture, and some applications of it.
- **Chapter 5** aims to answer the question of how rules can be encoded by the weighted-sum computation as used in the architecture. In so doing, this chapter looks into the question of causality and the question of how to capture commonsense causal reasoning in connectionist models through extending existing rule-based accounts. A new logical formalism is defined and formally compared with existing ones, showing that it is capable of dealing with very general rule-based reasoning; it is then applied to address the problems in causal reasoning, and fully demonstrates its usefulness in that regard. The formalism is shown to correspond directly to a connectionist architecture, and thus the two approaches converge and retain the benefits of both at the same time.
- **Chapter 6** discusses further issues related to inheritance reasoning, the generative capability in the architecture, and the knowledge acquisition for the architecture. Together it demonstrates that the architecture goes beyond traditional "symbolic" rule-based reasoning.
- **Chapter 7** discusses the problem of variable binding and its solution in the architecture, in order to extend its reasoning power. Some difficult issues in solving the variable binding problems are analyzed in detail.

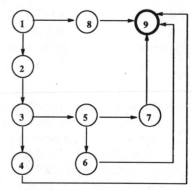

Figure 1.1. *Dependency among chapters.*

- **Chapter 8** reviews and compares related work, emphasizing the intellectual background that leads to this work. Three basic paradigms are explored: rule-based reasoning, connectionism, and case-based reasoning. It is shown that CONSYDERR is capable of taking advantage of each of these paradigms to a certain extent and avoiding some problems associated with each of them.

- **Chapter 9** summarizes the development and the discussion of the architecture, highlights the main points, and comments on the possible future research along its direction.

To facilitate the access of the book, some suggestions regarding how to get to the relevant parts of this book for people with different interests seem useful at this point. A "dependency graph" in Figure 1.1 shows the prerequisites for reading each chapter. For example, if there is an arrow from 5 to 7, Chapter 5 has to be read before Chapter 7.

For people interested in different topics, there are different ways of going through the book. Some road maps are presented in Figures 1.2 to 1.5:

- For those who are interested in accounting for commonsense reasoning data and for the common patterns embodied in it, Chapters 1, 2, 3, and 4 are the most relevant, as shown in Figure 1.2.

Figure 1.2. *Chapters regarding accounting for reasoning data.*

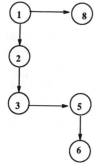

Figure 1.3. *Chapters regarding the relationship between reasoning, logic, and connectionism.*

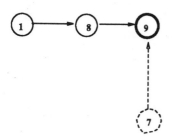

Figure 1.4. *Chapters regarding the philosophy behind this work. (The dashed line indicates a weak relation.)*

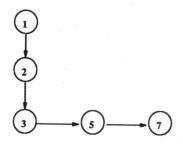

Figure 1.5. *Chapters related to connectionist models of rule-based reasoning.*

- For those whose primary interests are in the relationship between reasoning, logic, and connectionism, Figure 1.3 shows all the relevant chapters and their interdependence.
- For those who are concerned primarily with the theoretical ("philosophical") viewpoints advocated in this work but not all the technical details, Figure 1.4 shows the necessary chapters.
- Finally, for those who are only interested in connectionist models of rule-based reasoning, Chapters 1, 2, 3, 5, and 7 are relevant, as shown in Figure 1.5.

1.7 SUMMARY

In this chapter I have presented some background and a sketch of the model discussed in this book. Many important points or conclusions have been stated without much elaboration. In the rest of this book, starting with Chapter 2, I present detailed, step-by-step analyses of the issues involved and demonstrate and/or prove the aforementioned points.

CHAPTER 2 _____

Accounting for Commonsense Reasoning: A Framework with Rules and Similarities

All cases are unique, and very similar to others.
—T. S. Eliot, THE COCKTAIL PARTY

2.1 OVERVIEW

Theoretical developments require the support of real-world data. In this chapter I examine commonsense reasoning data and establish a basic framework, to facilitate the development of a computational architecture for commonsense reasoning. I start by introducing Collins' protocols and other examples, with a brief examination of the reasoning process involved in each of them (Section 2.2). I then expound on the data further to extract common characteristics and patterns from them (Section 2.3). Then the difficulties in accounting for these patterns by existing computational approaches are identified. This leads to a discussion of the brittleness problem of traditional "symbolic" AI in general (Section 2.4). Based on this discussion, a solution will be suggested and applied to the data (Section 2.5). Then some general discussions regarding rules and connectionism are presented in connection with the suggested solution (Section 2.6).

2.2 EXAMPLES OF REASONING

I will look into a set of examples of commonsense reasoning, most of which are protocols collected and analyzed by Allan Collins and his colleagues as in

Collins 1978, Collins and Michalski 1989.[1] Accounting for these examples, or more precisely accounting for common reasoning patterns in commonsense reasoning as embodied in these examples, is the starting point and the main goal of this work. In this section I present and examine briefly all the examples to be considered.

Let us examine these examples (protocols) one by one.

1. The first example shows uncertain, evidential reasoning:

Q: Do you think they might grow rice in Florida?
A: Yeah. I guess they could, if there were an adequate fresh water supply, certainly a nice, big, warm, flat area.

In this example, the person answering the question deduced an uncertain conclusion based on partial knowledge, with a piece of crucial information (i.e., the presence of fresh water) absent.

2. The second example is as follows:

Q: Is the Chaco the cattle country?
A: It is like western Texas, so in some sense I guess it's cattle country.

Here because there is no known knowledge (in other words, no applicable rules), an uncertain conclusion is drawn based on similarity with the known knowledge (or the known rules).

3. The third example is:

Q: Are there roses in England?
A: There are a lot of flowers in England. So I guess there are roses.

Here the inference is based on *property inheritance*. Namely, England *horticulture* flower; rose *is-a* flower; so England *horticulture* rose (to use the jargon of inheritance theory). The conclusion is only partially certain and is drawn because there is no information to the contrary (i.e., no *cancellation* of property inheritance).

4. The fourth example is:

Q: Is that [Llanos] where they grow coffee up there?
A: I don't think the savanna is used for growing coffee. The trouble is the savanna has a rainy season and you can't count on rain in general [for growing coffee].

[1] For matters related to protocol analyses, see, for example, Posner (1989).

This example shows a chain of reasoning: Llanos is a savanna, savanna has a rainy season, and rainy seasons do not permit coffee growing.

5. The fifth example is:

Q: Is Uruguay in the Andes Mountains?
A: It's a good guess to say that it's in the Andes Mountains because a lot of the countries [of South America] are.

Here there is no rule stating whether Uruguay is in the Andes or not. However, since most South American countries are in the Andes, the *default* is *in the Andes*. Uruguay just "inherits" this default value (though incorrectly).

6. The sixth example is:

Q: Can a goose quack?
A: No. A goose—well, it's like a duck, but it's not a duck. It can honk, but to say it can quack. No. I think its vocal cords are built differently. They have a beak and everything. But no, it can't quack.

Two patterns are present here. One is based on similarity between geese and ducks, independent of any knowledge directly associated with geese, yielding the conclusion that geese may be able to quack. Another pattern involves a rule: since geese do not have vocal cords built for quacking, they cannot quack.

7. The seventh example is:

Q: Is Florida moist?
A: The temperature is high there, so the water-holding capacity of the air is high, too. I think Florida is moist.

In this example the concepts involved are not all-or-nothing, but somehow graded (e.g., high, moist), so the conclusion must also be graded, in correspondence with the confidence values of known facts and rules.[2]

8. The eighth example is:

Q: Will high interest rates cause high inflation rates?
A: No. High interest rates will cause low money supply growth, which in turn causes low inflation rates.

---

[2] From this example on, I am no longer using Collins' protocols.

This example shows a forward chaining of rules: high interest rates will cause low money supply growth, and low money supply growth will cause low inflation rates, so high interest rates will cause low inflation rates.

9. The ninth example is:

Q: What kind of vehicles are you going to buy?
A: For carrying cargo, I have to buy a utility vehicle, but for carrying passengers, I have to buy a passenger vehicle. So I will buy a vehicle that is both a utility and a passenger vehicle. For example, a van.

This example shows the additive interaction of two rules: if carrying cargo, buy a utility vehicle; if carrying passengers, buy a passenger vehicle. The result is the combination of the two rules: something that is both a utility vehicle and a passenger vehicle.

10. The tenth example is:

Q: Do women living in that [tropical] region have short life expectancy?
A: Men living in tropical regions have short life expectancy, so women living in tropical regions probably have short life expectancy, too.

This is another case of using similarity because of the lack of direct knowledge.

11. The eleventh example is:

Q: Are all South American countries in the tropical region?
A: I think South American countries are in the tropical region, because Brazil is in the tropical region, Guyana is in the tropical region, Venezuela is in the tropical region, and so on.

Although the conclusion is incorrect, this example illustrates *bottom-up inheritance* (a form of generalization). Since there is no knowledge directly associated with the superclass *South American countries* as to whether they are in the tropical or not, subclasses are looked at, and a conclusion is drawn based on knowledge of the subclasses.

As pointed out by Collins and Michalski (1989), the task here is that of constructing a deep structural theory that is inspired by and extracted from the surface traces of the reasoning process (Chomsky 1980). One can observe from these data that (cf. Collins and Michalski 1989):

- The same patterns are present in many different situations (see, e.g., examples 2, 6, and 10).
- In these patterns, people attribute relative weights to different pieces of evidence that bear on their conclusion (as seen in many examples; see also Osherson et al. 1987).
- People are more or less certain about their conclusions, depending on the certainty of information (including rules and facts; see, e.g., examples 2 and 6).
- People have some means of encoding and applying existing knowledge (e.g., with rules) and some means of performing similarity matching when there is no directly applicable knowledge (many examples above indicate the existence of the two processes).

Judging from the analysis above, to model the examples, we need to determine the form of applying direct knowledge and the form of similarity matching. These are the necessary prerequisites for coming up with a "deep structural theory," namely a computational framework, for commonsense reasoning.

By now I have presented all the examples necessary for this study. In the next section I discuss how to account for these examples, which will lead eventually to a connectionist architecture.

2.3 PATTERNS OF REASONING

In this section I elaborate on a few points regarding the foregoing examples and the basic, recurrent *patterns* within them.

Collins and Michalski (1989) argue for the existence of *common patterns* of reasoning in their data instead of viewing them as a collection of unrelated instances of reasoning. I fully agree with this point of view. However, I find their analysis less than fully satisfactory. Moreover, in their work, there is no complete analysis of the algorithms used, no full characterization of the semantics, and no analysis of computational tractability. Therefore, I need to perform a different analysis in order to find a simple and uniform solution that can potentially be efficient computationally.

First, there is the question of the proper form of knowledge representation for applying existing, directly applicable knowledge (such as that in examples 1 and 7). Although there are many alternatives available, by all accounts, *rules* seem to be the best choice as an appropriate or even necessary form in expressing various kinds of knowledge.

Phenomenological evidence for the existence of rules in reasoning is mounting: Smith et al. (1992) present eight criteria for the existence of rules in cognition, and detailed experimental results are provided that show that the eight criteria can be satisfied by various data; thus it is argued that rules are an intrinsic part of cognition. Fodor and Pylyshyn (1988) argue that linguistic processes require systematicity which only symbol manipulation and rule-based reasoning can provide (but they ignored the possibility of implementing symbol manipulation and rule-based reasoning in connectionist models). Pinker and Prince (1988) show that phonological performance can be better modeled by utilizing rules, at least as a part of a mechanism.[3] In terms of commonsense reasoning data, the instances discussed above clearly indicate the existence of rules; for example, in the Florida case, there is undoubtedly a rule with four conditions (big area, warm area, flat area, and freshwater supply) and one conclusion (rice-growing area). Conversely, examining all the examples in Section 2.2, although there may be more than one ways for encoding some of them, all directly applied knowledge can be captured in rules rather naturally, as discussed earlier.

In addition, at the computational level, the following reasons support the use of rules:

1. Rules are the most common form of knowledge representation, used widely in all kinds of AI systems.

2. It has been argued convincingly that other knowledge representation schemes can be transformed into logic(rule)-based schemes (cf. Hayes 1977, Nilsson 1980, and Chomsky 1980).

3. Rules are precise but allow incorporation of confidence measures, uncertain knowledge, and plausible inference processes (Zadeh 1988, Pearl 1988).

4. Rules ensure modularity in representation, making the representation easy to construct and manipulate, which is important in developing flexible systems for commonsense reasoning that can incorporate new knowledge and change existing ones (although the detail of this aspect is not addressed in this work).

Having chosen rules as the form of representing direct knowledge, I need to determine the characteristics that the rule representation must possess to account for commonsense reasoning. Let us go back to a phenomenological level for this analysis. Phenomenologically, commonsense reasoning processes are *evidential*, which means that the existing knowledge, or rules, are not always deterministic, a priori, or transcendentally true. Rather, they are mostly empirical, inexact, and uncertain, based on the observations in Section 2.2 (see also Shultz et al. 1989, Pearl 1988). I further conjecture the following

---

[3]Some people may not agree with these opinions. I will not get into the controversy surrounding them.

in rule representation:

- Concepts or propositions involved in reasoning processes are often graded, that is, not all-or-nothing but fuzzy, possibilistic, or probabilistic (Dubois and Prade 1988). For example, "warm" is a fuzzy concept and there is no fixed boundary as to what is warm and what is not; similarly, the proposition "raining causes flooding" is probabilistic rather than deterministic. We can associate with each of these concepts and propositions a generic confidence measure that can be used to facilitate the reasoning process.
- As suggested by data (e.g., example 6), different pieces of evidence are weighted; that is, each of them may have more or less impact, depending on its importance or salience (see Osherson et al. 1987 for more evidence and arguments). We need a way of combining evidence from different sources with different weights, without incurring too much computational overhead (such as in probabilistic reasoning or the Dempster–Shafer calculus; cf. Pearl 1988, Shafer 1974).
- The evidential combination process is often cumulative; in other words, it "adds up" various pieces of evidence to reach a conclusion, with a confidence that is determined from the "sum" of the confidences of the different pieces of evidence. Knowing two conditions in a rule results in a larger confidence than knowing only one. For example, in the example regarding whether Florida is a rice-growing area, if we know all four conditions: warm, flat, big and freshwater supply, we can draw the conclusion with full confidence; when we know only three of the four conditions, we reach the same conclusion with less confidence. A cumulative evidential combination procedure is thus needed in rule representation.

The data above also clearly indicate the need for similarity matching (and analogy) in reasoning: in situations where there is no directly applicable knowledge (such as in examples 2 and 6), one can find similar concepts, propositions, or situations, and come up with some plausible conclusions based on their similarities. The confidence in the conclusion can also be determined based on the degree of similarity.

Phenomenologically, the comparison process that determines similarities is an intuitive, holistic and unstructured process, for the protocols and examples above do not indicate anything deliberative or analytical. This fact is also recognized by Dreyfus and Dreyfus (1987), Hinton (1990), and Smolensky (1988), based on theoretical and experimental observations (more discussion in Chapter 3). However, computationally, similarities can be implemented as rules (as in Collins and Michalski 1989) and thus only one process (rule application) is needed. Such an approach creates two problems: (1) one concept is similar to too many other concepts, and thus too many rules will have to be added into a system to capture all of these similarities; this tends to make systems for any reasonably large domain unwieldy (to say the least); (2) it will be difficult then to distinguish between strong rule-governed reasoning and mere associations based on similarities, whereas the distinction is rather clear commonsensically.

It is also evident that rule application and similarity matching are intrinsically mixed; for example, in the protocol about geese, the application of a rule regarding vocal cords is intertwined with the similarity matching with ducks. By combining the two processes, many interesting inferences can be made with relative ease. In other words, the interaction between the two processes creates interesting reasoning patterns (e.g., top-down inheritance, bottom-up inheritance, and cancellation; see Section 2.5). Therefore, it is important to study their interaction and to produce a computational model within which the interaction can be utilized.

Finally, there is evidence suggesting that reasoning processes with rules are parallel and spontaneous (see, e.g., Holland et al. 1986, Dreyfus and Dreyfus 1987). This is also the case with similarity matching (i.e., comparison of analogous knowledge; see, e.g., Waltz 1989), which should be taken into account in any theory of commonsense reasoning.

Admittedly, these examples can also be analyzed in other ways or from different perspectives. These patterns may be divided into the following categories, as in Collins and Michalski (1989):

- Derivation from mutual implication, in which particular values of different entities are related.
- Derivation from mutual dependence, in which functional relationships between two entities are exploited.
- GEN-based transformation, in which what is known about a particular class is generalized to its superclass.
- SPEC-based transformation, in which what is known about a class is specialized to a subclass.
- SIM-based transformation, in which what is known about a class is mapped to another class based on similarity.
- DIS-based transformation, in which what is known about a class is excluded from another class based on dissimilarity.

These categories can be combined in various ways.

2.4 BRITTLENESS OF RULE-BASED REASONING

In this section I characterize the difficulties in accounting for the common reasoning patterns. After looking at the above data, the first question one would ask is: Can traditional rule-based reasoning models be suitable for accounting for the reasoning above? My answer to this question is no. The past failure is a good indicator that pursuing this approach is counterproductive. There are a few obvious problems. First, similarity matching is hard to capture with traditional rule-based reasoning (as mentioned before and as argued more in Chapters 3 and 8; see also Dreyfus and Dreyfus 1987). Second, even for dealing with direct knowledge, it is difficult to capture the evidential, cumulative, and graded nature of commonsense reasoning in traditional rule-based reasoning in a computationally efficient manner within a unified framework (more details in Section 2.6).

Then the next question is: *Why* can't traditional rule-based reasoning do the job? My contention is that the inability of traditional rule-based models to account for these reasoning patterns is due to the brittleness of these models. To put it another way, the fact that these patterns exemplify various aspects of the brittleness problem makes them difficult to be accounted for by traditional rule-based models.

In fact, the term *brittleness* has been around for quite a long time, and different authors have ascribed somewhat different meanings to the word. But basically, "brittleness" suggests being easily breakable: the slightest deviation in input data from what is exactly known by a system can cause a complete breakdown of the system. Specifically, it can be qualified as the inability of a system to deal with, in a systematic way within a unified framework, the following aspects of reasoning:

- Partial information (e.g., the first example), in which not all relevant information is known but a conclusion has to be drawn.
- Uncertain or fuzzy information (e.g., the first example again), in which information is not known exactly and with absolute certainty, but a plausible conclusion has to drawn based on what is known.
- Similarity matching (e.g., the second example), in which rules describing similar but different situations are used due to the lack of directly applicable rules.
- Combinational rule interaction (e.g., the ninth example; see Chapter 6 for more details regarding this aspect), in which conclusions and conditions of multiple rules combine to produce strengthened, weakened, or entirely new results, made possible by the lack of consistency and completeness in a fragmented rule base.
- Top-down inheritance (e.g., the third example), in which information regarding superclasses is brought to bear on the subclasses.
- Bottom-up inheritance (e.g., the eleventh example), in which information regarding subclasses is brought to bear on the superclasses.
- Learning new rules, with which knowledge bases can be modified and new situations can be handled effectively.

These aspects are characteristic of commonsense reasoning. Thus the brittleness problem is more pervasive than one might think. With the exception of some extremely specialized narrow domains, it shows up in reasoning in various domains:

- The brittleness problem exists in *decision making*: when encountering a situation for which there is no rule with precisely specified conditions and decisions, a typical rule-based system cannot proceed without additional information or additional mechanisms for handling the case (cf. Hayes-Roth et al. 1983). So traditional rule-based systems are *brittle* when applied to this domain. To avoid this brittleness problem, every scenario of possible combinations of conditions and decisions needs to be analyzed and structured into a system, which is not always possible to do, especially for large problems.

- The brittleness problem exists in *diagnosis*. Diagnosis is the interpretation and classification of data (Hayes-Roth et al. 1983) and a conventional method is specifying *rules* for all possible interpretations. No matter how detailed a rule set is, there are in practice always some difficult situations or some unexpected interaction that may break down a system. For large systems, it is virtually impossible to test every possible situation, and this leads to brittle systems.

- The brittleness problem exists in *planning*. The classical planning paradigm is rule-based: a set of rules are supposed to specify all possible steps completely and to take into account all possible situations. Since rules are often insufficient in specifying situations completely, errors and dead-ends are inevitable, and we therefore need to perform search, or a trial-and-error process (although some partial remedies have been developed; Nilsson 1980, Hendler 1989). Solving the brittleness problem thus may well lead to a better, computationally more efficient planning paradigm.

The difficulty of traditional rule-based reasoning in dealing with all commonsense reasoning domains signifies the range and importance of the problem. A large number of attempts have been made to solve this problem in the past, yet it still seems far from having a satisfactory solution. It is paramount to deal more fully with this problem before we can develop truly intelligent systems capable of robust, flexible, and efficient reasoning.

Among all the aspects of the brittleness problem, learning new rules is really a separate issue and should be dealt with that way, as indicated in Chapter 1. While the remaining aspects of the problem still look like a disparate set of problems, they can all be characterized as reasoning with rules supplemented by similarity-based reasoning, as discussed next.

2.5 TOWARD A SOLUTION

In this section, the aspects of the brittleness problem are characterized as rule application plus similarity matching (the same for all the aspects). Thus a unifying framework can be established.

We need some precise definitions. Let me define rule application and similarity matching first. A **rule** is defined here to be a structure consisting a number of conditions and a conclusion; a numerical weight is associated with each condition. Whenever conditions are activated (to degrees commensurate with the confidence of the corresponding facts), the activation of the corresponding conclusion can be determined by multiplying the activation values of conditions by the weights and adding up the resulting products. This computation is commonly used (Shultz et al. 1989, Sun 1993e, Sun and Waltz 1991) and adopted here for its intuitive appeal and simplicity. The full justification is discussed in Chapter 5 and the connectionist implementation in Chapter 3.[4] I will denote a rule by $A \sim B$. (We will consider only a single condition for now.) And if A is activated, the activation of B due to A is denoted as $ACT_A * (A \rightarrow B)$, where ACT_A denotes the activation of A and $(A \rightarrow B)$ denotes the rule strength.

Similarity can be defined as a measure of the amount of overlap between the corresponding features (meanings) of the source and target concepts (a little simplistically, as a first approximation; detailed analyses and connectionist implementations appear later). I denote similarity by $A \sim B$, where B is the source and A is the target. So if A is activated (i.e., we want to know something about the concept A), the activation of B due to A (i.e., the projection from B to A) is denoted as $ACT_A * (A \sim B)$, that is, the activation of A times the similarity-matching measure between A and B.

Now I will analyze each aspect of the brittleness problem in turn, based on rules and similarities. Note that these aspects encompass all the data presented earlier.

1. When we have inexact information, the inexactness can be quantified with a confidence value, and it can be used in rules. Given a rule

$$A \rightarrow B$$

if A is activated to a degree commensurate with its confidence level, the confidence value of B can be determined by

$$ACT_B = ACT_A * (A \rightarrow B)$$

where ACT_A and ACT_B represent activations of respective concepts, $(A \rightarrow B)$ represents the weight from A to B (i.e., the numerical rule strength), and " $*$ " is multiplication.

2. When we have incomplete information (i.e., when we do not have all the requisite conditions to apply a rule), we can still deduce a conclusion, although with less confidence; for the confidence of a conclusion is determined by (vector) multiplications (i.e., inner products, a simple extension of

---

[4]The basic idea is that such a definition captures Horn clause logic and some other types of logics as special cases and also models commonsense causal reasoning. For uncertain reasoning in general, see, for example, Shultz et al. (1989), Heckerman (1986), and Hink and Woods (1987).

scalar multiplication). Suppose that we have a rule

$$ABC \rightarrow D$$

When the confidence values of A and B are given but C is unknown (zero confidence), D is inferred with less confidence than when the full confidence values of all of A, B, and C are given:

$$ACT_D = (ACT_A \ ACT_B \ ACT_C) * (ABC \rightarrow D)$$
$$= (ACT_A \ ACT_B \ 0) * (ABC \rightarrow D)$$

where $(ABC \rightarrow D)$ represents a vector of the three weights, and they are applied to the vector of the activation values of the conditions of the rule, $(ACT_A \ ACT_B \ ACT_C)$, to get the weighted sum (the inner product).

3. The similarity-matching situation (when there is no directly applicable rule) can be described as

$$A \sim B$$
$$B \rightarrow C$$

and the concept A is activated (i.e., the activation $A \neq 0$); in this case we want to know about A, but there is no rule directly applicable, besides a similarity with B. So we utilize the similarity between A and B and we have

$$ACT_B = ACT_A * (A \sim B)$$

where ACT represents the activation of the respective concept, $(A \sim B)$ represents the similarity-matching measure between A and B, and "$*$" is multiplication; furthermore, we utilize the knowledge C associated with B:

$$ACT_C = ACT_B * (B \rightarrow C) = ACT_A * (A \sim B) * (B \rightarrow C)$$

where $(B \rightarrow C)$ represents the weight (the rule strength).

4. For top-down inheritance, suppose that A is a subclass of B, A's property value is unknown, B has a property value C, and we need to know the corresponding property value of A; the situation can be described as[5]

$$A \sim B$$
$$B \rightarrow C$$

When A is activated, C is activated accordingly:

$$ACT_C = ACT_A * (A \sim B) * (B \rightarrow C)$$

In other words, C is inherited from B to A.

---

[5]The super/subclass relationship is a special case of similarity, and it is believed to be stronger than the general case (see Sun 1991a).

5. For bottom-up inheritance, suppose that B is a superclass of A, B's property value is unknown, and A has a property value D, and we want to know the corresponding property value of B^6; that is,

$$B \sim A$$
$$A \rightarrow D$$

When B is activated, D is activated accordingly (i.e., it is "inherited"):

$$ACT_D = ACT_B * (B \sim A) * (A \rightarrow D)$$

6. For cancellation of inheritance, suppose that A is a superclass (or subclass) of B, A has a property value D, and B has a property value C:

$$A \sim B$$
$$B \rightarrow C$$
$$A \rightarrow D$$

When A is activated, D should be activated more than C to "cancel" the inherited property value C.

7. In case of rule interaction, the situation can be described as

$$A \rightarrow C$$
$$B \rightarrow D$$
$$C \sim D$$

When A and B are both activated, the interaction of C and D might result in something else being strongly activated, depending on their mutual similarity (see example 9).

The foregoing description of the various patterns captures both their rigor and precision (in the sense explained in Chapter 1) and their flexibility. My main goal in this work is to develop a theory of commonsense reasoning with a proper balance and mixture of the two.

Note that the combination of rules and similarities bears some resemblance to case-based reasoning: retrieval of relevant cases, matching, and adaptation. In this case, retrieval is accomplished automatically—all existing knowledge is considered at the same time. Similarity matching for finding the best case is done in a massively parallel fashion—all cases are matched against the current one at the same time. Adaptation is done with changes in confidence values and rule interaction (which is discussed in Chapter 7). However, there are some significant differences between this framework and case-based reasoning, as will become evident along the way.

---

^{6}It is believed that bottom-up inheritance is less reliable than top-down inheritance, although they are both based on similarity. See Chapter 3.

It is useful at this point to compare this framework with Collins and Michalski's account. Collins and Michalski (1989) divide the patterns into the following categories (as explained earlier): derivation from mutual implication, derivation from mutual dependence, GEN-based transformation, SPEC-based transformation, SIM-based transformation, and DIS-based transformation. According to my analysis, the first two categories have little difference, so both can, to a large extent, be dealt with by rule application. The rest of the categories are similarity-based: generalization and specialization are special cases of similarity; therefore, they can be dealt with by similarity matching.[7]

In Collins and Michalski's work (1989), the confidence of a conclusion reached depends on a number of parameters:

- Conditional likelihood
- Degree of certainty
- Degree of typicality of a subset within a set
- Degree of similarity of one set to another
- Frequency of the referent in the domain of the descriptor
- Dominance of a subset in a set
- Multiplicity of the referent
- Multiplicity of the argument

According to my analysis, however, a smaller set of parameters can be identified: rule weights and similarity-matching measures. These two types of parameters can subsume the parameters used by Collins and Michalski: the first two—conditional likelihood and degrees of certainty—can be easily captured by rule weights; the rest can be accounted for by similarity-matching measures or a combination of rule weights and similarity measures.

Note that I do not intend to solve all the problems completely. Rather, my aim is a simple and elegant framework that can deal with some important and dominant aspects of the brittleness problem very effectively and efficiently. My contention is that this framework is conceptually simpler and computationally more efficient by combining and eliminating many parameters in Collins and Michalski's model. In other words, I have adopted a minimalist approach: making the framework as simple and as uniform as possible while capturing as wide a range of commonsense reasoning data as possible.

To summarize, a framework for commonsense reasoning has been outlined that involves both rule application and similarity matching. All the aspects of brittleness identified earlier (except learning) have been analyzed

---

[7]Dissimilarity-based inference is extremely unreliable: it is generally not the case that just because the things are different in some particular aspects, they are necessarily different in some other aspects. Therefore, this kind of inference is not considered here.

in this framework. The logical next step will be the development of a computational architecture that implements the framework. But before that, I will pause to take stock, that is, to have a brief look at what computational tools or components are available for such a purpose.

2.6 SOME REFLECTIONS ON RULES AND CONNECTIONISM

In this section some general reflections on rules and connectionism will be presented. Although this discussion is not necessarily limited to the problems discussed above, it has important bearings on further development of the solution. In a way, this discussion clears the stage for later development.

Rules (as in traditional rule-based reasoning) are efficient computational constructs for compact, modular representation and direct, efficient reasoning. They can be implemented in purely symbolic forms, such as in mathematical logic. This form has the advantage of having well-defined semantics, well-studied inference algorithms, and clearly definable axioms. However, this form lacks the inherent ability to handle inexact and incomplete information, which leads to severe brittleness. Inheritance can be handled with this form to a certain extent, but requires additional mechanisms and high computational costs. Another form is combined symbolic and numerical representation, for example, probabilistic reasoning, fuzzy logic, and the MYCIN certainty factor model, as mentioned in Chapter 1. These models deal with inexact and partial information to a certain extent, but none of them can really solve the brittleness problem since each deals only with one or two of the aspects discussed above: fuzzy logic (as in Zadeh 1988) does not deal with cumulative evidence, the probabilistic approach does not deal with graded concepts, and so on. As explained earlier, they are unwieldy for similarity matching and incapable of dealing with rule interaction (see Chapter 6). We need a more integrated approach.

Rule-based reasoning can be parallelized (e.g., for the purpose of speeding up reasoning processes to match the speed of human commonsense reasoning), but parallelization alone does not help to alleviate brittleness. Parallel rule-based systems are traditionally required to be serializable, and most of the parallel systems do nothing more than fire multiple rules at the same time when these rules do not interfere with each other. Thus there is no fundamental difference between serial and parallel rule-based systems.[8] We have to look elsewhere for the solution to the brittleness problem. I will term this view the *inadequacy of (traditional) rule-based reasoning thesis.*

Connectionism, as introduced in Chapter 1, advocates models having a large number of simple processing elements with extensive interconnections between those elements. Connectionist models are inherently massive paral-

---

[8]Massive parallelism in connectionist models, however, has a totally different flavor, as discussed in Chapter 3.

lel. They have the advantage of being robust, exhibiting generalization, graceful degradation, fault tolerance, and other useful properties. Connectionist reasoning and learning are often characterized as similarity-based: it usually involves utilizing previous similar cases, either individually or collectively in a statistical way (Rumelhart et al. 1986, Anderson and Rosenfeld 1988).

However, in its original simple form, connectionist models lack some elements necessary for high-level cognitive processes: rule application, compositionality, explanation, and so on. In other words, they do not have sufficient symbol processing capabilities (Fodor and Pylyshyn 1988, Pinker and Prince 1988). Inaccuracy results from this lack of symbolic capabilities: such models usually do not have precisely specifiable preconditions and conclusions, but only approximate mappings from input to output. I term this view the *inadequacy of simple connectionism thesis* and will elaborate on it further in Chapter 3.

Comparing rules and connectionism, we can see that they have complementary characteristics. Moreover, both have unique characteristics that are indispensable to modeling cognitive processes. Because of this complementary nature, it seems a good idea to combine the two. The question then is how to combine them so that they can supplement each other in modeling commonsense reasoning. Preferably, the two should be combined in a principled, not ad hoc way. The goal is to utilize the two respective approaches in a single unified framework.

It is important to note that I am not talking about the *forms* of rules and connectionist models, but the respective perspectives, approaches, and contents; for in terms of basic forms, they can be viewed as equivalent, as discussed in Chapter 5. Another way to see this is: both connectionist networks and rule-based systems (e.g., Prolog) are Turing equivalent, and therefore they are equivalent to each other.

It should also be cautioned that (1) most of the statements above (and some discussion in Chapter 3) are not of precise technical nature but are meant to be background intuitions that can lead to new investigations; (2) there are always some exceptions to generic statements such as those made above, which nevertheless should not be allowed to detract from the basic idea behind them; and (3) at some proper level, each paradigm can encompass almost everything else (e.g., rule-based reasoning is equivalent to any Turing-equivalent computation), but this is beside the point.

In summary, each of the two paradigms discussed above has some unique characteristics indispensable to modeling commonsense reasoning. Hence it is suggested that the two paradigms should be combined in a principled way.

2.7   SUMMARY

In this chapter I have introduced the problem of accounting for common patterns in commonsense reasoning. The Collins' protocols and other examples have been analyzed briefly. From this analysis, it has been concluded that traditional rule-based reasoning alone is not sufficient to account for the reasoning patterns embodied in these examples, and therefore other types of reasoning, mostly similarity-based reasoning, are also needed. The difficulty with traditional rule-based reasoning has been characterized as the brittleness problem. Various aspects of the brittleness problem are then characterized by two common themes: rule application and similarity matching; thus a solution has been outlined that involves both. Finally, I have stressed the need for combining rules and connectionisms in a principled way to form an integrated architecture.

The three goals for the rest of this book are:

- Accounting for the reasoning data and examples, dealing both with rule application and similarity matching and coping with the brittleness problem
- Devising a massively parallel (connectionist) architecture that carries out commonsense reasoning patterns in a natural way, by utilizing the synergy between rule application and similarity matching
- Developing and exploring various processing capabilities of such an architecture

In Chapter 3, I focus on the second goal, namely, the development of the architecture. In Chapter 4 I apply the architecture to account for the data. The third goal is addressed in Chapters 5, 6, and 7.

CHAPTER 3 _____

A Connectionist Architecture for Commonsense Reasoning

> *... Architecture,*
> *Existing in itself, and not in seeming*
> *A something it is not, surpasses them*
> *As substance shadow.*
>   —H. W. Longfellow, MICHAELANGELO

3.1 OVERVIEW

The framework proposed in Chapter 2 requires that both explicit *rule application* and fine-grained *similarity matching* (and the combinations of the two) be handled. In this chapter I develop a unified computational architecture for implementing this framework. In this development, the following questions are addressed:

- What components are needed in the computational architecture?
- How do these components interact?
- What constraints and requirements do the problems to be solved impose on the architecture?
- How can the parameters of the architecture be determined to satisfy the constraints imposed?

As will be shown in detail, the answers to these questions lead naturally to a connectionist architecture with dual representation.

In the rest of this chapter, first the need for (at least) two levels in this framework is identified; based on that, a generic connectionist architecture is outlined and gradually refined (Section 3.2). To set up structural parameters systematically, a set of constraints obtained from the characteristics of the problems to be solved (i.e., rule application, similarity matching, inheritance, etc.) are analyzed; the parameter values are then derived from those constraints (Section 3.3). Thus a complete computational architecture is specified. Some deeper theoretical questions, such as rule encoding, representational interaction, and inheritance hierarchies, are addressed in Chapters 5 and 6.

3.2   A GENERIC ARCHITECTURE

To come up with a computational architecture to implement the proposed framework, we must determine what is needed in such an architecture. In this process I take into consideration cognitive structures as we know them from related disciplines (e.g., psychology and philosophy), although I may not go very far in this regard, due to the lack of detailed understanding and consensus within these disciplines.

3.2.1   The Two Levels

Concept without intuition is empty. Intuition without concept is blind.
—E. Kant, A CRITIQUE OF PURE REASON

The first question is: What components are necessary in this framework? I present below arguments for two (or more) levels, each of which represents a qualitatively different cognitive processing capability, in models of commonsense reasoning.

Homogeneity   First, it is not satisfactory for me to have an ad hoc model composed of a set of randomly built components bearing no resemblance to any possible cognitive architecture. It seems that enough negative lessons have been learned from building AI systems by throwing together components (or subroutines) whenever a need for a particular computation arises. This tendency is aggravated by the ease with which one can write subroutine in LISP, or any other programming language for that matter. This practice results in a collection of separate, unrelated components (computer programs), each of which is designed ad hoc for a particular computation. Such a program (or a set of them) does not constitute a real theory of cognition, nor can it shed much new light on the actual cognitive processes (recall Marr's objection to programs as theories; Marr 1980).

On the other hand, connectionist models *are* homogeneous models with uniform representation (at least for most of them). However, it seems very unlikely that a fully uniform and homogeneous connectionist model can be a good model for accounting for the full spectrum of cognitive capabilities, as pointed out by many leading researchers (Pinker and Prince, 1988, Rumelhart et al. 1986, and others). The problems include, among others, the fact that one single homogeneous model does not facilitate (macro-level) functional specialization, multiple separate and simultaneous computations, or structured interaction of various functionalities, as seen in complex cognitive processes (cf. Posner 1989).[1]

So, between these two extremes (i.e., ad hoc structures and fully uniform structures), it is more desirable to have something somewhere in between: an architecture that has multiple components but is structured in a principled way, bearing (hopefully) close resemblance to cognitive structures. To achieve this end, we need to select, shape up, and combine existing models. Let us start with connectionist models, identifying their main problems and looking into ways of fixing these problems.

The Conceptual versus the Subconceptual   One particular criticism for connectionism is from Pinker and Prince (1988), against an early connectionist model for learning past-tense verb forms (Rumelhart et al. 1986). They point out that although this model exhibits interesting behaviors, it leaves much to be desired. One particularly acute problem is the lack of conceptual rules (that specify exactly the past-tense form of a particular verb), and the resulting lack of variables, bindings, and modularity, which are essential to human language capacities. This lack results in an inaccuracy in accounting for children's acquisition of past-tense forms. Specifically, the connectionist model relies on the correlational statistics (in the training data) between the forms of verb roots and their corresponding past-tense forms (statistical correlations are essential for conventional connectionist learning algorithms), which is not the case in human language acquisition. Some sort of rule representation and application, and some other high-level symbolic cognitive capabilities, are very much needed.

Another argument against homogeneous connectionist models as well as purely symbolic models is drawn from the distinction between conceptual and subconceptual processing. Smolensky in his "On the proper treatment of connectionism" (Smolensky 1988) argues for the need to model both conceptual and subconceptual processing. He points out that the processor for the conceptual level handles knowledge that possesses the following characteristics: (1) public access, (2) reliability, and (3) formality. He reaffirms the appropriateness of modeling such knowledge by symbolic processes (as numerous rationalist philosophers from Plato to Kant have done). But on the other hand, he recognizes that there are different kinds of knowledge, such

---

[1]Hidden units in a multilayer backpropagation network do develop some specialized processing capabilities, but this kind of micro-level specialization is far from macro-level functional specializations.

as skill, intuition, individual knowledge, and so on, that are not expressible in linguistic forms and do not conform to the three criteria prescribed above. It is futile to model such knowledge in symbolic forms, for the following reasons:

1. The resulting systems from the symbolic approach are often too brittle and inflexible.
2. There are major unsolvable difficulties in some important domains, such as natural language understanding, planning, and learning; "symbolic" systems used in these domains are far from comparable to human performance, despite tremendous efforts put into them.
3. "Symbolic" systems are too far removed from biological implementations in brains and thus they may not be able to capture some of the intrinsic properties.

Hence the conclusion that symbolic processing is not the sole appropriate framework seems plausible. Some of the capacities, such as skill, intuition, and individual knowledge, should be viewed as a different level in cognition, that is, the subconceptual level. The subconceptual level may be better dealt with by the connectionist approach, as argued for by many (Rumelhart et al. 1986, Anderson and Rosenfeld 1988).

From a different perspective, recognizing the inherent problems and pitfalls in "symbolic" AI, Dreyfus (1972, 1987) has repeatedly argued that symbolic AI studies only deliberative rationality (i.e., "analytical" knowledge), which is based on symbol manipulation and therefore is suitable to be modeled by the type of symbolic systems advocated in the *physical symbol hypothesis*. This approach leads to the failure of AI to account for intuition and situation-dependent reasoning, in which deliberative rationality must ultimately be rooted. Without intuition and situation-dependent reasoning, pure symbolic manipulation will not qualify as intelligence (as mentioned in Chapter 1). Dreyfus suggests that holistic, "holographic" similarity plays a large role in intuition. Due to its distributed nature, connectionist models may be better able to model intuition that symbolic AI fails to capture.

However, for connectionist models to qualify as a complete account of cognition, it is not enough to model only the subconceptual level; it is also necessary to address the conceptual level by developing symbolic capabilities in these models (as argued by Pinker and Prince 1988, as mentioned above). Along this line, some research has been conducted to explore symbolic processing capabilities in connectionist models. Among them, Touretzky and Hinton (1985) describe a connectionist production system based on distributed representation, with working memory, rule matching and selection, and rule firing mechanisms. Pollack (1988) presents a method of composing and decomposing structures with the back-propagation algorithm, demonstrating that connectionist models can exhibit some kind of compositionality (as demanded by Fodor and Pylyshyn 1988; see also Sun 1991c). Barnden (1988) describes a complex connectionist system hardwired in grid forms for performing syllogistic reasoning. Ajjanagadde and Shastri (1989) describe a connectionist system for performing backward-chaining rule-based reasoning. Sun (1989, 1992c) and Sun and Waltz (1991) model rule-based reasoning within a connectionist framework, emphasizing forward-chaining inference.

Another line of argument for the necessity of rules in connectionist models is made by Hadley (1990), in which the ease and speed with which one can learn and manipulate rules is used to show that there ought to be an explicit rule representation that can be manipulated consciously. Yet another argument is offered by Sun (1990b), in which conventional connectionist models are identified with sub/unconscious processing, due to the nature of implicit representation in conventional distributed connectionist models, and in which evidence is given for explicit, conscious rule application in cognition, in contrast to the nature of sub/unconsciousness; therefore, a conclusion is drawn that there should be separate components that can account for explicit conscious rule application in addition to conventional distributed connectionist processing.

A Proposal   In light of the foregoing arguments, the problem of modeling rules and similarities (in accordance with the previous framework) can be handled as follows: I propose that rule application should be modeled at the conceptual level by a symbolic process (which represents explicit, conceptual knowledge that is consciously accessible); and at the same time, fine-grained similarity matching should be modeled at the subconceptual level by an informal, holistic, structureless process (which may embody intuition). According to this proposal, on the one hand, there are symbolic processes, deliberative rationality (or reason), conceptual knowledge, and rules; on the other hand, there are subsymbolic processes, intuition, subconceptual knowledge, and similarity (see Figure 3.1). One advantage of this duality is that, by dividing a reasoning process into the two levels, we are able to explore the synergy between the two levels (that is, the synergy between *concepts* and *intuitions*, as summarized succinctly in the opening quote). This two-level structure and the synergy it generates may help to deal with the brittleness problem of traditional "symbolic" AI. (See the next two sections for a detailed analysis; see Chapter 4 for examples and Chapter 8 for some comparisons.)

Beside functional considerations as stated above, there is no definitive evidence as to why it has to be so. As for the actual anatomy of the brain, there is not enough known to have convincing evidence one way or the other, given the state of the art. However, this proposal seems to be a reasonable one by all accounts, in light of the arguments given above. Moreover, from the arguments above, it seems to me to be the best one in sight. One underlying hypothesis of the preceding proposal can be highlighted as

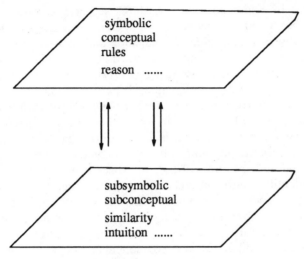

Figure 3.1. *The two levels.*

follows:

Dual-Representation Hypothesis   It is assumed in this work that cognitive processes are carried out in two distinct levels with qualitatively different processing mechanisms. Each level encodes a fairly complete set of knowledge for its processing, and the coverage of the two sets of knowledge encoded by the two levels overlaps substantially.[2]

This hypothesis is further developed and utilized later. According to the proposal, I outline in Figure 3.2 a very sketchy model of the architecture that we are aiming for.

3.2.2   Implementation of the Two Levels

Now I have to decide how each level should be implemented. This question can be reduced to the question of how the conceptual level should be implemented, since the subconceptual level has to be implemented in some types of connectionist models (based on the foregoing discussion). To determine the implementation of the conceptual level, let us examine some possible alternatives. There are hybrid systems, which are a mixture of a symbolic component (e.g., LISP code) and a connectionist component (e.g., a

---

[2]As explained earlier, the two distinct levels are the conceptual and subconceptual levels, which encode similar and comparable knowledge in different ways and utilize different processing mechanisms, so that they have qualitatively different flavors, but both can be used to tackle a task.

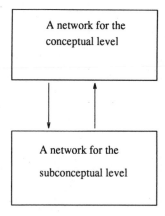

Figure 3.2. *Architecture 1.*

network). The problem with this approach is the difficulty of coupling them so as to carry out a rich two-way interaction in a massively parallel fashion. This difficulty stems from the inherent oddness of connecting two totally different components, that is, putting together a serial symbolic system with a parallel subsymbolic system.

A better approach is to implement both levels as connectionist networks. This approach allows the two levels to have similar representations and comparable structures, and allows both to work . in a massively parallel fashion, which opens the door for rich, complex, and multifaceted interaction between the two levels. It also corresponds well with the parallelism in human reasoning (Loftus and Collins 1980).

The approach may also have the advantage of being more cognitively plausible. Any conceptual level symbolic reasoning ultimately has to be carried out by a massively parallel "brainlike" structure in which each element does relatively simple processing but in which as a whole, through interaction of simple processing elements, complex, high-level reasoning can take place. Thinking in terms of low-level substrates instead of using knowledge-level (normative) analysis can help to narrow the search for plausible cognitive architectures and algorithms and reduce blind efforts in high-level modeling.[3] This is because cognitive processes are highly complex and the space of plausible architectures and algorithms, given currently available information, is too enormous to perform a brute-force search. Low-level considerations can play an important role in providing additional constraints (from low-level perspectives) with regard to what kinds of architectures are plausible. Furthermore, the *representational indeterminability conjecture* put forth by Anderson (1985) can imply an even more important role for low-level constraints, in that high-level representation may never be verified

---

[3]By no means is this to deny the need for work at the knowledge level or otherwise at a high level. What is meant is that we need to look at lower levels to complement the work at high levels.

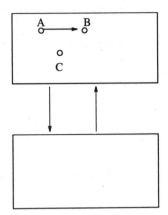

Figure 3.3. *Architecture 2. A, B, and C are concepts, and the link between A and B represents a rule A → B (e.g., A = Chaco, B = cattle-country, and C = western-Texas).*

functionally. In addition, an advantage of an architecture incorporating low-level considerations is the ease with which such an architecture can be coupled with low-level visual, sensory, and motor components. Therefore, for facilitating the interaction between the two levels and for being more cognitively realistic, I will adopt this approach.[4]

Since the network carries out reasoning at the conceptual level, the representation has to be explicit for concepts and reasoning processes to be consciously accessible and linguistically expressible. This leads directly to the idea of *local representation*. Note that local representation (or its opposite, distributed representation) is not a clearly definable concept, and usually it is taken to mean that each concept or proposition in a domain is represented by a single entity, for example, a single node in a network of nodes (cf. Feldman and Ballard 1982). Distributed representation, on the other hand, is more fine-grained, with each primitive entity (e.g., node) representing a feature (an element in the meaning) of a concept. Based on the idea of local representation, each concept forms an individual node in this network, and then rules can be implemented by, roughly speaking, links between nodes representing conditions and conclusions of a rule respectively.

For reasoning with rules, I prefer to have some sort of *computation in place* (David Waltz, personal communication), which means that there is no central data storage; reasoning does not involve indexing, retrieval, reorganization, and updating of large databases of facts; and computation is done where the data are. Those pairs of facts that are related by rules are connected together directly, and only local computation for passing on activations is needed for reasoning with rules. This approach eliminates the overhead for finding and selecting data and moving data around. In addition, this approach helps to achieve massive parallelism easily, and it is cognitively more plausible (see Minsky 1985). According to these ideas, I link up a node

---

[4] It also serves the purpose of further developing symbolic processing capabilities in connectionist models and devising new network constructs, as noted before.

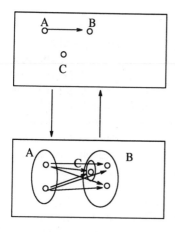

Figure 3.4. *Architecture 3. A, B, and C are concepts, and the link between A and B represents a rule A → B (e.g., A = Chaco, B = cattle-country, and C = western-Texas).*

that represents a fact in the condition of a rule with a node that represents a fact in the conclusion of the rule, as shown in Figure 3.3.

Rule encoding must also take into account the evidential, cumulative, and graded nature of commonsense reasoning (as has been discussed before). Hence a rule-encoding scheme for evidential reasoning is proposed in this work: FEL (for *"Fuzzy Evidential Logic"*), which uses only weighted sums as the main operation. It thus coincides with typical connectionist models and has an easy implementation in a connectionist network. FEL is explained in great length in Chapter 5, so that its explication (which is very long itself) will not interfere with my main line of presentation here.

At the subconceptual level, I adopt a distributed representation for carrying out similarity matching (as discussed before). Each node in the distributed representation corresponds to a feature, a fine-grained element in the meaning of a concept. Feature representation is *similarity-based*; that is, the amount of overlap between two sets of feature nodes representing two different concepts is closely related to the degree of similarity between these two concepts. The links at the subconceptual level are replications of the links at the conceptual level (which represent rules); that is, if there is a link between two nodes (or two concepts they represent) at the conceptual level, a link will be added between each node in the feature set of the first concept and each node in the feature set of the second concept (i.e., the full cross-product connection between the two feature sets), replicating diffusely the original link at the conceptual level. This is designed to capture the phenomenon of conceptual, "analytical" knowledge being incorporated into one's intuition in an inexact but flexible fashion (Dreyfus and Dreyfus 1987).[5] So we have a further refined working model, as in Figure 3.4.

---

[5]Dreyfus and Dreyfus (1987) propose a five-stage learning model, in which conceptual knowledge is assimilated into intuition through practice. The number of stages in their model may be questionable, but one point stands out: skills are acquired through obtaining conceptual knowledge and gradually turning it into intuition. See also Gelfand et al. (1989).

3.2.3   Interaction of the Two Levels

Now the question is how the conceptual level and the subconceptual level (or feature representation as a simple form of it) make contact with one another. The interaction is twofold: each concept at the first level should be connected to its corresponding features in the second level, and there should be both top-down influence—when concept nodes are activated, their feature nodes should also be activated to a certain extent; and bottom-up influence—when feature nodes are activated, the relevant concept nodes should be affected somehow. Furthermore, the interaction between the two levels can have a top-down path and a bottom-up path separately to have more flexibility. So we have a refined working model, as in Figure 3.5.

The temporal dimension of the interaction is also important. It is postulated here that the interaction between the two levels is not ever present. To see this, notice the psychological phenomenon that intuition and analytical thinking are in mutually independent processes, although they sometimes interact (see, e.g., Norman 1977, p. 590; see also Davidson and Davidson 1980 for psychobiological studies of consciousness in general). Taking this point into consideration, I will make the interaction *phasic* along the time line; that is, the two levels interact in certain time intervals in separate bottom-up and top-down phases, as a simplified way of approximating natural processes. One cycle in the interaction can be divided into three phases: the top-down phase, the settling phase, and the bottom-up phase, in which top-down flows occur only during the top-down phase and bottom-up flows occur only during the bottom-up phase. So we now have the working model shown in Figure 3.6.

I call this architecture CONSYDERR, which stands for a *"CONnectionist SYstem with Dual representation for Evidential Robust Reasoning."* I denote the conceptual level as CL (for *"Connectionist network with Local representation"*), and the subconceptual level as CD (for *"Connectionist network with Distributed representation"*).

Figure 3.5. *Architecture 4. A, B, and C are concepts, and the link between A and B represents a rule A → B (e.g., A = Chaco, B = cattle-country, and C = western-Texas).*

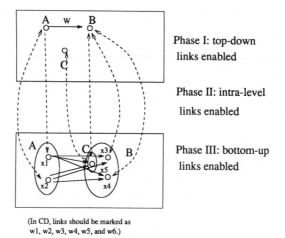

Phase I: top-down
links enabled

Phase II: intra-level
links enabled

Phase III: bottom-up
links enabled

(In CD, links should be marked as
w1, w2, w3, w4, w5, and w6.)

Figure 3.6. *Architecture 5. The top level is CL and the bottom level is CD. In the top level, a concept is represented by one node. In the bottom level, a concept is represented by a cluster of nodes. Corresponding nodes are connected via top-down and bottom-up links.*

3.2.4 Equations for the Two Levels

A set of equations for describing the computation during the three phases is as follows:

1. For the top-down phase,

$$ACT_{x_i}(t + 1) = \max_{x_i \in F_A} f(ACT_A(t))$$

where A is any node in CL that has $x_i \in F_A$, x_i is a node representing a feature in CD, t denotes the time period, ACT denotes the corresponding activation, and f is a monotonic increasing function; that is, a node in CD receives activations from the corresponding nodes in CL, and chooses the largest value.

2. For the settling phase,

$$\Delta ACT_A(t + 1) = \alpha \sum_i W_i I_i(t) - \beta ACT_A(t)$$

and

$$\Delta ACT_{x_i}(t + 1) = \mu \sum_i w_i i_i(t) - \nu ACT_{x_i}(t)$$

where W_i and w_i are link weights (which represent strengths or weights in FEL rules), and I_i and i_i are the activations of related facts (conditions or logical antecedents); that is, in this case, each node receives activations from other nodes at the same level and does a weighted sum for incrementing its own activation. α, β, μ, ν are parameters controlling the network dynamics: α and μ are rates of changes, and β and ν are decay rates.[6]

3. For the bottom-up phase,

$$ACT_B(t + 1) = \max\left(ACT_B(t), \sum_{x_i \in F_B} g\left(ACT_{x_i}(t)\right)\right)$$

where B is any node in CL, and g is a monotonic increasing function; that is, a CL node receives and sums up activations from its corresponding set of CD nodes, and chooses the result as its activation if it is greater than its original activation (in case there are negative activations, absolute values are used in comparisons).

To simplify the matter, in this work, I set $\alpha = \beta = \mu = \nu = 1$. So, derived from the equations above, the equilibrium-state equations for the settling phase are

$$ACT_A = \sum_i W_i * I_i$$

$$ACT_{x_I} = \sum_i w_i * i_i$$

where I_i's and i_i's are final converged inputs to the two nodes, respectively; these inputs are from other nodes that are linked to A and x_i; they eventually converge to some constant values, when external inputs are clamped to some nodes in the network and the network is given enough time to settle. The equilibrium equations for this architecture clearly amount to a simple weighted-sum computation. In the following discussion, I no longer make the distinction between the dynamics and the equilibrium state.

Similarly, to simplify the top-down phase equation and the bottom-up phase equation, I use a top-down weight td and a bottom-up weight bu. I simplify the top-down phase equation by setting $f(A) = td_A * A$, so that only a parameter td needs to be determined. To simplify the bottom-up phase

---

[6]The difference equations above can also be expressed as differential equations:

$$\frac{\partial ACT_A(t)}{\partial t} = \alpha \sum_i W_i I_i(t) - \beta ACT_A(t)$$

and

$$\frac{\partial ACT_{x_i}(t)}{\partial t} = \mu \sum_i w_i i_i(t) - \nu ACT_{x_i}(t)$$

As a matter of fact, it can easily be shown that at equilibrium, the two sets of equations will reach the same results.

equation, I set $g(ACT_{x_i}) = bu_B * ACT_{x_i}$, where $x_i \in F_B$; this reduces the function to one parameter, bu. So we now have the following: for the top-down phase,

$$ACT_{x_i} = \max_{x_i \in F_A} td_A * ACT_A$$

and for the bottom-up phase,

$$ACT_B = \max\left(ACT_B, \sum_{x_i \in F_B} bu_B * ACT_{x_i} \right)$$

One addition is needed in case there are multiple rules reaching the same conclusion. In such a case, each node in the architecture has one or more *sites*, each of which computes the weighted sum (or any other similar functions when needed) of the inputs. The maximum of the values computed by all the sites is taken to be the activation value of the node. This is important for combining results from different rules and for carrying out MAXs in the equations above. Sites can be added to the settling phase equations:

$$ACT_A = \max_j ACT_{A^j}$$
$$ACT_{A^j} = \sum_i W_i^j I_i^j$$

and

$$ACT_{x_l} = \max_j ACT_{x_l^j}$$
$$ACT_{x_l^j} = \sum_i w_i^j i_i^j$$

where W_i and w_i are link weights (representing strengths or weights in FEL rules), and I_i and i_i are the activation of related facts (conditions or logical antecedents); j denotes different sites. Each site is used to represent a different rule, so that activations resulting from different rules will not get mixed up.

A note about sites and the MAX operation used to combine results from sites is in order here. The idea of sites is proposed by Feldman and Ballard (1982), and is widely applied in localist models (e.g., Feldman and Ballard 1982, Shastri 1988, Sun 1989, Sun and Waltz 1991). It addresses the need for multiple modes in evidential combination: the weighted sum used within a site represents *accumulation*, and MAX used across sites represents *selection*. Although sometimes MAX is accomplished in connectionist models through a winner-take-all network, it is appropriate to include it here in a single node, because (1) this is customarily done in connectionist models as demonstrated by the work cited above; (2) the operation is no more difficult to implement than the weighted-sum operation, in digital or analog circuits, or in computer simulations; and (3) there is evidence indicating that some real neurons do perform such functions and thus it is not too farfetched to include such functions in abstract models.

3.2.5 Explanations

Applying the cycle above, first some nodes in CL get activated by external inputs (and clamped). Then the top-down phase activates (and clamps) the CD nodes corresponding to the active CL nodes. In the settling phase, links representing rules related to those activated nodes take effect in both CL and CD. Because of similarities, concepts may have overlapping CD representations, so some of the CD representations will be partially activated if a concept *similar* to them is activated in CD. Finally, in the bottom-up phase, fully or partially activated CD representations percolate up to activate the corresponding nodes in CL. The result can be read off from CL.

Notice the massive parallelism and spontaneity in the architecture specified above; activations are propagated, in a massively parallel and spontaneous fashion, from all pre-link nodes to all post-link nodes; each node receives inputs as soon as it can, and therefore fires as soon as it can, ensuring a maximum degree of parallelism in terms of rule application. For similarity matching, all similar concepts are activated (in their feature representations) immediately and simultaneously once an original concept is activated, and matched automatically with the original one (through top-down and bottom-up flows); thus the architecture is extremely efficient for similarity matching by employing the two-level structure. The parallelism and spontaneity in this architecture account well for the similar parallelism and spontaneity in human reasoning processes as identified before. The massive parallelism provides computational efficiency which no other existing models of reasoning (connectionist, rule-based, or case-based; see Chapter 8) can match.

To conclude, in this section I have developed a generic architecture dealing simultaneously with rule application and similarity matching in a massively parallel fashion. There are still some unspecified parameters in the architecture, which I discuss next.

3.3 FINE-TUNING — FROM CONSTRAINTS TO SPECIFICATIONS

In this section I consider the question of how to fine-tune (or set the values of the structural parameters in) CONSYDERR, so that the architecture will be able to perform the tasks ascribed to it earlier. In so doing, first I formally define the CONSYDERR architecture, pinning down all necessary details, and then I investigate data to be accounted for, requirements and constraints they impose, and theoretical considerations and desiderata.

3.3.1 A Formal Model

Let us formally define the CONSYDERR architecture.

Definition 3.1 A **node activation function** is a mapping between input vectors and the output value for a particular node, based on some weights and/or thresholds.

For example, weighted sums, thresholding, radial-basis functions, or even their combinations can be a node activation function (Rumelhart et al. 1986).

Definition 3.2 A **weighted-sum / MAX node activation function** is a node activation function in the form of

$$ACT_A = \max_j ACT_{A^j}$$

for node A, and

$$ACT_{A^j} = \sum_i w_i^j I_i^j$$

where ACT_{A^j} is a site activation value, w_i^j's are weights, and I_i^j's are inputs to a site.[7]

Definition 3.3 A **CL network** is a set of nodes and their connectivity: $\langle N, C \rangle$, where N is a set of nodes with weighted-sum/MAX node activation functions and C is a set of ordered pairs $\{(n_1, n_2) | n_1, n_2 \in N\}$ representing connectivity.

Definition 3.4 A **hierarchical CL network** is a CL network with a hierarchical structure, that is, acyclic connectivity.

We may want a network to be acyclic to avoid circular reasoning.

Definition 3.5 A **CD network** is a set of nodes and their connectivity: $\langle N, C \rangle$, where N is a set of nodes with weighted-sum/MAX node activation functions and C is a set of ordered pairs $\{(n_1, n_2) | n_1, n_2 \in N\}$.

This definition is identical to that of CL. The difference is in representational primitives.

Definition 3.6 A **hierarchical CD network** is a CD network with a hierarchical structure (i.e., acyclic connectivity).

---

[7]A thresholding mechanism can be added to the function but is not necessary.

Definition 3.7 A **CD network resulting from a mapping from CL** is a CD network satisfying the following condition: suppose that CL = $\langle N, C \rangle$ and CD = $\langle M, D \rangle$, and assume a one-to-many mapping $L: N \to M$; then $(m_1, m_2) \in D$ if and only if $(n_1, n_2) \in C$, $m_1 \in L(n_1)$, and $m_2 \in L(n_2)$.

This definition is meant to capture the idea regarding feature representation as discussed in Section 3.2. The question now is whether the CD network resulting from a one-to-many mapping from CL is still a hierarchical network. Generally speaking, the answer is no; but in specific applications, it can be made into a hierarchical network.[8]

Definition 3.8 **Interlevel connectivity** is the connection pattern in which a node in CL is connected to nodes in CD.

Definition 3.9 The **separate top-down and bottom-up interlevel connectivity** is the interlevel connection pattern in which for every link from a node in CL to a node in CD (top-down), there is a link going from the node in CD to the node in CL, and vice versa.

Definition 3.10 **Interlevel dynamics** is the way the interlevel connectivity is utilized, that is, the way CL and CD interact.

For example, the two levels could interact continuously, or they could interact in certain fixed time intervals, or they could interact in variable time intervals (e.g., when certain events occur).

Definition 3.11 The **phasic interaction interlevel dynamics** is as follows: using the separate top-down and bottom-up connectivity pattern, for each cycle, first the top-down connection is enabled (from CL to CD), then after an interval the connection is disabled and CL and CD work separately, and finally after both parts settle down the bottom-up connection is enabled (from CD to CL); that is:
For the top-down phase,

$$ACT_{x_i} = \max_{x_i \in F_A} td_A * ACT_A$$

For the bottom-up phase,

$$ACT_B = \max\left(ACT_B, \sum_{x_i \in F_B} bu_B * ACT_{x_i} \right)$$

---

[8]This is trivial, knowing that in CL we can always divide concept nodes into layers according to the links between them (provided that CL is hierarchical) and then can structure CD according to this layering so that only feature sets of the concepts that are at the same layer can share feature nodes and can thus overlap with each other.

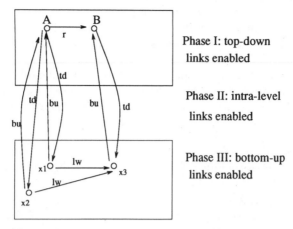

Phase I: top-down links enabled

Phase II: intra-level links enabled

Phase III: bottom-up links enabled

Figure 3.7. *Generic model. The top level is CL and the bottom level is CD. r is the link weight (the strength of a rule) in CL. lw is the link weight in CD, which diffusely replicates the CL link. Across CL and CD, bu is the bottom-up weight and td is the top-down weight. The operation of the model is divided into three phases.*

Definition 3.12 **CONSYDERR** is an architecture composed of a hierarchical CL and a hierarchical CD that is the result of a mapping from CL, with the weighted-sum/MAX node activation function, separate top-down and bottom-up interlevel connectivity, and the phasic interaction interlevel dynamics.

The reasons for the choices made here for CONSYDERR are all discussed in previous sections.

3.3.2 A Set of Constraints

In this section, in order to set up the structural parameters identified earlier, I work out a set of constraints and requirements concerning all the problems to be dealt with. From these constraints and requirements, the structural parameters are then derived.

Examining Figure 3.7, I need to specify the following: weights for links between any node in CL and any node in CD (i.e., cross-level links, both top-down and bottom-up, denoted as *td* and *bu*, respectively), and weights for links between two nodes in CD (denoted as *lw*). In contrast, links between two nodes in CL, and their associated weights (denoted as *r*), are taken as given, which represent rules.[9]

Now the question is: How should I delineate those parameters methodically, without being (or risking being accused of being) overly restrictive on the one hand or overly free-floating on the other. The approach I will take

---

[9]I explain in detail how the rule encoding works in Chapter 5.

here is: (1) first determining the range of problems to be solved, (2) studying the data and the problem characteristics and figuring out a set of quantitative constraints, and finally, (3) deriving the aforementioned parameters from those constraints.

The range of problems to be solved can be determined easily: according to the analysis in Chapter 2, the brittleness problem can be dealt with by rule application supplemented by similarity matching. **Similarity matching**, which I analyze first, has the following characteristics[10]:

- The degree of similarity from concept A to concept B[11] must depend on the amount of overlapping of the two corresponding feature sets, when everything else is equal. For example, suppose that A is a river-valley, lowland, temperate area, A' is a river-valley, lowland, tropical area, and B is a temperate lowland. Then obviously A matches B better than A' matches B.

- The degree of similarity from concept A to concept B must depend on the size of the feature set of B, when everything else is equal, because a larger feature set of B means that there are a lot of other features in B that do not match those of A. For example, supposing that B is a temperate plain and A is a temperate area, A matches B quite well. But if B' is a temperate prairie plain, A matches B' less well.

- The size of the feature set of A is not important in determining the similarity from A to B. For example, suppose that B is a temperate plain and A is a temperate area, and suppose further that A' is a temperate rainy area. The match from A to B is no less strong than the match from A' to B, because one extra feature in A does not make B''s properties more or less true for A. What is important is what gets matched about the target concept, not what does not get matched.

Another important consideration is whether similarity should be transitive, counter-transitive, or neither: that is, if A is similar to B and B is similar to C, should A be similar to C or not? There are two possibilities:

- There is something in common to all three: A, B, and C. In this case, A, B, and C are pairwise similar. So A *is* similar to C.

- There is something in common between A and B and something else in common between B and C. In this case, A is similar to B and B is similar to C, but A is *not* similar to C.

---

[10] For a general discussion of various similarity measures, see, for example, Tversky (1977), Thagard and Holyoak (1989), Sloman (1992), and Nosofsky (1986).

[11] Here similarity from A to B means that when there is no direct knowledge about the concept A that is available, concept B, which is similar to A, can be utilized to find plausible answers. Note that B is the source and A is the target. This situation can also be termed as similarity-based induction.

Therefore, similarity is neither transitive nor counter-transitive and should not be made to be either in implementation.

Similarly, $A \sim B$ is not commutative (symmetric), that is, $A \sim B \neq B \sim A$, as has been shown by Tversky (1977) as well as Grossberg (1987). Thus, similarity matching should not be made symmetric.

It should be noted that there are really no context-free universally applicable similarity measures. The considerations noted above, such as those regarding transitivity and symmetricity, are generalized from the examples (including Collins' protocols) and are suitable for some large classes of problems, including all the tasks to which I apply the measure (see Chapter 4 for details), but are not claimed to be universally correct.

Features used in similarity matching can be obtained from various sources and in various forms (as discussed with examples in Chapter 4): different kinds of features can be used for different domains and tasks; sometimes a prespecified set of features can be used for a specific reasoning task in a certain domain; sometimes features that are directly from perception or other low-level cognitive processes are used. Their exact form should not be part of the architectural specification. Using features makes potentially possible grounding reasoning processes in perceptions and other low-level primitive processes (including mapping the sensory similarity directly onto the representational similarity), and therefore interacting with internal and external environments naturally. In this way, concepts can be "defined" (at least in part) based on their similarities with related concepts, so that coherence, mutual constraints, and natural meanings of concepts are maintained in reasoning.

A parallel issue is how to deal with **rule application**, which involves the questions of how to represent rules and how to encode representation of rules in connectionist networks. For a rule in the form of $A \to B$, supposing that A has a confidence value of ACT_A and the rule has strength (or weight) r_{AB} as specified before, I want to be able to infer B with the confidence value $ACT_A * r_{AB}$ (i.e., the confidence value of the condition modulated by the confidence value of the rule). In order to keep the focus, I deal only with very simple rules here, that is, rules with one condition and one conclusion. (The justification and extension of this can be found in Chapters 5 and 7.[12])

I also need to deal with **mixed rule application** and **similarity-matching** situations. For example, in one case, supposing that $A \sim B$, $B \to C$, I want to make sure that if A is activated, then $ACT_B = ACT_A * s_{AB}$, and $ACT_C = ACT_B * r_{BC} = ACT_A * s_{AB} * r_{BC}$, where r_{AB} is the weight on the link between A and B and s_{AB} is the similarity from A to B. One instance of this is the following: Western Texas is similar to Chaco, Chaco is cattle country, so

---

[12] For a general discussion of rules in cognitive models, see, for example, Posner (1989), Buchanan and Shortliffe (1984), Newell and Simon (1972), and Klahr et al. (1989).

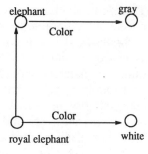

Figure 3.8. *Inheritance graph.*

western Texas is probably cattle country. Other cases include:

- $A \to B, B \sim C$
- $A \to B, B \sim C, C \to D$
- $A \to B, B \to C, C \sim D$
- $A \sim B, B \to C$
- $A \sim B, B \to C, C \to D$

and many other combinations. In all of these cases, an intuitively correct result analogous to the first case must be achieved. I do not consider cases where there are two or more successive instances of similarity matching, because I do not want similarity to propagate; that is, the fact that A is similar to B and B is similar to C does not necessarily mean that A is similar to C, according to the earlier discussion regarding transitivity.

I also need to deal with **inheritance** and **cancellation**: inferring information shared through the super-/subclass relationship. The reason for giving special consideration to this aspect, which seems to be just a mixture of rule application and similarity matching, is that inheritance and cancellation involve competition of mutually conflicting concepts (and their property values), which gives rise to some subtle requirements. (For a general discussion of this topic, see Touretzky 1985, Shastri 1988, and Yager 1989; Chapter 6 provides further details.)

I will formulate the inheritance problem as inheritance of property values. That is, an inheritance problem is expressed in an "inheritance graph," which is a directed acyclic graph in which nodes represent concepts and two types of conceptual links, *is-a* and *has-property-value*, are used to connect pairs of nodes, as in Figure 3.8.[13] This inheritance graph can be expressed as rules and similarities (and can eventually be transformed into the CONSYDERR representation). For example, Figure 3.8 can be described as

Elephants are gray, but royal elephants are white. Royal elephants are elephants.

---

[13]This is different from the problem formulation by Touretzky (1985); for details, see Chapter 6.

Here, one type of link, *has-property-value*, can be expressed as rules:

$$elephant \rightarrow color\text{-}gray$$

$$royal\text{-}elephant \rightarrow color\text{-}white$$

In such a rule, the condition of a rule is a concept node and the conclusion is a property-value pair (e.g., *color-gray*). In other words, I treat a property-value pair as an individual concept.

On the other hand, *is-a* links (the super/subclass relations, such as "royal elephants are elephants") are implemented implicitly through the containment relations in the corresponding feature sets of the two concepts; that is, the feature set of "royal elephant" is a superset of the feature set of "elephant," because "elephant" is a more general concept and hence has fewer features (less specificity) associated with it; and "royal elephant" is a subclass of "elephant" and hence contains all the features of "elephant" plus some other features that are unique to it. This is a well-known principle in philosophical logic (Leonard 1967): the larger the extension, the smaller the intension, and the extension of a concept with an intension that is a proper subset of the intension of another concept is a superset of the extension of the other concept. Here intension means the "meaning" or "definition" of a concept, or more precisely, a *finite* set of features that is common and jointly peculiar to a concept (see Leonard 1967); extension means the set of objects that are described by a concept (i.e., by the corresponding intension). Figure 3.9 shows an example inheritance graph, its description with rules and similarities, and its implementation in CONSYDERR (with rules in CL and feature set containment relations in CD).

Basically, CONSYDERR should deal with the following: inheritance of property values (top-down inheritance), percolation of property values (bottom-up inheritance), and cancellation of inheritance. Let A be a superclass of B (i.e., $A \supset B$); therefore, the feature set of A is a subset of that of B (i.e., $F_A \subset F_B$). Let us look into the following cases in detail (cf. Touretzky 1985).

- Suppose that A has a property value C and B has no specified property value. If B is activated, then C should be activated to a certain extent, from (top-down) inheritance. For example, temperate regions lie north of tropical regions in the northern hemisphere; subtropical regions constitute a subclass of temperate regions; so subtropical regions also lie north of tropical regions in the northern hemisphere.

- On the other hand, suppose that B has a property value D and A has no specified property value. If A is activated, D should be activated too, from the percolation of property values (bottom-up inheritance) from B, a subclass of A, to A. For example, given that subtropical regions lie north to tropical regions in the northern hemisphere, and that the

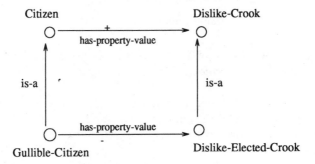

(1) Inheritance graph

Gullible-Citizen ~ Citizen
Dislike-Elected-Crook ~ Dislike-Crook

Citizen --> Dislike-Crook
Gullible-Citizen --> - Dislike-Elected-Crook

(2) Description

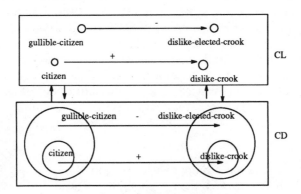

(3) Implementation

Figure 3.9. *Inheritance graph, its description, and its implementation with the two levels. In the figure, gullible-citizen* $\subset$ *citizen and* $F_{gullible\text{-}citizen} \supset F_{citizen}$. *dislike-elected-crook* $\subset$ *dislike-crook and* $F_{dislike\text{-}elected\text{-}crook} \supset F_{dislike\text{-}crook}$. *"+" represents a positive connection (with a weight 1). "−" represents a negative connection (with a weight −1). In CD, one arrow is drawn in place of pairwise connections.*

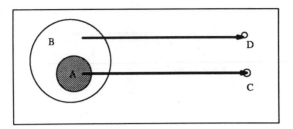

Figure 3.10. *Cancellation of inheritance case I. A ⊃ B. $F_A \subset F_B$. Only the feature sets of the respective concepts are shown here. One arrow is drawn in place of pairwise connections.*

subtropical regions are a subclass of temperate regions, when there is no information to the contrary, we can infer, with certain confidence, that temperate regions lie north to tropical regions in the northern hemisphere.

What is most difficult to deal with is the cancellation of property inheritance. I will discuss the following cases:

- As shown in Figure 3.10, A has a property value C and B has a property value $D \neq C$. If A is activated, C should win over D. For example, $A =$ a warm, flat, fertile area with ample freshwater supply, $C =$ a rice-growing area, $B =$ a warm, flat, fertile area with freshwater supply but rugged, mountainous, and $D =$ a non-rice-growing area. Given A, we should be able to deduce C, not D.
- As shown in Figure 3.11, A has a property value C and B has a property value $D \neq C$. If B is activated, D should win over C. For example, $A =$ a warm, flat, fertile area with freshwater supply, $C =$ a rice-growing area, $B =$ a warm, flat, fertile area with freshwater supply but rugged, mountainous, and $D =$ a non-rice-growing area. Given B, we should be able to deduce D instead of C.

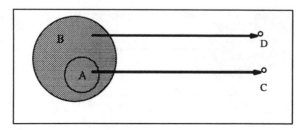

Figure 3.11. *Cancellation of inheritance case II. A ⊃ B. $F_A \subset F_B$. Only the feature sets of the respective concepts are shown here. One arrow is drawn in place of pairwise connections.*

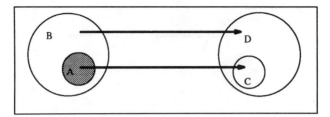

Figure 3.12. *Cancellation of inheritance case III.* $A \supset B$. $F_A \subset F_B$. $C \supset D$. $F_C \subset F_D$. *Only the feature sets of the respective concepts are shown here. One arrow is drawn in place of pairwise connections.*

- As shown in Figure 3.12, A has a property value C and B has a property value D that is a subclass of C. If A is activated, C should win over D. For example, A is a particular region (say, the south), B is a subarea of A (say, the southeast), C is a fruit-growing area, and D is an orange-growing area. So if A is given, C should have a higher confidence value than D.

- As shown in Figure 3.13, A has a property value C and B has a property value D that is a subclass of C. If B is activated, D should win over C. For example, A is a particular region (say, the south), B is a subarea of A (say, the southeast), C is a fruit-growing area, and D is an orange-growing area. So if B is given, D should have a higher confidence value than C. See also the work of Tversky and Kahneman (1983) for psychological evidence regarding this case.

I do not deal with multiple inheritance here, because it is not essential for the present purpose. (However, it is discussed in Chapter 6.)

In summary, a set of essential requirements and constraints from several major problems to be solved have been established. Based on these constraints, the structural parameters of CONSYDERR can be determined to complete the development of the architecture.

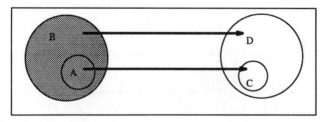

Figure 3.13. *Cancellation of inheritance case IV.* $A \supset B$. $F_A \subset F_B$. $C \supset D$. $F_C \subset F_D$. *Only the feature sets of the respective concepts are shown here. One arrow is drawn in place of pairwise connections.*

3.3.3 Specification of Parameters

The discussion above indicates that the architecture needs to deal with the problems of similarity matching, rule application, mixed similarity matching and rule application, property inheritance, property cancellation, and embedded properties. These problems impose various constraints, and these constrains can be used to derive the values of the structural parameters in the architecture, to enable the architecture to solve all the aforementioned problems. I will first state the results formally:

Theorem 3.1 CONSYDERR as defined in Section 3.1 can solve the similarity-matching problem as stated in Section 3.2, when all the structural parameters are set appropriately.

Theorem 3.2 CONSYDERR as defined in Section 3.1 can solve the rule application problem as stated in Section 3.2, when all the structural parameters are set appropriately.

Theorem 3.3 CONSYDERR as defined in Section 3.1 can solve the inheritance problem as stated in Section 3.2, when all the structural parameters are set appropriately.

These theorems state that this architecture can solve a set of problems when these problems are considered in isolation. In fact, I can prove a stronger result directly—a single system based on CONSYDERR architecture can solve them all:

Theorem 3.4 CONSYDERR can solve the similarity-matching problem, the rule application problem, and the inheritance problem, with the same set of (appropriately set) structural parameters.

Let me summarize the proof informally. The three structural parameters to be determined are the top-down weights (td), the bottom-up weights (bu), and the link weights in the CD level (lw). To determine these parameters, I utilize all the constraints available. Two cases of inheritance are analyzed first to come up with the link weights in the CD level, and two other cases of inheritance are then analyzed to determine the bottom-up weights. Based on the desiderata associated with similarity matching, I choose a simple formula. I then determine the top-down weights in relation to the similarity-matching formula and the other two parameters. Details of this derivation are given in the Appendix at the end of the chapter.

The derived parameters are as follows:

$$td_A = 1$$

$$lw_{AB} = \frac{r}{f(|F_A|)}$$

$$bu_B = \frac{1}{g(|F_B|)}$$

where f and g are monotonic increasing functions that are slower than but close to linear functions, and f is much closer to linear functions than g; $|F_i|$ denotes the size of the feature set for i; A is the CL node where the rule link originates, and B is the CL node where the rule link terminates; r is the rule strength between A and B (in CL). These parameters lead to a similarity-matching formula (which is easily obtained from the equations above)[14]:

$$(A \sim B) \approx \frac{|F_A \cap F_B|}{|F_B|}$$

The significance of this derivation lies in the fact that a connectionist architecture with a simple two-level structure can solve a wide range of representation and reasoning problems effectively and computationally efficiently in a massively parallel manner; moreover, everything here is accomplished within a unified framework. However, it is not a complete solution to all the problems within the scope; quite to the contrary, it is a solution to a subset of the most common reasoning problems that can be solved effectively and efficiently within an extremely simple computational framework. This is what connectionist models are good at: a simple and efficient architecture for a large set, but not necessarily the complete set, of important problems in a certain area (see Shastri 1988 for similar points). In view of this result, I postulate that by integrating extensional representation (at the conceptual level) and intensional representation (at the subconceptual level), and thus forming a two-level architecture, one can solve a number of problems that cannot be dealt with easily by utilizing the interaction between the two components. I believe the keys here are (1) the *intensional* representation (or

---

[14]This formula can be rewritten as

$$(A \sim B) = \frac{F_A \cdot F_B}{F_B^2}$$

where "·" refers to vector multiplication (inner products) and $F_B^2 = F_B \cdot F_B$. The latter formula is more general: each feature can be activated to a different degree. However, the former formula will be used for the sake of simplicity.

its simplest form, the feature representation), which can add much power to the extensional representation (which prevails in AI today),[15] and (2) the *synergy* between two types of representation, which enables the architecture to solve problems that neither type of representation alone can solve satisfactorily.

3.4 SUMMARY

In this chapter I have developed a computational architecture that utilizes the framework resulting from the analysis in Chapter 2 to account for the commonsense reasoning patterns. A two-level dual-representation connectionist architecture has been developed based on the dichotomy of the conceptual and the subconceptual processes. The problem of determining justifiably the structural parameters of the architecture is tackled. Quantitative constraints, requirements, and desiderata are identified to form a basis on which the connectionist architecture is fine-tuned to be fully capacitated to accomplish the task of modeling the common patterns in commonsense reasoning.

A connectionist architecture with a simple two-level structure has been shown to be able to solve a large range of representation and reasoning problems in an effective and computationally efficient way. Integrating extensional and intensional representation (and forming a two-level structure) enables the architecture to solve uniformly a number of problems that cannot be solved easily by either type of representation alone.

3.5 APPENDIX

3.5.1 Identifying Constraints

Similarity s_{AB} must satisfy all of the following requirements:

$$s_{AB} \propto |F_A \cap F_B|$$

$$s_{AB} \propto \frac{1}{|F_B|}$$

$$s_{AB} \not\propto \frac{1}{|F_A|}$$

[15]Note that the intensional representation enables meaning-oriented reasoning at a subconceptual level instead of purely syntactic symbolic manipulation.

Rules and Similarities   The following requirements must be satisfied (where $\sim$ represents similarity matching and $\rightarrow$ represents rule links):

1. $A \rightarrow B$. If A is activated, then $ACT_B = r_{AB} * ACT_A$, where r_{AB} is the weight on the link between A and B (the same below).
2. $A \sim B$, $B \rightarrow C$. If A is activated, then $ACT_B = s_{AB} * ACT_A$, and $ACT_C = r_{BC} * ACT_B$, where s_{AB} is the similarity between A and B (the same below).
3. $A \rightarrow B$, $B \sim C$. If A is activated, then $ACT_B = r_{AB} * ACT_A$, and $ACT_C = s_{BC} * ACT_B$.
4. $A \rightarrow B$, $B \rightarrow C$. If A is activated, then $ACT_B = r_{AB} * ACT_A$, and $ACT_C = r_{BC} * ACT_B$.
5. $A \rightarrow B$, $B \rightarrow C$, $C \rightarrow D$. If A is activated, then $ACT_B = r_{AB} * ACT_A$, $ACT_C = r_{BC} * ACT_B$, and $ACT_D = r_{CD} * ACT_C$.
6. $A \sim B$, $B \rightarrow C$, $C \rightarrow D$. If A is activated, then $ACT_B = s_{AB} * ACT_A$, $ACT_C = r_{BC} * ACT_B$, and $ACT_D = r_{CD} * ACT_C$.
7. $A \rightarrow B$, $B \sim C$, $C \rightarrow D$. If A is activated, then $ACT_B = r_{AB} * ACT_A$, $ACT_C = s_{BC} * ACT_B$, and $ACT_D = r_{CD} * ACT_C$.
8. $A \rightarrow B$, $B \rightarrow C$, $C \sim D$. If A is activated, then $ACT_B = r_{AB} * ACT_A$, $ACT_C = r_{BC} * ACT_B$, and $ACT_D = s_{CD} * ACT_C$.
9. $A \sim B$, $B \rightarrow C$, $C \sim D$. If A is activated, then $ACT_B = s_{AB} * ACT_A$, $ACT_C = r_{BC} * ACT_B$, and $ACT_D = s_{CD} * ACT_C$.

In all of the cases above, a correct node activation (ideally in both CL and CD, and in their final combined outcome) should result for each node involved. (I only deal with rules with a single condition here; rules with multiple conditions are just straightforward extensions of these cases, as shown in Chapter 5.)

Inheritance   Let A be a superset of B (i.e., $A \supset B$). The following cases must be handled:

1. Suppose that A has a property value C, and B has no specified property value. If B is activated, then C should be activated to a certain extent.
2. Suppose that B has a property value D, and A has no specified property value. If A is activated, D should be activated too.
3. Suppose that A has a property value C and B has a property value $D \neq C$. If A is activated, C should win over D.
4. Suppose that A has a property value C and B has a property value $D \neq C$. If B is activated, D should win over C.

5. Suppose that A has a property value C, which has a feature set F_C, and B has a property value D, which has a feature set F_D that is a subset of F_C. If A is activated, C should win over D.

6. Suppose that A has a property value C, which has a feature set F_C, and B has a property value D, which has a feature set F_D that is a subset of F_C. If B is activated, D should win over C.

Note that the exact magnitude of activation is immaterial here, since I can always use a *winner-take-all* network on top of the network that I am developing to decide which conclusion is more credible.

3.5.2 Deriving Parameters

Let us first direct attention to inheritance/cancellation. Assume in the following discussion that the weights of the rules in CL connecting a concept and its property values are all the same, that is, the maximal value 1, for the sake of simplifying the discussion. Consider the inheritance cases 3 and 4. When A is activated (but not B), I want C to be activated more strongly than D in CD. Then during the bottom-up process, these activation values will be transmitted to the corresponding concept nodes.[16] To make sure that C is activated more strongly than D, lw (weights on the links that diffusely replicate the link in CL) should be somehow inversely related to the size of the feature set of the originating concept. Assume that the original link weight is r, and the weights for links in the bottom level that replicate (diffusely) the original link is (uniformly) lw. Let A be the condition node and F_A be its feature set. Similarly, let C be the conclusion node and F_B be its feature set.

$$lw_{AC} = \frac{r}{f(|F_A|)}$$

for any A and C, where f is a monotonic increasing function, linear or otherwise. Similarly, when B is activated (but not A), I want D to be activated more strongly than C in the bottom level. Because the feature set of A is a subset of that of B (as explained before), the total activation transmitted to C or D should be related to the sizes of the respective feature sets. Otherwise, C and D will receive the same amount of activation, and therefore it will become impossible to differentiate the two. Since the total activation is equal to the size of the feature set of the originating concept times the activation transmitted along each individual link, to make sure that D is activated more strongly than C in this case, I must make f slower than

---

[16]I take the MAX of the corresponding top-level activation values and the bottom-up values, which represents the combination of the results of the concept level CL and the feature level CD.

linear, so that the total activation transmitted will be related to the size of the feature set of the originating concept.

It is easy to confirm that no matter what *bu* and *td* are used, with this *lw* function, C and D will have the right activation in both cases from the bottom-up flow. The details follow: suppose that A is activated, and let λ be the activation of the feature nodes of A due to top-down activation and *bu* be the bottom-up weight (which is the same for both C and D, because they both have only one feature node); assume that there is nothing going on in the top level, and all activations come bottom-up. Then

$$ACT_C = bu_C \sum_{F_A} lw_{AC}\lambda$$

$$= \delta|F_A|\frac{r}{f(|F_A|)}\lambda$$

$$ACT_D = bu_D \sum_{F_A} lw_{BD}\lambda$$

$$= \delta|F_A|\frac{r}{f(|F_B|)}\lambda$$

so C is activated more strongly than D. In the other case, if B is activated (with activation value λ for its feature nodes),

$$ACT_D = bu_D \sum_{F_B} lw_{BD}\lambda$$

$$= \delta|F_B|\frac{r}{f(|F_B|)}\lambda$$

$$ACT_C = bu_C \sum_{F_A} lw_{AC}\lambda$$

$$= \delta|F_A|\frac{r}{f(|F_A|)}\lambda$$

so D is activated more strongly than C, since f is slower than linear.

I am now ready to examine the inheritance cases 5 and 6, which are more complicated: because F_C is embedded in F_D (because C is a superclass of D, as explained before), it is imperative that I pick the right *bu* function that takes into account all effects, desirable or undesirable, of sizes of feature sets. Look at case 5 (Figure 3.12). In order to make C activate more strongly than D, I need to take into account the sizes of the feature sets of C and D (i.e., F_C and F_D) in determining *bu*. And *bu* should be inversely related to the size of the feature set of the node in the top level with which a particular *bu* is associated. For simplifying the discussion, assume that f is the identity function, since I can make it arbitrarily close to the identity function. Assume that all features of C and D are activated to the same degree, and F_C is embedded in F_D, or in other words, C has fewer features than D. If I use a uniform *bu* (equal to some δ), I will have an incorrect result (D being more strongly activated than C); that is,

$$
\begin{aligned}
ACT_C &= \sum_{F_C} bu_C * (\,activation\ of\ each\ node\ in\ F_C\,) \\
&= \sum_{F_C} bu_C \sum_{F_A} \lambda * lw_{AC} \\
&= |F_C| * \delta * |F_A| * \lambda * \frac{r_{AC}}{f(|F_A|)} \\
&= |F_C| * \delta * \lambda * r_{AC}
\end{aligned}
$$

where λ denotes the activations of the feature nodes of A, which are all the same;

$$
\begin{aligned}
ACT_D &= \sum_{F_D-F_C} bu_D * (\,activation\ of\ each\ node\ in\ F_D - F_C\,) \\
&\quad + \sum_{F_C} bu_D * (\,activation\ of\ each\ node\ in\ F_C\,) \\
&= \sum_{F_D-F_C} bu_D \sum_{F_A} \lambda * lw_{BD} + \sum_{F_C} bu_D \sum_{F_A} \lambda * lw_{AC} \\
&= |F_D - F_C| * \delta * |F_A| * \lambda * \frac{r_{BD}}{f(|F_B|)} + |F_C| * \delta * |F_A| * \lambda * \frac{r_{AC}}{f(|F_A|)} \\
&= \delta * \lambda * r_{AC} * |F_A| \left(|F_C| * \frac{1}{|f(F_A)|} + |F_D - F_C| * \frac{1}{f(|F_B|)} \right) \\
&= \delta * \lambda * r_{AC} \left(|F_C| + |F_A| * |F_D - F_C| * \frac{1}{|F_B|} \right)
\end{aligned}
$$

assuming that $r_{AC} = r_{BD}$. Comparing the two formulas, clearly $ACT_D > ACT_C$, which is wrong. So I cannot have a constant *bu*.

On the other hand, if I make *bu* inversely related to the size of the feature set of the CL node with which the *bu* is associated,

$$
bu_C = \frac{1}{g(|F_C|)}
$$

for all C. Then assuming that g is sufficiently close to the identity function, I have, obtained in the same way as before,

$$
\begin{aligned}
ACT_C &= \sum_{F_C} bu_C * \sum_{F_A} lw_{AC} * \lambda \\
&\approx r_{AC} * \lambda
\end{aligned}
$$

and

$$ACT_D = \sum_{F_C} bu_D * \sum_{F_A} lw_{AC} * \lambda + \sum_{F_D - F_C} bu_D * \sum_{F_A} lw_{BD} * \lambda$$

$$\approx \lambda * r_{AC} * \left(\frac{|F_C|}{|F_D|} + \frac{|F_D - F_C|}{|F_D|} \frac{|F_A|}{|F_B|} \right)$$

$$< r_{AC} * \lambda$$

Comparing C and D, I have $ACT_C > ACT_D$, which is correct.

In case 6 (Figure 3.13), I want the opposite: $ACT_D > ACT_C$. I can perform a similar analysis. In this case I would rather have as little influence from the sizes of the feature sets as possible, in contrast to the previous case. It is easy to see why: if I assume that bu is a constant (i.e., $bu = \delta$; in other words, $g(x)$ is a constant, equal to $1/\delta$), then, derived the same way as before, I have

$$ACT_C = \sum_{F_C} bu_C \sum_{F_A} \lambda * lw_{AC}$$

$$= |F_C| * \delta * |F_A| * \lambda * \frac{r_{AC}}{f(|F_A|)}$$

$$= |F_C| * \delta * \lambda * r_{AC}$$

and

$$ACT_D = \sum_{F_D} bu_D \sum_{F_B} \lambda * lw_{BD}$$

$$= |F_D| * \delta * |F_B| * \lambda * \frac{r_{BD}}{f(|F_B|)}$$

$$= \delta * \lambda * r_{AC} * |F_B| * |F_D| * \frac{1}{f(|F_B|)}$$

$$= \delta * \lambda * r_{AC} * |F_D|$$

provided that f is the identity function and $r_{AC} = r_{BD}$, where λ is the activation of the feature nodes of A, which are all the same. Comparing the two formulas, clearly $ACT_D > ACT_C$, which is correct. But if I try to have a linear function or a function faster than linear, I will not get the correct result. For example, let $g(x) = x$; that is,

$$bu_C = \frac{1}{|F_C|}$$

and

$$bu_D = \frac{1}{|F_D|}$$

I derive C and D in the same way as before:

$$ACT_C = \sum_{F_C} bu_C * \sum_{F_A} lw_{AC} * \lambda$$

$$= r_{AC} * \lambda$$

$$ACT_D = \sum_{F_D} bu_D * \sum_{F_B} lw_{BD} * \lambda$$

$$= r_{BD} * \lambda$$

Comparing C and D, I have $ACT_C = ACT_D$, which is wrong. So for this case, I must have a function g that is slower than the identity function (or slower than linear functions in general). It is easy to verify that with such a g, I will always have $ACT_D > ACT_C$.

Combining results from both cases, I conclude that g, as part of bu, has to be a function that is faster than constants (from case 5 of inheritance) but slower than linear functions (from case 6) and is sufficiently close to linear functions (an assumption used in case 5).

Although the derivation above assumes that $f(x) = x$, as I have shown before, $f(x)$ has to be slower than linear. To right the situation, I need to make $f(x)$ as close to linear as possible and much closer to linear than $g(x)$, so that the nonlinearity of $f(x)$ will not affect the relation obtained before ($ACT_C > ACT_D$ or $ACT_D > ACT_C$), given the possible ranges of $|F_A|$, $|F_B|$, $|F_C|$, and $|F_D|$. For example, I can choose $f(x) = x^{999/1000}$ and $g(x) = x^{9/10}$.

For the first two cases of inheritance, they can be handled by a mixture of rule application and similarity matching. Case 1 can be described as $B \sim A$, $A \rightarrow C$, and can be handled as mixed rule application and similarity matching. If B is activated,

$$ACT_C \approx ACT_B * s_{BA} * r_{AC}$$

Case 2 can be described as $A \sim B$, $B \rightarrow D$. If A is activated,

$$ACT_D \approx ACT_A * s_{AB} * r_{BD}$$

Let us look into similarity-matching cases. There are many different measures (cf. Tversky 1977, Posner 1989, Grossberg 1987), such as

$$s_{AB} = f_1(|F_A \cap F_B|) - f_2(|F_A - F_B|) - f_3(|F_B - F_A|)$$

namely, the contrast model (Tversky 1977). Or

$$s_{AB} = \frac{f_1(|F_A \cap F_B|)}{f_2(|F_A - F_B|) + f_3(|F_B - F_A|)}$$

namely, the ratio model (Tversky 1977). Still others include

$$S_{AB} = \frac{f_1(|F_A \cap F_B|)}{f_2(|F_A|) + f_3(|F_B|)}$$

$$S_{AB} = \frac{f_1(|F_A \cap F_B|)}{f_2(|F_A|) * f_3(|F_B|)}$$

$$S_{AB} = \frac{f_1(|F_A \cap F_B|)}{f_3(|F_B|)}$$

Many more models can be constructed. However, when I measure them against the previous desiderata, only the last one is acceptable, because it involves $|F_A \cap F_B|$ and $|F_B|$ but does not involve $|F_A|$.

Looking at the matter from a different perspective, considering implementation, I want as simple a formula as possible, not in terms of numbers of parameters or the time complexity of computation, but in terms of ease of implementing it in a connectionist fashion with a set of simple, autonomous, locally connected nodes. I want (1) all computation to be local, (2) only simple activations to be passed around, and (3) no extra nodes to be added (see Feldman 1986 for similar points). With these three criteria in mind, again only the last model can be selected (details are omitted).

In Figure 3.14, suppose that A is externally activated. The activation of A will go top-down to its feature nodes through weights td. Because of overlapping CD representations, some of the feature nodes of B are activated. Then at the bottom-up phase, the activations of the feature nodes of B go up to the node B in CL through weights $bu(= 1/g(|F_B|))$. According to

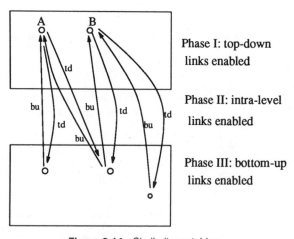

Phase I: top-down
links enabled

Phase II: intra-level
links enabled

Phase III: bottom-up
links enabled

Figure 3.14. *Similarity matching.*

what I have derived so far,

$$ACT_B = td_A * ACT_A * |F_A \cap F_B| * \frac{1}{g(|F_B|)}$$

To make the activation of B match what is obtained from a similarity matching formula, that is,

$$ACT_B = ACT_A * s_{BA} = ACT_A * \frac{|F_A \cap F_B|}{|F_B|}$$

I must choose td as

$$td_A = 1$$

for any node A in the top level, and I must choose g as close to the identity function as possible, to make $|F_A| \cap |F_B|/g(|F_A|) \approx s_{AB}$. Thus the last parameter, td, the weight for top-down transmission of activations, is determined. The requirements regarding rules and mixed rules/similarities can easily be shown to be satisfied (see Chapter 4).

CHAPTER 4 _____

Evaluations and Experiments

It is costly wisdom that is bought by experience.
—Roger Ascham, SCHOOLMASTER

4.1 OVERVIEW

In this chapter I present further evaluations and experiments that demonstrate the capability of the CONSYDERR architecture, to supplement, verify, and strengthen the earlier development and discussions of CONSYDERR. The plan for the bulk of this chapter is as follows:

- In the second section I discuss experiments in replicating the reasoning processes in the protocols and examples presented in Chapter 2.
- In the third section I present evaluations of the architecture, in terms of the generic cases discussed previously.
- In the fourth section I present experiments with systematically generated data.
- In the fifth section I discuss an important issue involved in commonsense reasoning, namely the issue of choice, focus, and context and its effect on reasoning.
- In the sixth section I describe a large-scale system GIRO for reasoning with geographical information.
- In the seventh section I discuss applications of the architecture in a number of other domains, to demonstrate the generality of the architecture.

4.2 ACCOUNTING FOR THE REASONING EXAMPLES

In this section I show how the reasoning embodied in the examples introduced in Chapter 2 can be accounted for by the CONSYDERR architecture. The basic steps taken in accounting for each of the examples are as follows: first, in each example, instances of rule application and similarity matching, as well as the ways in which these patterns are intermixed, are identified; these instances of rule application and similarity matching are described in the order as they appear in the data with the framework developed in Chapter 2; finally, the formulated patterns are translated in a straightforward way into representation in the CONSYDERR architecture; in so doing, concepts and features are identified and are inserted as nodes in the proper levels, and links are added to represent rules, with proper weights set. A methodological note is in order here: in describing different patterns, I use rules if conditions are mentioned and manipulated explicitly; I use similarity matching if none of the relevant conditions is mentioned explicitly (it is thus suggestive of a holistic process); when, in similarity matching, one concept is a superclass (or subclass) of the other, it is treated as a case of inheritance. (See, e.g., Posner 1989 regarding protocol analyses and modeling in general.)

4.2.1 The Examples Involving Rules Only

Let us look at examples 1, 4, 7, 8, and 9, all of which involve rule application but not similarity matching. CONSYDERR provides all the basic elements needed to account for these examples: specifically, to account for those rule-based inferences, CONSYDERR provides a way of encoding rules, which "implements" FEL, and of performing forward-chaining reasoning in a massively parallel fashion. Because of this massively parallel forward-chaining approach, the need to select from moment to moment a particular path to pursue and to backtrack when reaching dead ends no longer exists. Also, since this is not a study of reasoning in a particular domain, but a study of domain-independent patterns in commonsense reasoning, I will not be concerned too much with domain details.

Let us look at example 1 again:

Q: Do you think they might grow rice in Florida?
A: Yeah. I guess they could, if there were an adequate freshwater supply, certainly a nice, big, warm, flat area.

In this example, an uncertain conclusion is deduced based on partial information. The rule used is:

If an area is big, warm, flat, and has a freshwater supply, *then* it is a rice-growing area.

This can be handled by CONSYDERR: each node of CL represents a concept, including among other things "big-area," "warm-area," "flat-area," "freshwater-supply," and "rice-growing-area." The rules are represented by links between nodes:

big-area warm-area flat-area freshwater-supply → rice-growing-area

The weights on the links reflect degrees of confidence in the respective rules (or causal connections), as well as positiveness/negativeness of the rules. In this case the nodes representing the four conditions link to the node representing "rice-growing-area" at the *same* site, because they are part of the same rule, and weights for these links sum to be no more than 1 (see Chapter 5 for explanations). The reasoning process is as follows: the first three of the four conditions are activated to certain degrees (which reflect the corresponding confidence in these facts), then they send their activations to the node representing the conclusion ("rice-growing-area") and activate that node. Because of one missing condition, the activation, calculated with the weighted sum, will be less than 1 but still greater than zero. Therefore, a conclusion is reached that it *might* be a rice-growing area. Figure 4.1 depicts the entire reasoning process.

In the CD level, all the features necessary are included and are connected to the proper CL nodes. However, in this case, and in the subsequent cases involving only rule application, the CD level is not necessary for reaching the desired conclusions and it can be disregarded safely. (Therefore, details of CD are not shown in the aforementioned picture.)

The equilibrium state equation for CL is as follows:

$$ACT_E = ACT_A * w_{AE} + ACT_B * w_{BE} + ACT_C * w_{CE} + ACT_D * w_{DE}$$

where A = *big-area*, B = *warm-area*, C = *flat-area*, D = *freshwater-supply*, and E = *rice-growing-area*. In CD,

$$ACT_E = ACT_A * \frac{|F_A|}{f(|F_A|)} * \frac{|F_E|}{g(|F_E|)} * w_{AE} + ACT_B * \frac{|F_B|}{f(|F_B|)} * \frac{|F_E|}{g(|F_E|)} * w_{BE}$$

$$+ ACT_C * \frac{|F_C|}{f(|F_C|)} * \frac{|F_E|}{g(|F_E|)} * w_{CE} + ACT_D * \frac{|F_D|}{f(|F_D|)} * \frac{|F_E|}{g(|F_E|)} * w_{DE}$$

Overall,

$$ACT_E \approx ACT_A * w_{AE} + ACT_B * w_{BE} + ACT_C * w_{CE} + ACT_D * w_{DE}$$

Now let us look at example 4.

Q: Is that [Llanos] where they grow coffee up there?

A: I don't think the savanna is used for growing coffee. The trouble is the savanna has a rainy season and you can't count on rain in general [for growing coffee].

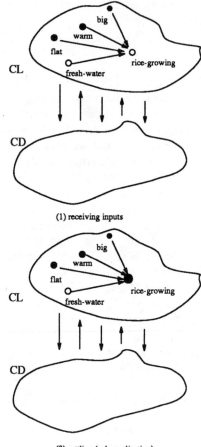

Figure 4.1. *Reasoning process for example 1.*

(1) receiving inputs

(2) settling (rule application)

This example clearly shows a chain of reasoning by applying three rules in sequence: Llanos is a savanna, a savanna has a rainy season, and rainy seasons prohibit coffee growing. This can be handled by CONSYDERR: each node in CL represents a concept, including "Llanos," "savanna," "rainy-season," "coffee-growing." The rules are represented by links between nodes:

$$Llanos \rightarrow savanna$$

$$savanna \rightarrow rainy\text{-}season$$

$$rainy\text{-}season \rightarrow \neg\, coffee\text{-}growing$$

The weights on the links reflect degrees of confidence in the implications. The reasoning process is as follows: first the node for Llanos is activated (to the maximum extent 1). Then it passes on activation to "savanna," then to "rainy-season," and finally, to "coffee-growing," all through the weighted-sum computation. The weight on the link from "rainy-season" to "coffee-growing" is negative, so the node representing coffee-growing will have a negative activation value. The conclusion is that there may not be any coffee growing in Llanos. Figure 4.2 depicts the entire process.

Now let us turn to example 7.

Q: Is Florida moist?

A: The temperature is high there, so the water-holding capacity of the air is high, too. I think Florida is moist.

There is a rule in this example:

if the temperature is high, *then* the water-holding capacity of the air is high;

and a fact:

the temperature is high in Florida.

The conclusion is that the water-holding capacity of the air is high (i.e., moist).

Again, nodes representing propositions such as "temperature-high" and "water-holding-capacity-high" are linked based on rules that relate them. The weights on the links represent the confidence of the rules. The reasoning is carried out by first activating the node representing "temperature-high" and then causing the subsequent activation of the node representing "water-holding-capacity-high." So the conclusion is that the water-holding capacity is high.

Now let us examine example 8:

Q: Will high interest rates cause high inflation rates?

A: No. High interest rates will cause low money supply growth, which in turn causes low inflation rates.

This example again shows the claiming of two rules:

High interest rates will cause low money supply growth
Low money supply growth will cause low inflation rates

The nodes in CL represent "high-interest-rate," "low-money-supply-growth," "low-inflation-rate," and other concepts. There are links from "high-interest-rate" to "low-money-supply-growth" and from "low-money-supply-growth" to "low-inflation-rate." After "high-interest rate" is activated, the activation will propagate to "low-inflation-rate" via "low-money-supply-growth." So the conclusion "low-inflation-rate" is obtained.

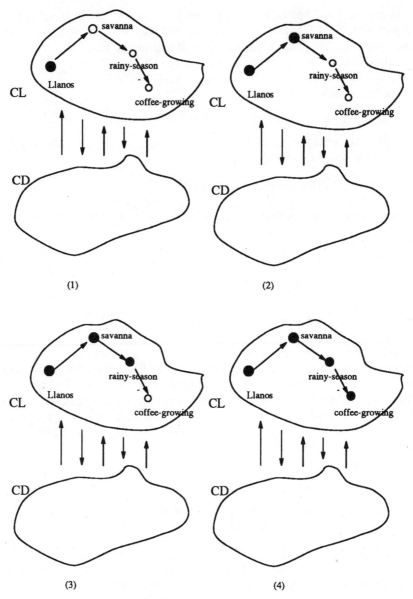

Figure 4.2. *Reasoning process for example 4 (the propagation of activation in CL).*

Finally, let us look at example 9.

Q: What kind of vehicles are you going to buy?

A: For carrying cargo, I have to buy a utility vehicle, but for carrying passengers, I have to buy a passenger vehicle. So I will buy a vehicle that is both a utility and a passenger vehicle: for example, a van.

This example uses two rules:

if carrying cargo, *then* buy a utility vehicle,

if carrying passengers, *then* buy a passenger vehicle.

Both rules are activated, given the inputs "carrying-cargo" and "carrying-passenger." So the results are both "buying-utility-vehicle" and "buying-passenger-vehicle." As explained in Chapter 6, the results from the two rules interact and the outcome is the "sum" of the two conclusions.

In CL, there are nodes representing "carry-cargo," "carry-passenger," "buy-utility-vehicle," and "buy-passenger-vehicle," and proper links representing rules between them. In CD, there are nodes representing all relevant features, which allow interaction between representations of various concepts to happen.

In these examples above, the networks based on CONSYDERR contain a large number of relevant and irrelevant nodes and links. How do we find the right links and nodes for a particular reasoning in this myriad? The answer is that the architecture is massively parallel and reasoning is spontaneous, so there is no need for searching a vast space to find a correct answer. As evident from the discussion and derivation in the previous chapters, when there are contradictory information around, the correct answer is certain to stand out amidst other related or unrelated answers. Because of the *massive parallelism* in the architecture, we can perform simple forward-chaining reasoning[1] to find all plausible answers efficiently, without the need for backtracking and without the need for somewhat awkward backward chaining as some other reasoning systems do (Hayes-Roth et al. 1983, Waterman 1985). Overall, we can see that CONSYDERR is well suited for accounting for the examples involving rule-based reasoning.

4.2.2 Examples Involving Rules and Similarities

Let us look into examples 2, 6, and 10 and see how they can be produced by the CONSYDERR architecture. These examples involve both rule application and similarity matching. In this type of reasoning, it is crucial to have a feature level. When conceptual knowledge is not enough for deducing a needed conclusion, feature similarity in the subconceptual level is explored and a plausible conclusion is reached through the interaction of the two levels.

Example 2 is as follows:

Q: Is the Chaco the cattle country?

A: It is like western Texas, so in some sense I guess it's cattle country.

---

[1]Goal components can be added to rules, so that reasoning will be more "goal-directed." See Sun and Waltz (1991) for details. Other devices similar to this are also possible.

Here, because there is no direct knowledge regarding Chaco, a plausible conclusion is drawn based on similarity with known knowledge. The knowledge is expressed in a rule:

$$western\text{-}Texas \rightarrow cattle\text{-}country$$

represented in CL by the two nodes, one for "western-Texas" and the other for "cattle-country," and the link between the two nodes. The similarity between the two areas

$$Chaco \sim western\text{-}Texas$$

is implemented through feature overlapping in CD. There are many different features, including those shared by "western-Texas" and "Chaco" such as temperate, grassland, and plain. And the CL links are diffusely replicated in CD. So the reasoning is as follows: First the node for "Chaco" is activated. In the top-down phase, the CD representation of "Chaco" will be activated and because of shared features, the CD representation of "western-Texas" is activated partially to a degree proportional to the similarity. Then in the settling phase, the links representing rules take effect in CD, so the CD representation of "cattle-country" is partially activated. Finally, in the bottom-up phase, the partially activated CD representation of "cattle-country" will percolate up to activate the node representing "cattle-country" in CL. The result, "cattle-country," can be read off from CL. (This is similar in a way to case-based reasoning as mentioned before; see, for example, Riesbeck and Schank 1989 regarding case-based reasoning; see Chapter 8 for reviews.) See Figure 4.3.

The equation combining CL and CD is as follows:

$$ACT_C = \frac{|F_A \cap F_B|}{f(|F_B|)} * \frac{|F_C|}{g(|F_C|)} * w_{BC} * ACT_A$$

where A stands for *Chaco*, B for *western-Texas*, and C for *cattle-country*. Now let us look at example 6.

Q: Can a goose quack?

A: No. A goose—well, it's like a duck, but it's not a duck. It can honk, but to say it can quack—no. I think its vocal cords are built differently. They have a beak and everything. But no, it can't quack.

This example shows two patterns. I will explain one of them here, which is based on the similarity between "goose" and "duck," and it can be described

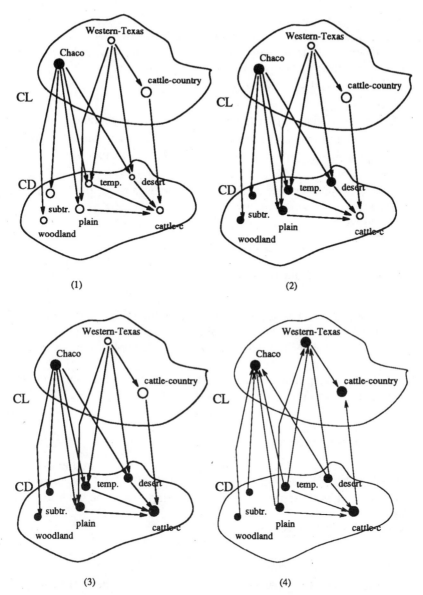

Figure 4.3. *Reasoning process for example 2: (1) receiving inputs, (2) top-down, (3) settling (rule application), and (4) bottom-up.*

by the following:

$$goose \sim duck$$
$$duck \rightarrow quack$$

All the concepts involved, "goose," "duck," and "quack," are represented by nodes in CL and are connected to their corresponding features in CD. Therefore, when "goose" is activated, the activation will be passed to "quack" through similarity with "duck," in the same way as before. So we conclude (wrongly, as in the data) that a goose can quack.

Now let us look at example 10.

Q: Do women living in that region have short life expectancy?

A: Men living in tropical regions have a short life expectancy, so probably women living in tropical regions have a short life expectancy, too.

This example is another case of using similarity because of the lack of direct knowledge. It can be described by

$$women\text{-}in\text{-}tropical \sim men\text{-}in\text{-}tropical$$

$$men\text{-}in\text{-}tropical \rightarrow short\text{-}life$$

Each concept involved is represented by a node in CL and a number of (shared) features in CD. Therefore, when "women-in-tropical" is activated, "short-life" will be activated partially, through rule application and similarity matching carried out in CD.

Overall, the system handles mixed rule application and similarity matching well, through the interaction between the two levels of CONSYDERR.

4.2.3 Examples Involving Inheritance

Let us now look into examples 3, 5, and 11. These examples involve inheritance, which is a combination of rule application and similarity matching but is dealt with separately because it imposes some additional constraints.

Example 3 is as follows:

Q: Are there roses in England?

A: There are a lot of flowers in England. So I guess there are roses.

The reasoning based on property inheritance is as follows:

England *horticulture*[2] flower; rose *is-a* flower; so England *horticulture* rose.

---

[2]*Horticulture* here is a property, but can be viewed as a link like *is-a*. See Chapter 6 for detailed explanations. The same goes for other properties.

It can be described by rules and similarities[3]:

$$England \rightarrow h\text{-}flower$$
$$h\text{-}flower \sim h\text{-}rose$$

Therefore, in the same way as before, this can be implemented in CONSY-DERR with the two-level dual representation and their interaction. See Figure 4.4.

Example 5 is as follows:

Q: Is Uruguay in the Andes Mountains?

A: It's a good guess to say that it's in the Andes Mountains because a lot of the countries (of South America) are.

Formally, according to inheritance theory,

South-American-country *mountain* Andes; Uruguay *is-a* South-American-country; so Uruguay *mountain* Andes.

Describing it with rules and similarities[4]:

$$Uruguay \sim South\text{-}American\text{-}country$$
$$South\text{-}American\text{-}country \rightarrow in\text{-}Andes$$

Therefore, in the same way as before, this can be implemented in CONSY-DERR through the interaction between the two levels.

Example 11 is as follows:

Q: Are all South American countries in the tropical region?

A: I think South American countries are in the tropical region, because Brazil is in the tropical region, Guyana is in the tropical region, Venezuela is in the tropical region, and so on.

This example illustrates bottom-up inheritance—a form of generalization. According to inheritance theory,

Guyana *is-a* South-American-country; Guyana *weather* tropical; Brazil *is-a* South-American-country; Brazil *weather* tropical; Venezuela *is-a* South-American-country; Venezuela *weather* tropical; so South-American-country *weather* tropical.

---

[3]Although it is not shown explicitly in the following formalism, in this case we actually have $h\text{-}flower \supset h\text{-}rose$ and $F_{h-flower} \subset F_{h-rose}$.

[4]In this case, we have *South-American-country* $\supset$ *Uruguay* and $F_{South\text{-}American\text{-}country} \subset F_{Uruguay}$.

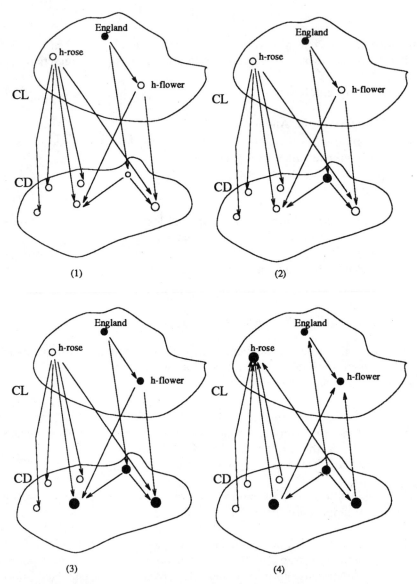

Figure 4.4. *Reasoning process for example 3: (1) receiving inputs, (2) top-down, (3) settling (rule application), and (4) bottom-up.*

Describing the knowledge with rules and similarities:

$$South\text{-}American\text{-}country \sim Brazil$$

$$Brazil \to w\text{-}tropical$$

$$South\text{-}American\text{-}country \sim Guyana$$

$$Guyana \to w\text{-}tropical$$

$$South\text{-}American\text{-}country \sim Venezuela$$

$$Venezuela \to w\text{-}tropical$$

Therefore, in the same way as before, the conclusion is drawn that "South-American-country" is in the tropical region. This can be implemented in CONSYDERR with two-level dual representation. Overall, CONSYDERR deals successfully with this type of reasoning. (See also Chapter 6 for more discussions of inheritance in CONSYDERR.)

4.3 EVALUATIONS OF THE ARCHITECTURE

I shall evaluate the architecture in terms of (1) the aspects of the brittleness problem, (2) the constraints and requirements for similarity matching, rule application, and inheritance, and (3) psychological evidence for similarity matching.

4.3.1 Aspects of the Brittleness Problem

I will sketch below how CONSYDERR handles the various aspects of the brittleness problem as identified in Chapter 2. After all, the goal of CONSY-DERR is to deal with these aspects.

1. Given inexact information for a concept A, the node representing the concept can be partially activated, to a degree commensurate with its certainty. Suppose that there is a rule in the form of

$$A \to B$$

and the weight on the link between A and B is w_{AB}. According to the CONSYDERR equations, the activation of B due to the rule application is as follows: From CD,

$$ACT_B = ACT_A * \frac{|F_B|}{g(|F_B|)} * \frac{|F_A|}{f(|F_A|)} * w_{AB}$$

From CL,

$$ACT_B = ACT_A * w_{AB}$$

So overall,

$$ACT_B \approx ACT_A * w_{AB}$$

That is,

$$ACT_B = ACT_A * (A \rightarrow B)$$

as prescribed in Chapter 2.

When there are multiple conditions in the rule, such as

$$ABC \rightarrow D$$

with weights w_{AD}, w_{BD}, and w_{CD}, the activation of the conclusion D is

$$ACT_D \approx ACT_A * w_{AD} + ACT_B * w_{BD} + ACT_D * w_{CD}$$

or

$$ACT_D = (ACT_A \ ACT_B \ ACT_C) * (ABC \rightarrow D)$$

given the partial activations (inexact and uncertain information) of A, B, and C, namely, ACT_A, ACT_B, and ACT_C.

2. When the given information is incomplete (i.e., not all conditions in a rule are known), the weighted-sum computation above can still be applied to reach a (weaker) conclusion. Suppose that

$$ABC \rightarrow D$$

with weights w_{AD}, w_{BD}, and w_{CD}, and B and C are known (i.e., $ACT_B = 1$ and $ACT_C = 1$), but A is unknown ($ACT_A = 0$). The conclusion D can still be reached, according to the CONSYDERR equations:

$$\begin{aligned} ACT_D &\approx ACT_A * w_{AD} + ACT_B * w_{BD} + ACT_D * w_{CD} \\ &\approx w_{BD} * ACT_B + w_{CD} * ACT_D \\ &\approx w_{BD} + w_{CD} \end{aligned}$$

That is,

$$\begin{aligned} ACT_D &= (ACT_A \ ACT_B \ ACT_C) * (ABC \rightarrow D) \\ &= (0\,1\,1) * (ABC \rightarrow D) \end{aligned}$$

The situation in which the known conditions (such as B and C above) are inexact can be handled similarly, combining this method with the previous.

3. When there is no rule applicable, similarity matching is utilized to reach a conclusion. Given the concept A, and the knowledge

$$A \sim B$$
$$B \rightarrow C$$

That is, A and B share features (in CD) and there is a rule from B to C (in CL and CD). Apply the equations in Chapter 3: From CD,[5]

$$ACT_B = ACT_A * \frac{|F_A \cap F_B|}{g(|F_A|)}$$

$$\approx ACT_A * s_{AB}$$

$$ACT_C = ACT_B * \frac{|F_B|}{f(|F_B|)} * w_{BC}$$

That is,

$$ACT_C \approx ACT_B * w_{BC} \approx ACT_A * s_{AB} * w_{BC}$$

so

$$ACT_C = ACT_A * (A \sim B) * (B \rightarrow C)$$

Other cases can be handled similarly, such as when A is similar to a number of other concepts and those concepts are linked to many other concepts via rules, which can be handled by straightforward extensions of this method, or when the rules used have a number of other (unknown) conditions, which can be handled by incorporating the previous method.

4. Top-down inheritance can be described as

$$A \sim B$$
$$B \rightarrow C$$

in which A is a subclass of B (so $F_A \supset F_B$), and C is a property value (such as *color-red*) of B. It is obvious that this is a special case of case 3, so it can be handled in exactly the same way. I should note, however, that in this case, $s_{AB} = |F_A \cap F_B|/g(|F_B|) = |F_B|/g(|F_B|) \approx 1$, because $F_A \supset F_B$. And if we assume that $w_{BC} = 1$ (the same for all property-value rules), the resulting activation of C (representing the confidence that A has property value C) is

$$ACT_C \approx ACT_B * w_{BC} \approx ACT_A * s_{AB} * w_{BC} \approx ACT_A$$

so

$$ACT_C = ACT_A * (A \sim B) * (B \rightarrow C) = ACT_A$$

---

[5]CL can be ignored, because node activation in CL are less strong than node activations in CD since slower-than-linear functions are used in CD.

5. The bottom-up inheritance is similar:

$$B \sim A$$
$$A \rightarrow D$$

in which, however, different from the preceding case, B is a superclass of A (so $F_B \subset F_A$), and D is a property value of A. This is also a special case of case 3, so it can be handled in the same way. In this case, we have $s_{BA} = |F_B \cap F_A|/g(|F_A|) \approx |F_B|/|F_A| < 1$, because $F_B \subset F_A$. If we assume that $w_{AD} = 1$ (the same for all property-value rules),

$$ACT_D \approx ACT_A * w_{AD} \approx ACT_B * s_{BA} * w_{AD} < ACT_B$$

which represents the partial confidence based on the evidence from the subclass B. So

$$ACT_D = ACT_B * (B \sim A) * (A \rightarrow D) < ACT_B$$

6. Cancellation of top-down inheritance is as follows: suppose that A is a subclass of B, A has a property value D, and B has a property value $C \neq D$ (assuming that C and D have one feature node each). Then

$$A \sim B$$
$$B \rightarrow C$$
$$A \rightarrow D$$

When A is activated, D should be activated more than C to cancel the inherited property value C. Assume that $w_{AD} = w_{BC} = 1$. From CD,

$$ACT_D = ACT_A * |F_A| \frac{w_{AD}}{f(|F_A|)}$$

$$= ACT_A * \frac{|F_A|}{f(|F_A|)}$$

$$ACT_C = ACT_A * |F_A \cap F_B| \frac{w_{BC}}{f(|F_B|)}$$

$$= ACT_A * w_{BC} * \frac{|F_A \cap F_B|}{f(|F_B|)}$$

$$= ACT_A * w_{BC} * \frac{|F_B|}{f(|F_B|)}$$

$$= ACT_A * \frac{|F_B|}{f(|F_B|)}$$

where $F_A \supset F_B$ and $|F_A| > |F_B|$. Since f is a monotonic increasing function, slower than linear, $ACT_D > ACT_C$ (by a small margin).

7. Cancellation of bottom-up inheritance is similar: suppose that B is a superclass of A, B has a property value C, and A has a property value $D \neq C$. Then

$$B \sim A$$
$$A \to D$$
$$B \to C$$

When B is activated, C should be activated more strongly than D. Assuming again that $w_{AD} = w_{BC} = 1$, from CD,

$$ACT_C = ACT_B * |F_B| \frac{w_{BC}}{f(|F_B|)}$$

$$= ACT_B * \frac{|F_B|}{f(|F_B|)}$$

$$ACT_D = ACT_B * |F_B \cap F_A| \frac{w_{AD}}{f(|F_A|)}$$

$$= ACT_B * w_{AD} * \frac{|F_B \cap F_A|}{f(|F_A|)}$$

$$= ACT_B * w_{AD} * \frac{|F_B|}{f(|F_A|)}$$

$$= ACT_B * \frac{|F_B|}{f(|F_A|)}$$

where $F_B \subset F_A$ and $|F_B| < |F_A|$, and f is slower than but close to linear. So we have $ACT_C > ACT_D$.

8. Rule interaction can be described as

$$A \to C$$
$$B \to D$$
$$C \sim D$$

When A and B are both activated, the interaction C and D might result in something else being strongly activated. Assuming that $F_E = F_C \cup F_D$ and $F_C \cap F_D = \varnothing$, we have in CD

$$ACT_E = |F_E - F_D| \frac{1}{g(|F_E|)} ACT_C + |F_D| \frac{1}{g(|F_E|)} ACT_D$$

if $ACT_C = ACT_D$,

$$ACT_E = ACT_D(|F_E - F_D| + |F_D|)\frac{1}{g(|F_E|)}$$

$$= ACT_D * |F_E| * \frac{1}{g(|F_E|)}$$

So we have $ACT_E > ACT_D$ and $ACT_E > ACT_C$. Other cases can be dealt with similarly, such as when $E = C \cap D$ or when $E = C - D$.

4.3.2 Constraints and Requirements

Let us see how CONSYDERR satisfies other constraints and requirements, including similarity matching, rule application, and inheritance.

Similarity Matching As discussed in Chapter 3, similarity matching should have a number of characteristics. The similarity-matching formula used in CONSYDERR can satisfy these constraints: that is,

$$A \sim B \approx \frac{|F_A \cap F_B|}{|F_B|}$$

- Depends on the amount of overlapping of the two corresponding feature sets
- Depends on the size of the feature set of B
- Does not depend on the size of the feature set of A

Note that here *similarity* refers specifically to *reasoning based on similarity matching* (or *similarity-based induction*), not generic similarity.

Another consideration is that similarity matching is neither transitive nor counter-transitive. By the same token, similarities are not symmetric. The similarity-matching formula in CONSYDERR fits these requirements also.

Rule Application As mentioned in Chapter 3, CONSYDERR should deal correctly with the following cases of rule application and mixed rule application/similarity matching.

1. For $A \rightarrow B$, $B \sim C$, if A is activated, then in CD

$$ACT_C = \sum_{F_B \cap F_C} \frac{1}{g(F_C)} \sum_{F_A} ACT_A \frac{w_{AB}}{f(F_A)}$$

$$= \frac{|F_B \cap F_C|}{g(F_C)} \frac{|F_A|}{f(F_A)} * w_{AB} * ACT_A$$

$$\approx ACT_A * w_{AB} * s_{BC}$$

that is,

$$ACT_C = ACT_A * (A \rightarrow B) * (B \sim C)$$

2. For $A \rightarrow B$, $B \rightarrow C$, if A is activated, then according to the CONSYDERR equations,

$$ACT_C = \sum_{F_A} ACT_A \frac{w_{AB}}{f(F_A)} \sum_{F_B} \frac{w_{BC}}{f(F_B)} \sum_{F_C} \frac{1}{g(F_C)}$$
$$\approx ACT_A * w_{AB} * w_{BC}$$

that is,

$$ACT_C = ACT_A * (A \rightarrow B) * (B \rightarrow C)$$

3. For $A \rightarrow B$, $B \rightarrow C$, $C \rightarrow D$, if A is activated, then according to the CONSYDERR equations,

$$ACT_D = \sum_{F_A} ACT_A \frac{w_{AB}}{f(F_A)} \sum_{F_B} \frac{w_{BC}}{f(F_B)} \sum_{F_C} \frac{w_{CD}}{f(F_C)} \sum_{F_D} \frac{1}{g(F_D)}$$
$$\approx ACT_A * w_{AB} * w_{BC} * w_{CD}$$

that is,

$$ACT_C = ACT_A * (A \rightarrow B) * (B \rightarrow C) * (C \rightarrow D)$$

4. For $A \sim B$, $B \rightarrow C$, $C \rightarrow D$, if A is activated, when

$$ACT_D = \sum_{F_A \cap F_B} ACT_A \frac{w_{BC}}{f(F_B)} \sum_{F_C} \frac{w_{CD}}{f(F_C)} \sum_{F_D} \frac{1}{g(F_D)}$$
$$\approx ACT_A * s_{AB} * w_{BC} * w_{CD}$$

that is,

$$ACT_D = ACT_A * (A \sim B) * (B \rightarrow C) * (C \rightarrow D)$$

5. For $A \rightarrow B$, $B \sim C$, $C \rightarrow D$, if A is activated, then

$$ACT_D = \sum_{F_A} ACT_A \frac{w_{AB}}{f(F_A)} \sum_{F_B \cap F_C} \frac{w_{CD}}{f(F_B)} \sum_{F_D} \frac{1}{g(F_D)}$$
$$\approx ACT_A * w_{AB} * s_{BC} * w_{CD}$$

that is,

$$ACT_D = ACT_A * (A \rightarrow B) * (B \sim C) * (C \rightarrow D)$$

6. For $A \rightarrow B$, $B \rightarrow C$, $C \sim D$, if A is activated, then

$$ACT_D = \sum_{F_A} ACT_A \frac{w_{AB}}{f(F_A)} \sum_{F_B} \frac{w_{BC}}{f(F_B)} \sum_{F_C \cap F_D} \frac{1}{g(F_D)}$$
$$\approx ACT_A * w_{AB} * w_{BC} * s_{CD}$$

that is,

$$ACT_D = ACT_A * (A \rightarrow B) * (B \rightarrow C) * (C \sim D)$$

7. For $A \sim B$, $B \rightarrow C$, $C \sim D$, if A is activated, then

$$ACT_D = \sum_{F_A \cap F_B} ACT_A \frac{w_{BC}}{f(F_B)} \sum_{F_C \cap F_D} \frac{1}{g(F_D)}$$
$$\approx ACT_A * s_{AB} * w_{BC} * s_{CD}$$

that is,

$$ACT_D = ACT_A * (A \sim B) * (B \rightarrow C) * (C \sim D)$$

Note that although I only discuss rules with a single condition, rules with multiple conditions are straightforward extensions of these cases (see Chapter 5).

Inheritance   In addition to the cases of inheritance discussed earlier, there are the following two cases of inheritance cancellation (Touretzky 1985) that are more complicated but need to be handled correctly. Assume that A is a superclass of B, and thus $F_A \subset F_B$. Suppose that A has a property value C and B has a property value D that is a subclass of C (and therefore, $F_D \supset F_C$). If A is activated, C should win over D.

In CONSYDERR, where A is activated, from CD,

$$ACT_C = |F_C| * \frac{1}{g(|F_C|)} * |F_A| * \frac{1}{f(|F_A|)} * ACT_A$$
$$\approx ACT_A$$

and

$$ACT_D = ACT_A * \left(\frac{|F_C|}{g(|F_D|)} + \frac{|F_D - F_C|}{g(|F_D|)} \frac{|F_A|}{f(|F_B|)} \right)$$

$$< ACT_A$$

because $|F_C|/g(|F_D|) < 1$, $|F_D - F_C|/g(|F_D|) < 1$, and $|F_A|/f(|F_B|) < 1$. So $ACT_C > ACT_D$.

In the other case, suppose that A has a property value C and B has a property value D that is a subclass of C (and therefore, $F_D \supset F_C$). If B is activated, D should win over C. In CONSYDERR, from CD,

$$ACT_C = |F_C| * \frac{1}{g(|F_C|)} * |F_B| * ACT_B * \frac{1}{f(|F_B|)}$$

and

$$ACT_D = |F_D| * \frac{1}{g(|F_D|)} * |F_B| * ACT_B * \frac{1}{f(|F_B|)}$$

Since $|F_D| > |F_C|$, we have $ACT_D > ACT_C$.

4.3.3 Psychological Evidence for Similarity Matching

There are some existing psychological experimental data that can be used to support the formula used in CONSYDERR for similarity matching. The closest counterpart of such similarity matching in the psychological literature is *feature-based induction* (which I would rather refer to as similarity-based induction or simply similarity matching). The psychological data discussed below are mostly from work of Osherson et al. (1990) (and also Sloman 1992). The discussion of these data will be at a qualitative level, without quantitative data fitting and equations. One normative assumption that I will utilize is that concepts have comparable and equally rich feature representations; in particular, a subclass has all the features of its superclasses plus some features unique to it (note that this is not necessarily true, psychologically).

Let us look into several cases, one by one.

1. *Source–Target Similarity.* Psychological data show that the strength of a similarity-matching argument (i.e., a similarity-matching measure) depends on the extent to which the concepts in the source are similar to the concepts in the target. Here, for $A \sim B$, the source concept refers to B and the target concept refers to A. According to CONSYDERR, the similarity between A and B is related to the size of the intersection of the two respective feature sets and is inversely related to the size of the feature set of the source

concept. This case is readily explained by the formula used in CONSY-DERR: the more similar the target concept is to the source concept, the more overlapping there tends to be between the source and the target feature sets; with more overlapping, the conclusion is stronger. See the equations concerning similarity matching in Chapter 3.

2. *Source Diversity*. Psychological data also show that the less similar sources are to each other, the stronger the similarity-matching argument (measure) tends to be. In CONSYDERR, this is due to the fact that the more diverse the sources are, the more support the sources will lend to the target, because more features are involved in rules leading to the conclusion (provided that all the sources lead to the same conclusion and their evidential supports are added up).

3. *Source Typicality*. When the source concepts are subclasses of the target concept, the more typical the source concepts are of the target concept, the stronger the argument is. This is because the more typical the source concepts are of the target concept, the more alike their feature sets tend to be. According to CONSYDERR, the strength of an argument is related to the size of the intersection of the two respective feature sets and is inversely related to the size of the feature set of the source concept. In this case, the intersection of the two feature sets is the same as the feature set of the target concept (because it is a superclass) and the size of the feature set of the source concept is inversely related to its typicality: the more typical the source concept is, the fewer extraneous features it has. Therefore, the more typical the source concepts are, the stronger the argument is.

4. *Target Specificity*. When source concepts are properly included in the target concept (as a subclass), the more specific the target concept is, the stronger the argument is. This psychological phenomenon can be explained in CONSYDERR by the fact that the more specific the target is, the more overlap there is between the source and the target feature sets, since source concepts are subclasses of the target concept (and therefore the intersection of the source and target feature sets are the same as the feature set of the target concept) and the similarity does not depend on the size of the target feature set.

5. *Source–Target Asymmetry*. Switching source and target concepts can result in different argument strengths (i.e., asymmetric arguments). This psychological phenomenon can easily be explained by the similarity-matching formula used in CONSYDERR: it is asymmetric in that it depends on the size of the source feature set but not the target feature set.

6. *Source–Target Identity*. Arguments with identical sources and targets are perfectly strong. This phenomenon matches perfectly the similarity-matching formula used in CONSYDERR.

7. *Source Monotonicity*. Adding a new source concept that is chosen from the lowest-level category that includes both the old source concepts and the target concept will increase the argument strength. According to CONSY-

DERR, adding new sources always tends to increase the argument strength because, with the added concept, there will be more evidential support for a particular conclusion (provided that all the source concepts lead to the same conclusion).

8. *Feature Exclusion.* A source concept that has no overlap with the target concept should have no effect on the argument strength, even if it leads to a more diverse set of sources. This phenomenon can result directly from the similarity-matching formula used in CONSYDERR.

9. *Source–Target Inclusion.* Arguments in which the target concept is a subclass of the source concept is perfectly strong. This is because if the target concept is a subclass of the source concept, it has all the features of the source concept, and the intersection of the two feature sets are the same as the source feature set. According to CONSYDERR, the similarity is 1.

It should be noted, however, that there are a number of phenomena that cannot easily be explained by the similarity-matching model used in CONSYDERR. More mechanisms or additional explanations are necessary in these cases (see Osherson et al. 1990 and Sloman 1992 for details).

4.4 SYSTEMATIC EXPERIMENTS

CONSYDERR has many useful properties, as demonstrated earlier. The architecture also has shown its utility by accounting for the reasoning data. However, we have not yet studied the entire spectrum of its behavior and do not know how the architecture and its components fare when applied to a wide range of situations. Therefore, it is necessary to explore its characteristics with systematic experiments. Specifically, I need to design test cases that can cover rule application functions, similarity-matching functions, top-down weights, bottom-up weights, CD link weights, and other parameters to see how they work under a variety of circumstances. In the rest of this section, test cases and test results are presented in three categories: similarity matching, rule application, and inheritance.

4.4.1 Similarity Matching

Let us look into the case of similarity matching. Similarity matching is calculated with

$$s_{AB} = \frac{|F_A \cap F_B|}{|F_B|}$$

This formula is implemented (approximately, as explained in Chapter 3) with the two-level structure of CONSYDERR.

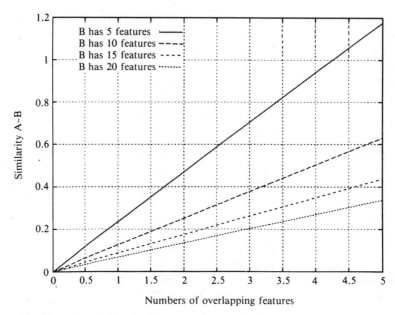

Figure 4.5. *Similarity matching in CONSYDERR when A has 20 features and B has small variable numbers of features, where* $S_{AB} = |F_A \cap F_B| / |F_B|^{9/10}$.

To test similarity matching in CONSYDERR, I collected the data shown in Figures 4.5 and 4.6. In these two figures, A is a concept with 20 features in CD; B is another concept, with varying number of features in CD. When A is activated, based on the similarity between A and B, B will be activated to a certain degree, that is, $ACT_B = ACT_A * s_{AB}$. The two figures demonstrate the difference in the final similarity-matching outcome when one or more of the following three parameters change: $|F_A|$ (the number of features of A), $|F_B|$ (the number of features of B), and $|F_A \cap F_B|$ (the number of overlapping features). The results show that each curve is almost straight, just as we wanted, while in fact a slower than linear (but very close to linear) function is used concerning $|F_B|$ (as an approximation to the linear function, as explained in Chapter 3). When the size of the feature set of B, $|F_B|$, grows large, the addition of features in B has less effect on the similarity-matching outcome. The size of the feature set of A, $|F_A|$, has no effect on the similarity-matching outcome.

These figures show what happens when a novel input is encountered (where A is a novel input and B is an existing concept that shares some features with A). If we assume that the novel input A is activated to its full extent (having activation 1), the figures show the activation of a similar concept B, where B has different numbers of features and shares different numbers of features with A. The activation of B (which is similar to the novel input A) brings to bear on A the knowledge associated with B, so that

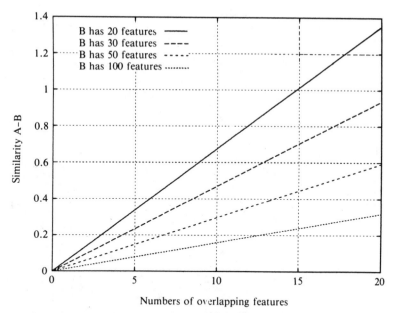

Figure 4.6. *Similarity matching in CONSYDERR when A has 20 features and B has large variable numbers of features, where* $S_{AB} = |F_A \cap F_B| / |F_B|^{9/10}$.

the system will not break down due to the lack of directly applicable rules as in typical rule-based systems. As in case-based reasoning, when dealing with a novel situation, we utilize existing similar cases and adapt previous solutions to the new situation, although in this case I deal only with very simple and highly abstract "cases."

4.4.2 Rule Application

Let us look into the case of rule application. In CONSYDERR, activations at equilibrium resulting from rule application are determined by

$$ACT_B = \sum_i W_i * ACT_{A_i}$$

$$ACT_{x_l} = \sum_i w_i * ACT_{x_i}$$

where $W_i = r_{A_iB}$ and $w_i = lw_{A_iB}$ are link weights (representing strengths of FEL rules). These two formulas are implemented at the two different levels of CONSYDERR, respectively.

To test rule application in CONSYDERR, I collected activation data in Figure 4.7. Note that the figure shows the different activations of the conclusion B with different numbers of conditions activated (and to different

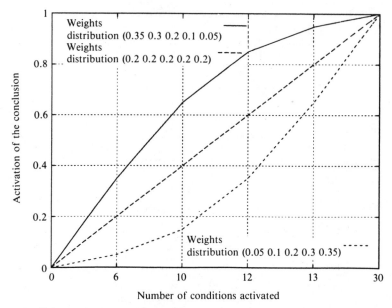

Figure 4.7. *Rule application in CONSYDERR: activations of the conclusion relative to the number of conditions activated, with different weight distributions.*

degrees), A_1, A_2, A_3, A_4, and A_5, in a fixed order but with different weight distributions.

What the figure demonstrates is that rules in CONSYDERR can be activated partially with a partial satisfaction of conditions by input. Depending on weight distributions, a rule with a certain portion of its conditions activated can reach its conclusion partially, with varying degrees of confidence (the activations of the conclusions), as shown in the figure.

4.4.3 Inheritance

Let us look into the case of inheritance. Inheritance is carried out in CONSYDERR with mixed similarity matching and rule application: that is, classes are represented as concept nodes and feature nodes, property-value pairs are represented as separate concept nodes and feature nodes, and links between them indicate which class has what property values. Concepts and features are implemented with the two-level structure of CONSYDERR.

To test inheritance in CONSYDERR, we can examine Figures 4.8 to 4.11. These figures are for bottom-up inheritance, top-down inheritance, bottom-up inheritance with cancellation, and top-down inheritance with cancellation, respectively. Suppose that $A \supset B$, $F_A \subset F_B$, $|F_B| = 10$, and either $A \rightarrow C$ (in case of bottom-up inheritance) or $B \rightarrow D$ (in case of top-down inheritance) exists, or both (in case of cancellation), with the weights equal to 1. When A is fully activated, the figures show the activations of the property-values (C or D, or both). In these figures, I assume that $g(x) = x^{9/10}$ (used in *bu*) and

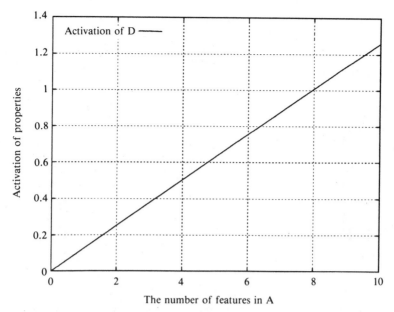

Figure 4.8. *Inheritance in CONSYDERR: activations of property values relative to the number of features in A, when A is fully activated, where A ⊃ B, $F_A \subset F_B$, $|F_B| = 10$ and B → D, with the weight equal to 1.*

$f(x) = x^{999/1000}$ (used in *lw*). Note that the activation values can be slightly higher than 1, in order for comparison of property values to take place. This is not a problem: a winner-take-all network can be placed on top of pairs of conflicting concepts (e.g., *color-red* versus *color-white*) to decide the final activations (0 or 1) for these concepts (see the next section). I look only at cases where each property value is represented by a distinct single feature node in CD. Other cases are similar.

These figures demonstrate that CONSYDERR handles inheritance properly. When there is inheritance without cancellation, the situation is handled the same way as in the case of simple similarity matching: the property value of a similar class is activated. When there is cancellation, the canceled property value always has a weaker activation than the right property value, as guaranteed by the selection of the structural parameters (namely, *td*, *bu*, and *lw*; see the derivation in Chapter 3).

4.5 CHOICE, FOCUS, AND CONTEXT

For many are called, but few are chosen.
—Matthew XXII

Because similarity matching obviously is not context-free and not all features are relevant to a particular task, a question that naturally comes to mind

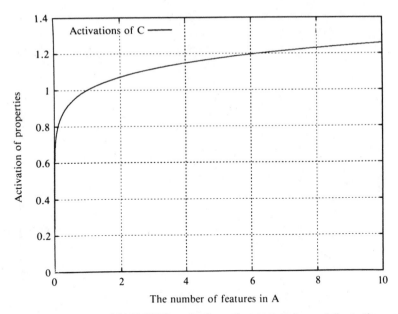

Figure 4.9. *Inheritance in CONSYDERR: activations of property values relative to the number of features in A, when B is fully activated, where $A \supset B$, $F_A \subset F_B$, $|F_B| = 10$, and $A \rightarrow C$, with its weight equal to 1.*

when looking at the preceding experiments is: How do we select the right features to focus on? A related question is: After reaching a number of conclusions about a situation, how do we sort them out, that is, pick out the most plausible and relevant ones and discard contradictory and irrelevant ones?

These problems are, more or less, ubiquitous; that is, most AI systems encounter these problems one way or another. Dreyfus (1972) considers the inability of symbolic AI in dealing with the problem of utilizing similarity in relation to contexts as a major obstacle toward real intelligence. Dennett (1983) discusses a complementary issue—what he terms the "smoking gun" problem—how one can decide which of the features in a particular situation can safely be ignored. Clearly, I do not have a generic solution to these problems; what I propose in this section is a specific mechanism for a specific task; the mechanism is very preliminary.

The problem of **choice** is how to choose the right answer out of many similar, contradictory, or complementary results reached by a system, such as a connectionist network. Because of the nature of the forward-chaining reasoning in CONSYDERR, all reachable results, direct or indirect, will be reached within a fixed amount of time, though some of them may be weak in activation. Given the large number of conclusions, a system is faced with the daunting task of sorting out useful information from them. One way to do

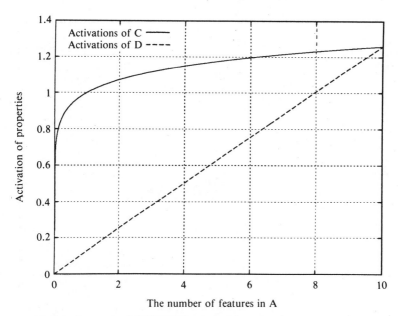

Figure 4.10. *Inheritance in CONSYDERR: activations of property values relative to the number of features in A, when A is fully activated, where $A \supset B$, $F_A \subset F_B$, $|F_B| = 10$, and $A \to C$, $B \to D$, with the weights equal to 1.*

this is by forming *subject sets*, each of which is a set of concepts that are relevant in a given context and with regard to a particular goal. The relationships among those concepts in a particular subject set include: *contradiction* (e.g., color-gray versus color-white), *complementation* (e.g., color-gray and size-large), and *no-relation* (e.g., color-white and music-classic). To deal with these different relationships, we need to further divide a subject set into *core subject sets*, each of which contains only those concepts that are contradictory to each other. Then after reaching all the conclusions in a core subject set, the results can be passed on to a *winner-take-all* network (i.e., a separate network), which uses competition to determine the most plausible conclusion. Each WTA network for each core subject set can then be examined to gather the final results.

Subject sets and core subject sets are formed dynamically, after the current context is given (or inferred). With different contexts, those sets are different—it is the context that determines the formation and structure of each of those sets.

The problem of **focus** is, in similarity matching, how to attend to those features that are relevant in the current context with regard to current goals. One natural result of dividing representation into the two levels is that the feature set of a concept can be modified dynamically by suppressing some and highlighting others in the feature level, independent of conceptual

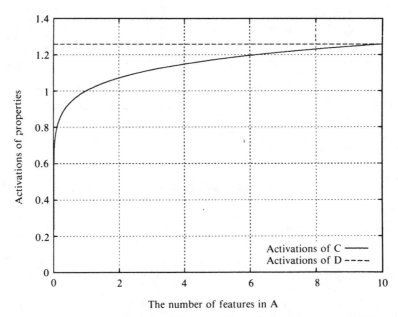

Figure 4.11. *Inheritance in CONSYDERR: activations of property values relative to the number of features in A, when B is fully activated, where $A \supset B$, $F_A \subset F_B$, $|F_B| = 10$, and $A \rightarrow C$, $B \rightarrow D$, with the weights equal to 1.*

structures in the concept level. This modification can be done by an *attention-focusing module*, which is attached to but is external to the CONSYDERR architecture. In such a module, the contextual effect is attained through "context rules," which, given a particular context (or a query as in the examples), will highlight those features that are relevant to the current context and will suppress others. For example, if a query is "Is Florida a rice-growing area?", only those features that are related to agricultural products should be used, that is, climate, landform, vegetation, and so on. If a query is "What is the most important mineral deposit in Texas?", features regarding landform but not those regarding climate will be highlighted. See Figure 4.12. Such "context rules" need not be discrete rules; in general, they can form a multilayer feedforward connectionist network, with past and current queries as input and feature focusing (suppressing and highlighting)

Context	Context Rule
agriculture	rice-growing $\longrightarrow$ tropical subtropical temperate ...... plain highland ....
mining	mineral-deposit $\longrightarrow$ plain highland coastal rugged ....

Figure 4.12. *Examples of context rules.*

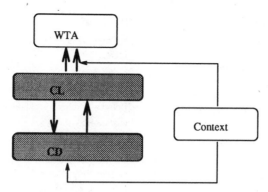

Figure 4.13. *Overall architecture with feature and result selections.*

control as output. In a network form, an attention-focusing module can be trained through standard connectionist learning algorithms. This is similar to the idea of drive input (as described in Levine 1991). Core subject sets explained above can be formed in a similar way.

Incorporating these mechanisms, the overall architecture is shown in Figure 4.13. Because of the fact that these mechanisms are domain specific, they are not part of the CONSYDERR architecture, but are add-on mechanisms.

4.6 REASONING WITH GEOGRAPHICAL KNOWLEDGE

In this section I look into a system for reasoning with geographical information: GIRO, which stands for *a "system for Geographical Information Reasoning and Organization."*

In the foregoing discussion of how CONSYDERR accounts for the reasoning data, the question of sizes and scalability arises naturally: What if there are a large number of nodes in each level? What if there are a lot of similar concepts, rules, and features? In order to show that systems for reasoning in a particular domain can be constructed systematically based on the CONSYDERR architecture and that they will work reasonably despite the existence of interference, distractions, and a large number of nodes, I have developed the system GIRO, which stores a large amount of knowledge extracted from encyclopedias and reasons about agricultural characterizations of regions.

4.6.1 The Structure of GIRO

GIRO is based on the two-level, dual-representation architecture of CONSYDERR, with structural parameters as derived in Chapter 3. Knowledge

"Chaco"	"Honduras"
"Uruguay-coastal"	"Uruguay-plateau-highland"
"Mendoza"	"Llanos"
"w-Peru"	"c-Peru"
"e-Peru"	"Bolivia-orient-grassland"
"Bolivia-orient-rainforest"	"Bolivia-cordillera-occidental"
"e-Paraguay"	"w-Paraguay-forest"
"w-Paraguay-savanna"	"Panama-lowland"
"w-Texas"	"Guiana-pgs"
"Guiana-hilly-country-forest"	"Guiana-hilly-country-savanna"
"Guiana-plain"	"Bolivia-SW-highlands"
"Brazil-cw"	"Brazil-s"
"Brazil-saopaulo"	"Brazil-e"
"Brazil-ne"	"Brazil-n"
"Chile-n"	"Chile-s"
"Chile-c"	"Argentina-ne"
"Argentina-pampa"	"Argentina-Patagonia"
"Argentina-andeanhighland"	"Columbia-w"
"Columbia-e"	"Columbia-basin"
"Ecuador-coast"	"Ecuador-highlands"
"Venezuela-Llanos"	"Venezuela-coastalplain"
"Suriname-coastalplain"	"Suriname-plateau"

Figure 4.14. *Geographical regions included in GIRO.*

representation of GIRO utilizes the two-level idea in the CONSYDERR architecture by dividing the geographical knowledge represented in the system into two categories: concepts, which include basic geographical regions and regional characterizations (such as "cattle-country"), and features, which include primitive geographical descriptions of regions, such as "highland," "mountainous," and "tropical." Concepts are represented in CL, and features are represented in CD. Each geographical region in CL is connected to its corresponding features in the CD level, and because features are shared by similar concepts, the CD representation is similarity-based: that is, two concepts have overlapping CD representations if and only if the two are similar and the amount of overlapping is proportional to the degree of the similarity between them, as alluded to before. Each region is also connected by links to concepts representing its characterizations, if the knowledge is available to the system.

To give a clear idea of what is available in GIRO, I tabulate some of the data stored in the system. Figure 4.14 lists some of the geographical regions included in the system. Most of them are in South America, which is chosen

"cotton-producing-area"
"coffee-growing-area"
"wine-producing-area"
"potato-growing-area"
"rubber-producing-area"
"goats-area"
"rice-growing-area"
"wheat-growing-area"
"soybean-growing-area"
"rubber-producing-area"
"sheep-country"
"producing-banana"
"producing-tropical-fruits"
"corn-growing-area"
"sugar-producing-area"
"fruit-veg-growing-area"

Figure 4.15. *Regional characterizations included in GIRO.*

as an example. Figure 4.15 lists concepts for characterizing geographical regions in terms of agricultural products, such as "rice-growing-area," "cattle-country," and "sheep-country." Figure 4.16 lists some features used in CD.

4.6.2 The Knowledge Acquisition for GIRO

Having described the structure of GIRO, I turn next to the question of how to acquire all the necessary data to build up such a system. The problem of knowledge acquisition is ubiquitous. Much research in AI has been concentrated in this area. Although this work does not contribute any general technique for knowledge acquisition, it is worth noting that the process of knowledge acquisition for GIRO is straightforward and systematic, and nothing is tuned arbitrarily just for getting one outcome or the other.

temperate	arctic	woodland	plain	Mediterranean
plateau	Mts	coastal-land	lake	tropical
lowland	hill	river-valley-basin	swamp	rainforest
evergreen	deciduous	highland	upland	sparsely-populated
densely-populated	fertile	infertile	flood	prairie
dependable-rainfall	scrub	farming	rugged	subtropical
rainy	savanna	dry-arid	grassland	desert

Figure 4.16. *Geographical features included in GIRO.*

Specifically, the knowledge in GIRO is obtained from encyclopedias, such as *Encyclopaedia Britannica* or *Encyclopedia Americana*, in the form of a basic geographical region (a region with relatively uniform characteristics), its agricultural characterizations, and its geographical features. Since those types of information are well documented and rather extensive in source books, the task is straightforward, although it is extremely tedious and time consuming.

For example, a typical entry is as follows:

```
Peru—Montana:
lowland, tropical, woodland
```

This is extracted from the following descriptions:

- *Peru—Montana*. From west to east the major surface features of Peru are (1) the desert coast, (2) the Andes highlands, (3) the Montana.

- *Montana*. The Montana is the remote region containing the lower, densely forested slopes of the eastern Andes and flat, tropical Amazon plains called Selva. The region experiences high temperatures and abundant rains throughout the year. The natural vegetation cover is a tall tropical rainforest, with a leafy canopy shading a damp, open forest floor. Grasses grow in poorly drained areas, while coarse grasses and brush grow on sandy, porous soils and rocky slopes.

In extracting information from source books, there are some subtleties that have to be taken into consideration. Each article describing a particular region is written by a particular researcher familiar with that region, and varies in depth, presentation, amount of detail, and emphasis. This diversity in style, resulting from the diversity in the authorship of these articles, inevitably has adverse effects on the accuracy of the specification. The problem is the lack of details on the one hand and too many details on the other hand. When there are not enough details from one sourcebook, I can find another sourcebook and try to fill in what is needed. In case of too many details, I have to be very careful in selecting the most important and the most relevant information out of the tangled web of irrelevant descriptions. As a rule of thumb, I usually disregard information associated with phases such as "plus," "in addition," "besides," "although," "a small portion of," "mostly . . . but . . . ." A problem is that few regions are absolutely geographically homogeneous. What I want is a description that is applicable to the largest portion of a region, expressing its *essential* characteristics, without having irrelevant information or descriptions that can be applied only to a small part of that region. There is certainly a tension between (1) capturing important characteristics of a region, and (2) excluding information applicable only to a small part of a region. The trade-off between these two aspects helps us to decide what primitive geographical regions are and what information is to be included for each such region.

After extracting the necessary pieces of information, we need to encode them into the connectionist architecture. As explained before, each geographical region is represented by a single node in the CL level, each feature is represented by a single node in the CD level, and appropriate links are established between the two levels. All agricultural characterizations are also represented in the CL level and are replicated in the CD level. Links are established to indicate agricultural characterizations associated with each region. All CL links have weights 1. CD link weights are obtained from the corresponding CL link weights in accordance with the specifications in Chapter 3.

4.6.3 The Working of GIRO

Now I am ready to describe the working of the system: in GIRO, once the name of a geographical region is given to GIRO, as when a query is imposed, GIRO will provide us with its agricultural characterizations, such as "cattle-country," "rice-growing-area," or "rubber-producing area," through rule application or similarity matching, or a combination of both.

For example, suppose that I choose to reason about "Brazil-north," which is described as "tropical rainforest hilly plateau." I start by giving GIRO a query: What is the main agricultural product of "Brazil-north"? This amounts to activating the node representing "Brazil-north." To answer this question, I let GIRO run to perform its reasoning. The output from GIRO is as follows:

```
>(consyderr 0)

TITLE:  GEOGRAPHY
focusing on context AGRICULTURE : remove feature NIL
setup done
starting running
top down
cl propagating
cd propagating
bottom up

the average activation is 0.1213409896658248
( 2, ''cattle-country'', 0.1249998807907104 )
( 10, ''fruit-veg-growing-area'', 0.1249998807907104 )
( 12, ''producing-banana'', 0.1249998807907104 )
( 13, ''producing-tropical-fruits'',
     0.1249998807907104 )
( 20, ''rubber-producing-area'', 0.9999990463256836 )
( 29, ''c-Peru'', 0.125 )
( 32, ''Bolivia-orient-rainforest'',0.125 )
( 40, ''Guiana-pgs'', 0.125 )
```

```
( 41, ''Guiana-hilly-country-forest'',
    0.1666666666666667 )
( 42, ''Guiana-hilly-country-savanna'', 0.125 )
( 45, ''Brazil-cw'', 0.125 )
( 50, ''Brazil-n'', 1 )
( 60, ''Columbia-basin'', 0.1666666666666667 )
( 61, ''Ecuador-coast'', 0.125 )
( 66, ''Suriname-plateau'', 0.125 )
```

The result shows that it is a "rubber-producing-area" for certain (with confidence value qual to 0.999999), and it is similar, to a small extent, to "Guiana-hilly-country-forest" (with confidence value 0.167) and "Columbia-basin" (with confidence value 0.167), and there is a small chance that it produces bananas (with confidence value 0.125) and tropical fruits (with confidence value 0.125), etc. If we want to choose one answer out of many, we can simply use a winner-take-all network on top of this, but this is not an intrinsic part of GIRO and is not needed in this case. Despite the appearance of mere information retrieval, those conclusions actually result from rule-based and similarity-based reasoning from the top-down, bottom-up, and settling flows. For example, tracing the reasoning process of the system, we see that "producing-banana" (0.125) is obtained based on the following reasoning: "Ecuador-coast" produces bananas, and "Brazil-north" is similar to "Ecuador-coast" to a small extent, so there is a small chance that "Brazil-north" might produce bananas. The conclusion of "rubber-producing-area," on the other hand, is obtained based on straightforward rule application: *Brazil-north* → *rubber-producing-area*. Other outcomes are obtained in various similar fashions. See Figure 4.17.

Another example is as follows: Suppose that I want to know about the Ecuador coastal region. I give GIRO a query: "What is the main agricultural product of the Ecuador coastal region?" by activating the node representing "Ecuador-coast." To answer this question, I let GIRO run to perform its reasoning. The output from GIRO is as follows:

```
(consyderr 0)

TITLE:  GEOGRAPHY
focusing on context AGRICULTURE : remove feature NIL
setup done
starting running
top down
cl propagating
cd propagating
bottom up

  the average activation is 0.1433035089856102
  ( 6, ''Uruguay-coastal'', 0.1666666666666667 )
```

```
( 10, ''fruit-veg-growing-area'', 0.2499997615814209 )
( 12, ''producing-banana'', 0.9999990463256836 )
( 13, ''producing-tropical-fruits'',
  0.2499997615814209 )
( 30, ''e-Peru'', 0.1666666666666667 )
( 32, ''Bolivia-orient-rainforest'', 0.1875 )
( 60, ''Columbia-basin'', 0.1666666666666667 )
( 61, ''Ecuador-coast'', 1 )
```

The result indicates that the region produces banana (with confidence value equal to 0.99999), from applying a rule: *Ecuador-coast → producing-banana.* And it is very likely producing tropical fruits and other fruits/vegetables (with confidence value equal to 0.25), inferred from mixed similarity matching and rule application: for example, we have *Ecuador-coast → producing-banana* and *producing-banana ~ producing-tropical-fruits*), so one of the conclusions reached is *producing-tropical-fruits.* "Ecuador-coast" is also similar, in some way, to "Uruguay-coastal" (with activation 0.16), "eastern-Peru" (with activation 0.16), and "Columbia-basin" (with activation 0.16), due to similarity matching (feature overlaps) between "Ecuador-coast" and each of these regions. See Figure 4.18.

As yet another example, let us examine "Brazil-south." I give GIRO a query: "Does Brazil-south produce cattle?" by activating the node representing "Brazil-s" and looking for "cattle" in the results. The output from GIRO is as follows:

```
(consyderr 0)

TITLE: GEOGRAPHY
focusing on context AGRICULTURE : remove feature NIL
setup done
starting running
top down
cl propagating
cd propagating
bottom up

  the average activation is 0.1492545754568917
  ( 2, ''cattle-country'', 0.9999990463256836 )
  ( 11, ''sheep-country'', 0.9999990463256836 )
  ( 46, ''Brazil-s'', 1 )

The Result ----
( 2, ''cattle-country'', 0.9999990463256836 ) --- end
  of results
```

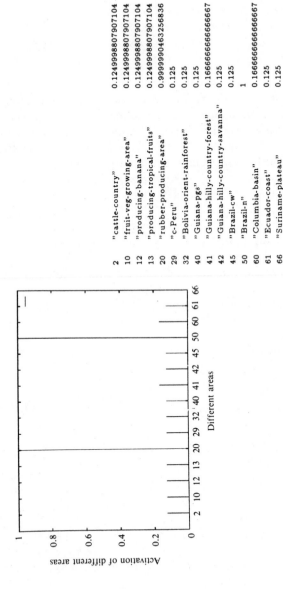

2	"cattle-country"	0.1249998807907104
10	"fruit-veg-growing-area"	0.1249998807907104
12	"producing-banana"	0.1249998807907104
13	"producing-tropical-fruits"	0.1249998807907104
20	"rubber-producing-area"	0.9999990463256836
29	"c-Peru"	0.125
32	"Bolivia-orient-rainforest"	0.125
40	"Guiana-pgs"	0.125
41	"Guiana-hilly-country-forest"	0.1666666666666667
42	"Guiana-hilly-country-savanna"	0.125
45	"Brazil-cw"	0.125
50	"Brazil-n"	1
60	"Columbia-basin"	0.1666666666666667
61	"Ecuador-coast"	0.125
66	"Suriname-plateau"	0.125

Figure 4.17. Output from GIRO: Case 1.

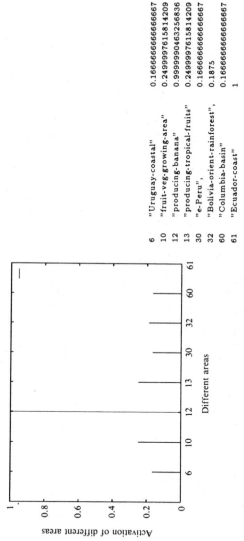

6	"Uruguay-coastal"	0.166666666666667
10	"fruit-veg-growing-area"	0.249999761581209
12	"producing-banana"	0.999999046325836
13	"producing-tropical-fruits"	0.249999761581209
30	"e-Peru",	0.166666666666667
32	"Bolivia-orient-rainforest",	0.1875
60	"Columbia-basin"	0.166666666666667
61	"Ecuador-coast"	1

Figure 4.18. *Output from GIRO: Case 2.*

113

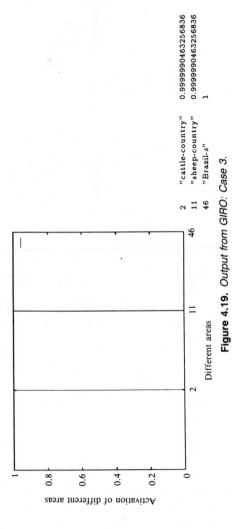

Figure 4.19. *Output from GIRO: Case 3.*

2	"cattle-country"	0.999999046325836
11	"sheep-country"	0.999999046325836
46	"Brazil-s"	1

The result indicates that the region does produce cattle and sheep, due to the respective rules that lead to these results: *Brazil-s* → *cattle-country* and *Brazil-s* → *sheep-country*. Nothing else in the network fires strongly, or distinguishably, in this case, due to the lack of other relevant rules and similarities. See Figure 4.19.

Yet another example is about "Argentina-Andean-highland": Is it a cattle country? I activate the node representing the region, and the output from GIRO is as follows:

```
(consyderr 0)

TITLE: GEOGRAPHY
focusing on context AGRICULTURE : remove feature NIL
setup done
starting running
top down
cl propagating
cd propagating
bottom up

the average activation is 0.0861359060756744
( 40, ''Guiana- pgs'', 0.125 )
( 52, ''Chile- s'', 0.1666666666666667 )
( 53, ''Chile- c'', 0.1666666666666667 )
( 57, ''Argentina- Andea- highland'', 1 )
( 58, ''Columbia- w'', 0.1666666666666667 )
( 62, ''Ecuador- highlands'', 1 / 4 )

The Result ----
( 2, ''cattle- country'', 0.08333325386047362 ) ---- end
    of results
```

This result shows clearly that it is not a cattle country, due to the lack of relevant rules and the lack of strong similarities with any cattle-producing area. See Figure 4.20.

To conclude, a system (GIRO) for reasoning about geographical characteristics of certain regions is developed, which organizes relevant knowledge into concepts, features, and rules (and similarity matching that emerge from the feature representation) according to the CONSYDERR architecture. The knowledge in the system is extracted from source books, without any arbitrary hand-tuning. Various examples show that the system works reasonably despite the large number of data items stored in the system, and the interferences/distractions that may result from the large number of data items.

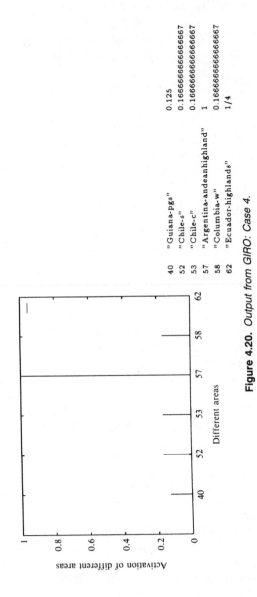

Figure 4.20. *Output from GIRO: Case 4.*

40	"Guiana-pgs"	0.125
52	"Chile-s"	0.166666666666667
53	"Chile-c"	0.166666666666667
57	"Argentina-andeanhighland"	1
58	"Columbia-w"	0.166666666666667
62	"Ecuador-highlands"	1/4

4.7 APPLICATIONS TO OTHER DOMAINS

Now the question is: Can the method demonstrated in Section 4.6 be applied to other domains where no natural division of knowledge into concepts and features (as in the geographical domain) seems to exist? I will look into this question and show that the same method does work for some other domains.

Because this is outside my main focus, I will not be concerned with all the details of the domains involved or conduct a thorough study of them. Only some brief hints as to how this architecture may be applied to these other domains are provided.

4.7.1 Applications to Natural Language Understanding

Natural language understanding is an area in which commonsense reasoning is crucial. Some discussion, through an example, will be useful in clarifying how the CONSYDERR architecture might be applied to this important area.

In applying CONSYDERR, it is important to identify concepts involved and rule sets needed (i.e., the set of rules that connect all the related concepts identified); it is also important to identify all the features associated with the concepts identified, with or without specific meanings (i.e., interpretations) attached. I do not have generic answers ready for how to handle all of these aspects, for they are highly domain specific. For practical purposes, I can either perform a thorough domain analysis to identify useful features, or use some statistical methods to determine similarities and, based on similarities, construct the CD representation (which may not be interpretable as in the earlier experiments). (See the Appendix at the end of the chapter for details.) It is also important to focus on relevant features in a specific context, as mentioned earlier, which implies the need for a specification of the relationship between contexts and features.

One of the most difficult problems in natural language understanding is that of lexical disambiguation (Waltz and Pollack 1985, Bookman 1989, Pustejovsky 1993). One simple example that lends itself to our discussion is "pot," taken from the work of Lange and Dyer (1989). I adopted the problem but provide a different solution. The problem can be stated as follows: normally, the word "pot" should be interpreted as "cooking pot," but under certain circumstances, given some pertinent clues, it should be interpreted as marijuana. Given the sentence,

John put the pot inside the dishwasher because the police are coming.

what does the word "pot" mean? Depending on contexts and/or clues given, a reasoner with proper knowledge should be able to give correct answers.

I set up a set of additional tests (which are not in Lange and Dyer 1989), to further verify the capability of CONSYDERR.

1. The first test is:

   John put the pot inside the dishwasher.

   The word "pot" should mean "cooking pot" in this case.

2. The second test is:

   John put the pot inside the dishwasher because the police are coming.

   The word "pot" means "marijuana" in this case.

3. The third test is:

   John put the pot inside the dishwasher because the police are coming and John wants to make the kitchen clean.

   The solution should be "cooking pot" in this case.

4. The fourth test is:

   John put the pot inside the dishwasher because John wants to make the kitchen clean.

   The solution should be "cooking pot" in this case.

5. The fifth test is:

   John put the pot inside the dishwasher when the police come for the bank robbery across the street.

   The situation is ambiguous, and the system could interpret it as "marijuana."

6. The sixth test is:

   John is cleaning the kitchen, putting the pot inside the dishwasher, when the police come for the bank robbery across the street.

   The solution should be "cooking pot" in this case.

I constructed a system that can handle the problem and pass the six tests, based on the CONSYDERR architecture, as follows: each concept involved in the problem description is represented by one node in CL. Rules are extracted from commonsense knowledge. Rules that are put into the systems include:

1. Pot is cooking pot.
2. Pot could be marijuana.
3. Marijuana is illegal.
4. Cleaning kitchens implies cleaning cookware.
5. Using dishwashers implies cleaning cookware.
6. If one has marijuana and the police are coming, the police will see it.
7. Police seeing illegal substance results in someone being arrested.
8. To avoid arrests, prevent the police from seeing illegal substances.
9. To prevent somebody from seeing something, hide it.
10. Putting something in a dishwasher is for washing it.

11. Putting something in a dishwasher could be for hiding it.
12. If there is a bank robbery going on and the police are coming, they are here to stop the bank robbery.

On the other hand, CD is basically a distributed version of CL by sharing nodes among related concepts. This CD structure is constructed according to STSIS (see the Appendix at the end of the chapter). Each node is vaguely interpretable. The rules in CL are duplicated diffusely in CD.

When all the weights are set appropriately, the system performs the task correctly. It gives correct answers to all the tests, distinguishing subtle differences through rule application and similarity matching.[6]

The advantage of this solution, using both rule application and similarity matching instead of using only rules, is that it increases the expressive and reasoning power of the system by enabling analogous knowledge to be used (as discussed before). Although this example is very simple and cannot possibly capture all the intricacy involved, it does point out, to a small extent, an alternative way of dealing with lexical ambiguity and with natural language understanding in general.

4.7.2 Applications to Mundane Reasoning

Mundane reasoning is another area in which commonsense knowledge is heavily involved. Mundane reasoning is used to refer to the type of reasoning that we do daily regarding mundane matters, for example, which chair to sit in, when to eat, whom to talk to, and so on. The goal of such mundane reasoning is to come up rapidly with an interpretation of a situation or to make a quick decision, given the current situation. Therefore, it involves a lot of subconceptual reasoning ("subcognition"; Hofstadter 1985).

In applying CONSYDERR to this area, we have to identify for CL all the concepts and rules involved in a particular task. We also have to identify all the features associated with the concepts. I will look into the "Ted" example from Derthick (1988). Again, I adopted the problem, but provide a different solution: instead of doing constraint satisfaction as in Derthick (1988) or as in Thagard (1989), I perform rule application plus similarity matching; for, in addition to other reasons, massively parallel rule application and similarity matching are much more efficient computationally than constraint satisfaction, which is slow and costly in terms of computational resources (see Chapter 8). This way the results are also less susceptible to small changes in

---

[6]Note that some subtle linguistic elements are not taken into account in the present implementation, for example, "*when* the police are coming" versus "*because* the police are coming." When finer distinctions are needed, more nodes will have to be added to the system, along with possibly other mechanisms, to take those elements into consideration.

weight values. the problem can be stated as follows (Derthick 1988):

> Ted is seen walking along a pier, dressed like a sailor. Ted launched into an excited monolog on the influence of TV programming. It seems reasonable to conclude that Ted is a professional sailor, and that he is interested in television. But another possibility is that Ted is a TV tycoon and a millionaire playboy and has a hobby of sailing.

Depending on the clues given, a reasoner with proper knowledge should be able to give correct answers.

The knowledge used for performing this reasoning is encoded in the following rules:

1. *dressed-like-sailor talks-like-sailor walks-like-sailor → sailor*
2. *talk-about-TV-business → interested-in-TV*
3. *talk-about-TV-business → in-TV-business*
4. *in-TV-business ↛ sailor*
5. *dressed-like-sailor → hobby-sailor*
6. *hobby-sailor → rich-people*
7. *rich-people ↛ sailor*

In CD, distributed representation is used and similar concepts have shared features. CD is constructed according to STSIS, and each node is vaguely interpretable. The rules implemented in CL are duplicated diffusely in CD.

I devise a set of tests to verify the correctness of the system in the same way as before. The system works as expected; that is, when given the input that Ted is dressed up like a sailor (in the form of activating nodes "dressed-like-sailor"), the system will indicate that Ted is a sailor (in the form of activating the node "sailor" strongly); when given the input that Ted is dressed up like a sailor but talks a lot about TV business (in the form of activating nodes "dressed-like-sailor" and "talk-about-TV-business"), the system will indicate hobby sailors (in the form of activating the node for "hobby-sailor" more strongly than the node for "sailor"). Overall, the CONSYDERR approach works well and should prove to be of use in this area.

4.7.3 Applications to Planning

Planning is yet another area in which commonsense reasoning is important. I am concerned mainly here with commonsensical planning activities, not formal planning based on strict mathematical models. Since I have not implemented anything in this area, I will only discuss some speculations related to the usefulness of CONSYDERR in this area.

The most important issue here is the sequential nature of planning, which has to be dealt with adequately. Planning is inherently sequential: a plan is formed from a sequence of steps, and moreover, steps can interfere with each other in the form of undoing what was accomplished before or disabling what should be done later, and so on. To deal with sequences, some notions of temporality have to be incorporated in order to express sequences; actions, conditions, and results have to be associated with temporal measures.

The question now is how to account for temporality in CONSYDERR. So far, CONSYDERR is nonsequential. So we need some other means. This is where the idea of *temporal simulation* comes into play. By temporal simulation, I mean actually carrying out plan steps temporally inside CONSY-DERR, when forming a plan. Since the system can infer what the next step should be within a system cycle when given the current state, another cycle can infer yet another step, with the previously inferred state as the current one. This process can go on and on until desired states are reached.

One planning paradigm that alleviates the need for sequences altogether is *universal plans*. According to Schoppers (1989): "Universal plans classify possible situations; naturally cover the entire domain; place no restrictions on what possible situations might become actual and in what order; and use sensory information to identify the class of possible situations, hence redeciding what to do from moment to moment." CONSYDERR can provide a computational framework in which this type of planning can be implemented. In planning, with a network model instead of a symbolic model, more realistic structures, constraints and processes can be explored. On the other hand, the notion of universal plans provides the conceptual framework in which CONSYDERR can be applied to planning problems.

Rules and similarities are used readily in planning. Rules are used to encode the relationship between the plan step taken within the current context and the new state after the step is performed, and the relationship between the current state and the next step to take. Similarities are used for dealing with situations not precisely specified in the rule set, to reach plausible conclusions. It is also useful to have interaction in representation, as discussed in Chapter 6.

Some issues arise in such a system. For one thing, a planning system based on CONSYDERR should preferably be able to adapt itself to new situations, new actions, and so on. Although similarity matching is one possible way of doing this, we may need more complex similarity-matching measures, and perhaps more complex types of features, in the CONSYDERR architecture. Another issue is how to focus on relevant aspects in the feature representation of a concept. Something like goals of a plan and purposes of a step can help in this regard, but a lot more work has to be done for concrete solutions. Yet another issue is how to revise plans upon receiving feedback regarding the outcome of current actions—the network equivalent of searching the state space. Some kinds of feedback links are needed, and these links have to be structured in such a way that they can help to identify steps to be avoided or to be favored, along with other considerations.

4.8 SUMMARY

This chapter covers evaluations and experimental studies of the CONSY-DERR architecture. I have shown that this architecture can deal very well with, in a massively parallel fashion, rule application (including issues such as partial match, incomplete information, and uncertain knowledge), similarity matching, and inheritance, the most common elements in commonsense reasoning. A large-scale system GIRO is designed for reasoning with geographical information extracted from encyclopedias. It shows that the CON-SYDERR architecture can scale up to a reasonable size and perform useful tasks. Finally, I extend the domain of applications, and look into such areas as natural language understanding, mundane reasoning, and planning.

4.9 APPENDIX: DETERMINING SIMILARITIES AND CD REPRESENTATIONS

STSIS, or a *"Statistical Test-Score procedure for determining Intensional Similarity,"* is a procedure for determining, by empirical means, the feature (intensional) similarities in CD and for constructing CD representations.[7] This procedure can be applied to build CD for systems based on CONSY-DERR, without performing a thorough domain analysis to determine all relevant features (because not all areas have a set of features well analyzed, as in geography).

Assume that there is a set of concepts $c = \{c_1, c_2, c_3, \ldots, c_n\}$, and $\bar{c}$ is the vector composed of all these concepts. The matrix M_2 measures the pairwise similarities between elements of the vector $\bar{c}$, that is,

$$M_2 = S(\bar{c} \times \bar{c})$$

where $\times$ denotes the outer product and S is the similarity-matching measure: $S([x]) = [S(x)]$. (In other words, the similarity of a matrix is a matrix of the similarities of its elements). For each matrix element,

$$S(a, b) = \frac{\sum_{i=1}^{n} S_i'(a, b)}{n}$$

where $S_i'(a, b)$ is an empirical measure (i.e., a subjective rating) of the similarity matching between a and b, ranging from 0 to 1. We can also calculate the mean squared error:

$$\delta(a, b) = \sqrt{\sum_{i=1}^{n} (S - S_i')^2}$$

[7]For similar procedures, see, for example, Zadeh (1983).

Then for higher-order similarities (involving more than two concepts), we have

$$M_3 = S(\bar{c} \times \bar{c} \times \bar{c})$$

and

$$M_4 = S(\bar{c} \times \bar{c} \times \bar{c} \times \bar{c})$$

and so on.[8]

One problem with this approach is that there are too many entries to fill in each matrix, especially in higher-order ones. One way to deal with this problem is determining which entry will be zero beforehand and thus avoiding computing that entry; for a large number of entries in these matrices will be zero, which can be determined by examining related entries in the lower-order ones: if one of the related entries is zero, then the entry is zero. (*Related entries* are defined to be entries that contain a subset of the concepts involved in the original entry.)

Another problem is when we should stop, because obviously we do not want too many M matrices (we can produce as many matrices as the number of concepts). There is no theoretical result determining when to stop. However, we can set up some empirical criteria. For example, we can limit the number of matrices to be no more than half the number of the concepts involved.

Once the similarity-matching measures are obtained, a pseudo-code description of the algorithm for constructing CD representations based on the similarity-matching measures is as follows: suppose that we have the following matrices: $M_1, M_2, \ldots, M_m$. Let the total number of nodes in CD be L. Let the number of nodes for c_i be L_i (ideally, $L_i = |F_{c_i}|$).[9] Define S_i to be L_i.

```
Let i = 2
Repeat if i ≠ m
    For each set of entries (e.g., Mᵢ(a,b) = Sₐb, and
    Mᵢ(b,a) = Sᵦₐ), allocate an appropriate number of
    nodes shared among those concepts in the entires,
    and subtract the same number of nodes from each of
    the node pools established for the related entries
    of the next-lower-numbered matrix
    i = i + 1
```

Here *related entries* mean entries consisting of a set of concepts that is a subset of the original concept, for example, $(a\,b\,c)$ for $(a\,b\,c\,d)$. *An appropriate number of nodes* means the number of nodes proportional to the

---

[8]Ideally, we should have $S_{ab} = |F_a \cap F_b|/|F_b|$, $S_{abc} = |F_a \cap F_b \cap F_c|/|F_c|$, $S_{abcd} = |F_a \cap F_b \cap F_c \cap F_d|/|F_d|$, *and so on.*
[9]L_i is determined based on the principle of similarity-based representation: the more general a concept is, the fewer feature nodes there are for representing it.

similarity-matching measure in question. For example, suppose that $M_i(a, b) = S_{ab}$ and $M_i(b, a) = S_{ba}$, so the appropriate number of nodes will be $S_{ab} * L_b = S_{ba} * L_a$. According to the definition of similarities above, the equality always holds. It is because $S_{ab} * L_b = |F_a \cap F_b|/|F_b| * L_b = |F_a \cap F_b|$, and $S_{ba} * L_a = |F_a \cap F_b|/|F_a| * L_a = |F_a \cap F_b|$. However, in reality this equality may not hold: because human similarity judgments and measurements are always error-prone, inconsistency is inevitable (Tversky 1977). Random noises alone are enough to upset the equality. When inconsistency is encountered, we can use the average of the two, instead, in the formula.

An issue is the subtraction of nodes from the node pools of the related entries in the lower-order matrices. Because of the fact that a high-order similarity is part of some lower-order similarities, the (feature) nodes used in the high-order similarity are part of the node pools of the lower-order similarities. When we allocate nodes for a high-order entry, we must subtract the same number of nodes from each of the related lower-order entries. Since we establish node pools for similarities iteratively, from the lowest order up, each time we only need to subtract from the related entries of the closest lower-order matrix.

The question of which nodes to remove from a pool of nodes can be answered partially by considering constraints we have, that is, the fact that we have to preserve the established similarities (i.e., node-sharing situations). When the constraints we have are not enough to determine a uniquely correct way of removing nodes, we can make a tentative decision and backtrack later if necessary, that is, performing a search over the space of all possible ways of removing nodes, until a test shows that all similarity-matching measures are implemented correctly.

CHAPTER 5 _____

More on the Architecture: Logic and Causality

Behind the coarse effect is a fine cause. ...
—R.W. Emerson, ESSAYS, FIRST SERIES: CIRCLES

5.1 OVERVIEW

In my previous derivation and specification of the CONSYDERR architecture, some of the questions regarding rule encoding and FEL (*fuzzy evidential logic*)[1] still linger:

- What is FEL exactly?
- How are rules encoded with FEL and implemented in CONSYDERR?
- Why is this encoding advantageous?

In this chapter I investigate these issues.

For any rule-based reasoner, it is important, or even crucial, to be able to represent commonsense causal knowledge: reasoning is largely causal-based, and conversely, the capability of capturing commonsense causal knowledge renders much power to a rule-based reasoner. The requirement of capturing commonsense causal knowledge provides useful constraints as to what kind

---

[1]Here the word *fuzzy* is used to refer to the gradedness or the continuous inexactness of a concept, not necessarily referring to Zadeh's notion of fuzziness based on linguistic variables.

of rule encoding is desirable, therefore helping in the understanding of representation in connectionist models.

I first discuss causality in very general terms and its importance in representation and reasoning. I then analyze a *causal theory* and its advantages and shortcomings in dealing with commonsense causal knowledge; this analysis will provide some hints as to possible ways of obtaining a better model. Based on this, I define FEL formally, with a connectionist "implementation" in mind, and I look into its logical capability and equivalence, and its realization in CONSYDERR. I then look into the relationship between FEL and causality in general and show that FEL is suitable for dealing with commonsense causal reasoning and requires nothing more than the weighted-sum connectionist model as defined before. Finally, I look into the issue of weights in FEL, which are yet to be specified, and provide some interpretations. In short, in this chapter I show that connectionist models using the weighted-sum computation are a natural way of "implementing" rules and a suitable framework for capturing commonsense causal knowledge.

To summarize the plan:

- In the second section I look into causality and causal models in general.
- In the third section I discuss a particular *causal theory* and problems associated with it.
- In the fourth section I present FEL formally, as a potential solution to the identified problems.
- In the fifth section I discuss how FEL deals with commonsense causality.
- In the sixth section I explain weights involved in the formalism.

The material in this chapter is quite technical, but ample informal explanations are provided in each section.

5.2 CAUSALITY IN GENERAL

Every why has a wherefore.
        —W. Shakespeare

In order to explain rule encoding in CONSYDERR in a broader context, I need to take a detour. In this section I examine the issue of causality, its relationship to reasoning, and its role in representation. Causality has long been widely studied in philosophy and more recently in AI, but its essential nature is still in question. Its role as the "cement of the universe" (Hume 1740) signifies the scope of the problem and may explain the difficulty in understanding it. Although I do not expect to resolve this issue outright in this short treatment, I do wish to shed some new light on it and in the process establish a foundation for rule encoding in CONSYDERR.

Here I want to bring forth the distinction between "scientific" causality and commonsense causality, which I believe will help to clarify somewhat the notion of causality. In the literature, there are clearly two (maybe more) divergent approaches in studying causality (although sometimes they are intermixed). One approach tries to abstract, sanitize, and make crisp the notion of causality, which I term "scientific" causality, since it tends to describe the notion(s) of causality used in physical sciences. According to such a notion, causality is crisp, determinate, and precise. The other approach, on the contrary, treats causality as inexact, indeterminate, and dynamic phenomena, which corresponds better with the notion of causality in commonsense reasoning.

Let us examine some existing theories. Hume attempted to define causality logically as "an object followed by another, and where all the objects, similar to the first, are followed by objects similar to the second. Or in other words where, if the first object had not been, the second would never had existed" (Hume 1740). This notion of a *ceteris paribus* sufficient and/or necessary condition as a definition of causes does capture some scientifically motivated aspects of causality. However, it has long been recognized as problematic in various other aspects (see Mackie 1975, Lewis 1975). Philosophers of science tried various ways to amend this definition, including introducing more advanced logics.

Bunge (1963) also tries to cleanse causality of any uncertain or statistical notions. He defines causality as necessary, constant, and unique (in common terms, necessary and sufficient) production, and views it as one special type of determination amidst many other types of determination (such as statistical determination, structural determination, teleological determination). His theory emphasizes *production*, the dynamic character that he believes is missing in Hume's definition. By restricting the scope of causality this way, Bunge thoroughly analyzes this type of "scientific" causality.

On the AI side, Iwasaki and Simon (1986) and de Kleer and Brown (1986) show how causal relations can be identified in device behavior (as well as in economics and thermodynamics; Simon 1965) out of quantitative descriptions. It is argued by Iwasaki and Simon that analyses of a set of algebraic or differential equations that describes the behavior of a device can produce an ordering of variables, which entails causal relatedness and causal directions, and thus can identify causality in such a device. De Kleer and Brown, on the other hand, insist on analyzing qualitative behavior of devices directly and thus obtaining causal relations. Both proposals handle "scientific" causality: deterministic and qualitative causal relations between a set of clearly defined variables without provisions for accommodating vague concepts and indeterminate relationships.

Shoham (1987) developed a modal logic formalism for causality in which some events are necessary and some others are also needed for a given event to occur but are less important. According to this theory, we do not have to worry about relevant but nonessential events in causal reasoning, as long as their potential falsehood is not obvious. Thus causal conditions are divided into two types: causes and enabling conditions. The theory follows logical traditions but tries to accommodate certain commonsense concerns with the introduction of modalities. However, it draws too clear a distinction between causes and enabling conditions (more on this later); it cannot deal with partial information, uncertain causal connections, and vagueness of concepts, which are all essential to commonsense reasoning (as discussed before).

There is a trend toward viewing causality as a complex and indeterminate (or probabilistic) process in the philosophical literature (Suppes 1970, Sosa 1975, Salmon 1984). Salmon (1984) proposes the concept of a "process" as a basic entity rather than the concept of an event as in more traditional theories. A causal *process* transmits energy, information, and causal influence. Salmon defines the principle of marker transmission, the principle of structural transmission, and the principle of propagation of causal influence, which states: "A process that transmits its own structure (transmitting changes in structure) is capable of propagating a causal influence from one space time locale to another." This theory attempts to capture a commonsensical notion of causality. One problem with this theory is that it does not address the issue of how to identify a cause out of a myriad of co-occurring events. A second problem with this theory is its lack of a concise and accurate representation.

Suppes (1970) advocates a probabilistic view of causality. He recognizes the *uncertainty* in the world; according to Suppes, causes are, simply put, a set of events that precede the effect event and that enable one to predict the effect event with a higher probability. In case there are multiple causes, the real cause is the *earliest stronger predictor*, defined by Suppes (1970) with a precise mathematical treatment. He distinguishes, based on the definition, prima facie causes, spurious causes, genuine causes, and so on. Hempel (1965) proposes a statistical relevance theory of scientific explanation. According to this view, causal explanation is inductive-statistical, and the deductive-normological explanation is viewed as a special (limiting) case of causality. Although both theories tend to extend "scientific" causality rather than fully embrace the commonsense causality, some of their ideas are important and applicable. From a cognitive point of view, they both make too strong an assumption—the axioms for probabilistic structures—making a well-defined probabilistic structure a prerequisite for identifying causality.

Along a different line, Putnam (1992) advocates a subjective view of causality, in which causal structures are not "physical" in the sense that they are not built into the external reality; as a matter of fact, causality neither exists independent of the mind nor is cast onto the external world from the mind, but exists with the observer and the physical reality together. This view, in my opinion, supports a subjective, commonsensical approach to the study of causality, in that any notion of causality has to deal with the cognitive agent itself.

These theories have their problems, as debated in the philosophical literature, of which space does not permit a detailed examination. Among the theories described, I share with Putnam the view that causality should be studied in an observer-related way (with a more subjective, commonsensical approach), I share with Salmon the view that causality can be studied and modeled as a complex process, I share with Suppes the view that causality need not be deterministic (especially for commonsense reasoning), and finally I share with Shoham the view that causality can be determined by a (large) number of different conditions each of which is of different importance playing a different role (although I find the clear distinction between them to be an overidealization). Synthesizing and generalizing these views can lead to models that better account for commonsense causality.

Let us look into the relationship between causality and reasoning in general. Reasoning, to a large extent, can be viewed as the formation, modification, and manipulation of an internal model of the world (the environment). This internal model captures commonsense knowledge of the world and allows one to predict, anticipate, and meditate upon an outcome of a current event, possible consequences of an action, and future directions resulting from the interaction of various current events. Based on this internal model, people can reason about a given situation and set up goals, and in order to achieve a certain goal, people can form a plan for the best course of actions, carry out necessary steps, and handle exceptions. An internal model of causality seems to be an essential part of what is underlying this precise, yet flexible, reliable, but fallible process. Based on a causal model, reasoning can utilize artificial causation, changing the model without actually affecting the real world (cf. Sowa 1982).

An internal causal model can be modeled in a network fashion, capturing causal relations between elements of the world; that is, each element of the model corresponds to an element in the world, and each causal link represents a direct causal relation between elements in the world; indirect causes are captured in the chaining of direct causal links (Shoham and Dean 1985). Reasoning can be viewed as a search, either rule-governed or spreading activation (or both), in a network of causal connections. The advantage of using a network model is that causal relations can be represented explicitly and compactly which can allow efficient local processing and modification with minimum global control.

For the operation of a causal model, a rule-based approach is preferred over spreading activation (Collins and Loftus 1975). Collins and Loftus observe (rightly) that the sequential firing of rules or other symbolic structures is much too slow to account for some psychological data and cannot account for the speed, automaticity, and simultaneity exhibited by human reasoning; so spreading activation over a network of prewired links representing associations seems to be a remedy. What is wrong with this picture, I believe, is the following: (1) when talking about sequential operations of rules, they actually have in mind a von Neumann computer, which does go through a slow serial process of fetch, process, and store, one data item at a time, but this is not the best model available today; and (2) there are too many different things in this world associated with too many different other things, so that a fully automatic spreading of activation will not be able to distinguish strong causes from weak associations. (A limited model in a toy domain might work well when associations are fully controlled for the task, but in the real world a vast network with numerous connections will be a totally different situation.) On the other hand, a massively parallel computational architecture can handle many rules at the same time. When rules in some logical form (such as FEL) representing the causality of the world are incorporated into a massively parallel computational architecture (such as CONSYDERR), they behave *as if* the operation were an automatic spreading of activation. However, this "spreading of activation" is rule-governed or rule-directed (see Holland et al. 1986 for similar points).

In summary, causality not only provides a scientific framework in which the physical world is explained (such as in physics, which is an abstraction and an idealization of the commensense notion of the physical world), but also provides a cognitive model of the commonsense world (which is of course murkier), indicating what to expect under a given type of circumstance. A causal model can be represented explicitly in a network fashion, facilitating commonsense reasoning with rules and other mechanisms.

5.3 SHOHAM'S CAUSAL THEORY

Based on the general discussion of causality in Section 5.2, in this section I examine specifically the causal theory of Shoham (1987) in terms of representing commonsense causality.

5.3.1 The Theory

Shoham's theory is undoubtedly one of the most notable contemporary accounts of causality with rule-based formalisms. It utilizes ideas from temporal logic, modal logic, and nonmonotonic logic, and provides a synthesis from a semantic (model-theoretic) viewpoint. The resulting formalism has a close resemblance to Horn clause logic, and therefore is very suitable for use in rule-based AI systems (although all of his algorithms are devised based on the semantics of the logic).

An informal description of Shoham's causal theory (CT) is as follows: causes are primary conditions that together with some secondary conditions, will bring about the effect. In reasoning, as long as we know that the primary conditions (*causes* or *necessary conditions*) are true and that there is no information that the secondary conditions (*enabling conditions* or *possible conditions*) are false, we can deduce that effects will follow. This definition makes the theory nonmonotonic, because if later one of these secondary conditions become known to be false, the reasoning somehow has to be retracted. Shoham insists on using temporal notations in the logic to make sure that causes always precede the effect; thus causality is strictly one-directional. The theory is described in terms of modal logic, with one basic modal operator ($\Box$ or *necessity*) for specifying primary conditions. Another modal operator ($\Diamond$ or *possibility*) for specifying secondary conditions is defined based on the first one (*necessity*).[2]

The formal definition is as follows:

Definition 5.1 A **causal theory** is a set of formulas of the following form:

$$\wedge_i \Box n_i a_i(t_{i1}, t_{i2}) \wedge_j \Diamond n_j b_j(t_{j1}, t_{j2}) \rightarrow \Box c(t_1, t_2)$$

where n_i's are either $\neg$ or nothing, t denotes time, $t_2 > t_{i2}$ for all i's, $t_2 > t_{j2}$ for all j's, a_i's, b_j's, and c are all propositional atoms, $n_i a_i$'s are necessary conditions (causes), and $n_j b_j$'s are possible conditions (enabling conditions). c is concluded iff all $n_i a_i$'s are known to be true and all $n_j b_j$'s are not known to be false.[3]

From the standpoint of modeling commonsense causal knowledge, this model has the following advantages:

- It provides a simple and elegant formalism with efficient inference algorithms. (Shoham (1987) has shown that the problem of inferring all results that are true in all minimal models in CT is polynomial.)
- It is easily representable (and implementable), judging from its Horn clause–like appearance, despite the fact that it synthesizes several radically different approaches: modal logic, temporal logic, nonmonotonic logic, and casual reasoning.
- It has certain compatibility with philosophical accounts of causality in the form of incorporating some important points of Mackie, Lewis, and Suppes (Shoham 1987).

5.3.2 Problems with the Theory

On the other hand, this model is intended only to be a *normative* description of causal reasoning and, as a consequence, it ignores or discounts many

---

[2]Note that the terms *necessary/possible* conditions could be misleading; they do not, in this context, mean what they literally mean. Also note that there is no need for nested modal operators in this logic, since it is for modeling causal conditions (which do not embed in each other) rather than nested beliefs.

[3]This process is described formally by Shoham (1987) with a *minimization* principle.

aspects of commonsense causal reasoning. Below, I discuss one by one the reservations I have about the theory.

1. All propositions in this theory are binary: either true or false; there is no sense of gradedness. Commonsense knowledge, on the other hand, is certainly not limited to true/false only. Inexactness is evident from various psychological data and theories (e.g., Shultz et al. 1989, Hink and Woods 1987, Collins and Michalski 1989), yet it is often absent, ironically, from models aimed at capturing commonsense reasoning.

For example, "the dry weather during that period caused the loss of crops later" can be expressed in CT as

$$\Box \, dry(t, t+1) \;\rightarrow\; \Box \, crop\text{-}loss(t+1, t+2)$$

However, "dry" is a fuzzy concept, and there is no well-defined cutoff point as to what is dry and what is not.

2. Beside the inexactness of individual concepts, reasoning processes in reality are also inexact and evidential. Specifically, the evidential combination process is cumulative (as observed in the data; see Chapter 2). The more conditions we know, the more confidence we have in the conclusions. Moreover, different pieces of evidence are weighted; that is, each of them may have more or less impact, depending on its importance or salience, on the reasoning process and the conclusions reached. There is a need to find a computationally efficient method for combining evidence from different sources cumulatively with weights, without incurring too much computational overhead, such as in probabilistic reasoning or Dempster–Shafer calculus (Pearl 1988, Shafer 1974). (As will be seen later, connectionist weighted-sum computation, viewed simply as a computation, apart from any network implementation, provides just such a method.)

3. Because of the lack of gradedness, the model will make projections too far along a chain of reasoning (or too far into the future). An example from Shoham (1987);

$$\Box \, alive(t_0, t_0)$$

$$\Box \, shoot(t, t) \;\rightarrow\; \Box \, \neg \, alive(t+1, t+1)$$

$$\Box \, alive(t,t) \Diamond \neg \, shoot(t, t) \Diamond \neg \, otherwise\text{-}killed(t, t) \;\rightarrow\; \Box \, alive(t+1, t+1)$$

which means that if one is alive at time t_0, one will continue to be alive as long as one is not shot or otherwise killed. So if there is nothing known about "shoot" and "otherwise-killed," then according to the minimal model approach, we will predict that

$$\Box \, alive(t, t) \quad where \, t \to \infty$$

This is certainly not true.

The problem results from the neglect (in Shoham's formalism) of the fact that along a chain of inference (as well as in temporal projections), the confidence for the conclusions reached should be weakened, as in human reasoning. Moreover, the weakening should occur gradually, and there should not be any sudden transition from predicting *alive* to predicting *not alive*. However, we can weaken confidence along the way only when gradedness is reinstated into causal theories. (This constitutes another reason why we need a model that accommodates gradedness.)

A counterargument is that without other possible causes for death being given, it is reasonable to conclude that the person will live forever. This assertion is, in my opinion, based on the a priori conviction to the absolute certainty (exactness) of the logical approach, which requires that everything has to be accounted for by an exact cause. As a comparison, a human reasoner does not need to know any particular illness in order to predict that someone 88 years old is more likely to die than someone 25 years old—the cause can be unknown or uncertain. The key here is *uncertainty* (inexactness) in causality: (1) the uncertainty of an event (e.g., "60% chance of a cancer"), (2) the uncertainty of causal connections (e.g., "cancer may cause death" or "cancer causes death 80% of the time"), and after all, (3) the uncertainty of actual causes (e.g., "an 88-year-old is likely to die of some illness"). The logical approach fails to handle the third type of uncertainty as well as the first two types.

4. The clear-cut distinction between *necessity* and *possibility* is problematic. In reality, there is little, if any, qualitative difference between *causes* and *enabling conditions*. The difference is more quantitative (as illustrated in Section 5.5), and sometimes the two are interchangeable. For example, "he is shot dead" is expressed as

$$\Box \, shoot(t, t) \land \Diamond \neg \, wearing\text{-}bulletproof\text{-}vest(t, t) \ldots \to \Box \, dead(t + 1, t + 1)$$

and "his failure to wear the bulletproof vest caused his tragic death" is expressed as

$$\Box \, \neg \, wearing\text{-}bulletproof\text{-}vest(t, t) \land \Diamond \, shoot(t, t) \ldots \to \Box \, dead(t + 1, t + 1)$$

So one fact can be both a cause and an enabling condition. This also suggests that enabling conditions have a more important role in causal reasoning than Shoham's model presupposes.

One counterargument is that the second sentence does not really specify causality, but an English "emphatic device". The attribution here of the use of causal terms to surface linguistic features rather than to the expression of causality seems unfounded in that (1) it is not backed up by any established linguistic theories, (2) it is not based on well-defined criteria regarding what is causality and what is not, and (3) it goes against the goal of capturing the commonsense notion of causality as used in everyday discourse (instead of "scientific" causality).

5. Although the model distinguishes two different types of conditions, it does not explain the distinction, that is, why some conditions are necessary and some conditions need only to be possible.

6. According to the model, it is necessary to list all causes and all enabling conditions, in order to guarantee correct results. This could be hard to do in practice, because the number of conditions could be infinite. For example, there are too many reasons why someone is not dead after being shot at: the gun did not work and therefore did not actually fire, the person was wearing a bulletproof vest, there happened to be a stone in front of the person, another stray bullet deflected the bullet aimed at that person, and many others.

7. The causal connection between events in the left-hand side of a causal statement (conditions) and events in the right-hand side of the same statement (conclusions) may not be deterministic. It could be probabilistic, or otherwise uncertain (as discussed before; see Suppes 1970).

8. There are reasons to believe that the temporal aspect of causality is more involved than Shoham's model admits. In commonsense reasoning, it seems to me not the case that causes *must* precede effects in time, especially in terms of the subjective perception of time by a cognitive agent. The effect can be perceived before the cause. For example, in the case of thunder and lightning, people normally think that thunder is the cause of lightning, although lightning is always perceived before thunder, and there is no need to invoke complex scientific theories to explain away the problem (such as "light travels faster than sound"). My goal is precisely the modeling of such commonsense causality. Also notice that up to now, there is no consensus regarding this issue in the philosophical literature. This fact also suggests the complexity of the issue. Lewis (1975) explicitly supports anachronistic causality and believes that there are legitimate physical hypotheses that posit backward or simultaneous causation.

Therefore, it will be better off to discuss causality atemporally, based on the following considerations: (1) most existing formulations of causality are atemporal (e.g., Hume 1740, Mackie 1975, Pearl 1988, Iwasaki and Simon 1986), (2) I need to concentrate on other important issues and therefore must avoid being bogged down by this single issue (which requires more in-depth studies), (3) theoretically, I can do whatever reasoning in an atemporal logic the temporal logic is capable of by introducing different atoms for propositions at different time intervals, and an atemporal version can be extended into the temporal one, after I resolve other important issues, and (4) temporality should be treated the same way as other heuristics, most of which are not dealt with by the logic-based models (including Shoham's), such as *spatial contiguity* and *similarity* (see, e.g., Shultz 1982, Anderson 1990).

In view of these problems, in the following sections I propose a new formalism, which is somewhat an extension of Shoham's formalism that fixes the aforementioned problems.

5.4 DEFINING FEL

In this world, nothing is certain but death and taxes.
—Benjamin Franklin

In this section I first present formal definitions of FEL (including FEL_1 and FEL_2—two versions of *fuzzy evidential logic*) and then analyze its relations to Horn clause logic and Shoham's logic. (The use of FEL in dealing with causality is discussed later in Section 5.5.)

FEL is presented here in a logical framework, but it is based on the most commonly used connectionist model—the weighted-sum model. In a way it can be viewed as simply an interpretation of connectionist models in terms of logics; in other words, FEL provides a semantics for connectionist models based on logics. Like Shoham's formalism, FEL is defined around rules, which are encoded with the weighted-sum computation. FEL is meant to capture, among other things, gradedness and evidentiality of commonsense reasoning, in a cognitively motivated way (instead of dwelling on mathematical details that have little to do with cognitive reality).

5.4.1 Definitions

Definition 5.2 A **fact** is a propositional atom or its negation, represented by a letter (with or without a negation symbol) and having a value between l and u (e.g., $l = -1$ and $u = 1$). The value of an atom is related to the value of its negation by a specific method, so that knowing the value of an atom results in immediately knowing the value of its negation, and vice versa.[4]

Definition 5.3 A **rule** is a structure composed of two parts: a left-hand side (LHS), which consists of one or more facts, and a right-hand side (RHS), which consists of one fact. When facts in LHS get assigned values, the fact in RHS can be assigned a value according to a weighting scheme.[5]

Definition 5.4 A **weighting scheme** is a way of assigning a weight (between -1 and 1) to each fact in the LHS of a rule, with the total weights (the sum

---

[4]I view the value of a fact as a generic confidence measure. Later I characterize this measure further.

[5]When the value of a fact in the LHS is unknown, assume its value to be zero (in case $l = -1$ and $u = 1$) or whatever value represents *unknown*.

of the absolute values of all the weights) less than or equal to 1, and of determining the value of the fact in the RHS of a rule by a thresholded (if thresholds are used) weighted sum of the values of the facts in the LHS (or inner products of weight vectors and vectors of values of LHS facts). When the range of values is continuous, the weighted sum is passed on if its absolute value is greater than the threshold. When the range of values is binary (or bipolar), the result will be one or the other depending on whether or not the weighted sum (or the absolute value of it) is greater than the threshold.[6]

The justifications for using the weighted-sum computation here are the following:

- It weighs different pieces of evidence, giving different weights to facts of different importance, the necessity of which is argued in Chapter 2.
- It accumulates evidence; that is, knowing more pieces of evidence resulting in higher confidence, as demonstrated before in Chapter 2.
- It is the simplest computation one can find that has the two characteristics above.

Next, I define the notion of a theory:

Definition 5.5   A **theory** is a 4-tuple: $\langle A, R, W, T \rangle$, where A is a finite set of facts, R is a set of rules, W is a weighting scheme for R, and T is a set of thresholds each of which is associated with one rule in R (thresholds are optional for rules in R).

One issue that needs to be clarified is how to handle multiple rules reaching the same conclusion (i.e., the same fact is on the RHS of more than one rule and they are all activated), in which case we have to combine the results somehow. In choosing an operator, I can rule out simple ADD, because there is no guarantee that the result will be within the range of $[-1, 1]$ or the like. I cannot use the weighted sum either, because it is used for combining evidence within a rule—the weighted sum represents accumulation of evidence, while this operator should take care of the selection of evidence. One way to accomplish the selection of evidence is to take the MAX of values from various rules. Other operators may also be usable (there are infinitely many possible operators), although I can rule out some of them one way or the other (for details, see Chapter 6). As shown below in relation to other logics, MAX is sufficient for accomplishing what I need to do here and is thus chosen.

---

[6]This weighting scheme can be generalized, as discussed later.

Therefore,

Definition 5.6 A **conclusion** in FEL is a fact and its value, calculated from rules and facts by doing the following:

(1) For each rule having that fact in its RHS, obtain conclusions of all the facts in its LHS (if any fact is unobtainable, assume its value to be zero or whatever value represents the unknown); and then calculate the value of the fact in question using the weighting scheme.

(2) Take the MAX of all these values associated with the fact that are calculated from different rules or are given initially.

Note that *conclusion* is defined here recursively. Thus depending on the structure of a particular theory, this definition may or may not make sense (e.g., in case of recursive structures in a theory). I can restrict the structure of the theories allowed.

Definition 5.7 A rule set is said to be **hierarchical** if the graph depicting the rule set is acyclic; the graph is constructed by drawing a unidirectional link from each fact (atom) in the LHS of a rule to the fact (atom) in the RHS of the rule.

Making a rule set hierarchical avoids circular reasoning. (This is optional, though; circular reasoning may occur in commonsense reasoning.) Now FEL can be defined as follows:

Definition 5.8 A **fuzzy evidential logic** (FEL) is a 6-tuple: $\langle A, R, W, T, I, C \rangle$, where A is a set of facts (the initial values of which are assumed to be zero or whatever represents "unknown"), R is a set of rules, W is a weighting scheme for R, T is a set of thresholds each of which is for one rule, I is the initial condition: a set of elements of the form (f, v) (where f is a fact and v is the value of f), and C is a procedure for deriving conclusions (i.e., computing values of some facts on the basis of the initial condition I).

In other words, it consists of a theory $\langle A, W, R, T \rangle$ (as defined before), a set of initial conditions I, and an inference procedure C (to be determined).

I differentiate FEL into two versions: FEL_1 and FEL_2, which differ in their respective ranges for values of facts.

Definition 5.9 FEL_1 is FEL when the range of values is restricted to between 0 and 1 (i.e., $l = 0$ and $u = 1$), and the way the value of a fact is related to the value of its negation is

$$a = 1 - \neg a$$

for any fact a.

Definition 5.10   FEL$_2$ is FEL when the range of values is restricted to between -1 and 1 (i.e., $l = -1$ and $u = 1$), and the way the value of a fact related to the value of its negation is

$$a = - \neg a$$

for any fact a.

Different ranges of values entail different interpretations of the meaning of a particular value. For example, if the range is between -1 and 1, 0 is viewed as *unknown*. But if the range is between 0 and 1, 0 is viewed as *not*. As a matter of fact, the two different formalisms FEL_1 and FEL_2 can be transformed into one another. Let v_1 stand for a value of a fact in FEL_1, and let v_2 stand for a value of the same fact in FEL_2; then

$$v_1 = \frac{v_2 + 1}{2}$$

In the rest of this book, I will in general use FEL_2 in my discussion.

5.4.2 Special Cases

As an illustration of its capability, I will first show that FEL can implement Horn clause logic as a special case (only the propositional version is considered here; for discussions of first-order cases, see Chapter 7). Let me define Horn clause logic first (cf. Chang and Lee 1973):

Definition 5.11   **Horn clause logic** is a logic in which all formulas are in the form

$$p$$

or

$$p_1 \wedge p_2 \wedge \cdots \wedge p_n \rightarrow q$$

where the p's and q are propositions.

Binary FEL can simulate Horn clause logic:

Definition 5.12   A **binary FEL** is a reduced version of FEL (either FEL_1 or FEL_2), in which values associated with facts are binary (or bipolar), each weight is positive, the total weights of each rule sum to 1, and all thresholds are set to 1.

Here is the theorem for the equivalence (see the Appendix for proofs):

Theorem 5.1 The binary FEL is sound and complete with respect to Horn clause logic.

I also want to show that FEL can simulate Shoham's causal theory as another special case, to explore further the logical capability of FEL. (FEL_2 will be used in the following discussion.) Let me first redefine the causal theory:

Definition 5.13 A **causal theory** is a set of formulas of the form

$$\wedge_i \, \Box \, n_i a_i \, \wedge_j \Diamond n_j b_j \, \rightarrow \, \Box \, c$$

where n_i's are either $\neg$ or nothing, a_i's, b_j's, and c are all propositional atoms, $n_i a_i$'s are necessary conditions (causes), and $n_j b_j$'s are possible conditions (enabling conditions). c is concluded iff all n_{ii}'s are know to be true and none of $n_j b_j$'s are known to be false.

This is a nontemporal version of CT; that is, I strip away all temporal notations and treat the same proposition in the original definition with different temporal variables as different propositions (and represent them with different letters).[7]

I need to find a weighting scheme that can equate FEL to causal theory. But before that, I need to find a mapping between truth values of formulas in causal theory and confidence values of facts in FEL. Since in CT and in FEL, there is no logical OR, we only need to be consistent with regard to logical equivalences without OR connectives, such as $\Box a = \neg \Diamond \neg a$, and so on. Therefore, I use a mapping as follows, which can easily be verified to satisfy these equivalences and the requisite axioms (see the Appendix at the end of the chapter)[8]:

$$M(f) = \begin{cases} 1 & \text{if } f = \text{true} \\ -1 & \text{if } f = \text{false} \\ 0 & \text{if } f \text{ is unknown} \end{cases}$$

$$M(\neg f) = \begin{cases} 1 & \text{if } f = \text{false} \\ -1 & \text{if } f = \text{true} \\ 0 & \text{if } f \text{ is unknown} \end{cases}$$

$$M(\Diamond f) = \begin{cases} 1 & \text{if } M(f) = 0, 1 \\ -1 & \text{if } M(f) = -1 \end{cases}$$

---

[7]The original definition of CT requires it to be irreflexive and antisymmetric, but I will take a stronger position here, that is, a CT has to be hierarchical (or, equivalently, the transitive closure of a CT is irreflexive and antisymmetric; Shoham 1990). To be sure that it is not overrestrictive, it suffices to point out that this stronger position is logically implied by the definition of the temporal version of CT.

[8]Note that this mapping amounts to a S5 system (Hughes and Creswell 1968), but I can easily make the mapping a K45 (or weak S5) system (see the Appendix for details).

$$M(\Box f) = \begin{cases} 1 & \text{if } M(f) = 1 \\ -1 & \text{if } M(f) = 0, -1 \end{cases}$$

$$M(f_1 \wedge f_2) = \begin{cases} 1 & \text{if } M(f_1) = 1 \text{ and } M(f_2) = 1 \\ -1 & \text{if } M(f_1) = 0 \text{ or } M(f_2) = 0 \\ 0 & \text{otherwise} \end{cases}$$

$$M(f_1 \rightarrow f_2) = \begin{cases} 1 & \text{if } M(f_1) = M(f_2) = 1 \text{ or } M(f_1) = -1 \\ -1 & \text{if } M(f_1) = 1 \text{ and } M(f_2) = 0 \\ 0 & \text{otherwise} \end{cases}$$

where f represents an atom or a formula.

The translation of the *modus ponens* inference rule is:

Given $f_1 \rightarrow f_2$:

$$M(f_2) = \begin{cases} 1 & \text{if } M(f_1) = 1 \text{ and } M(f_1 \rightarrow f_2) = 1 \\ 0 & \text{otherwise} \end{cases}$$

I can implement this mapping in FEL in accordance with the behavior of causal statements in CT. However, in FEL, there are only representations for atoms such as a, b, m, n, but not for $\Box a$ or $\Diamond b$, and so on. There are two ways of dealing with this:

- Extending and making more complex the weighting scheme that transforms values for atoms to values for atoms with modal operators.
- Adding nodes that can be used to represent atoms with modal operators.

I will adopt the first approach here (the second approach will also work, and the difference is insignificant; see the Appendix). For a formula in causal theory,

$$\wedge_i \Box n_i a_i \wedge_j \Diamond n_j b_j \rightarrow \Box c$$

Arbitrary weights can be assigned to atoms: a_i's and b_i's, as long as their absolute values sum to 1 (if there is a negation, the corresponding weight is negative; otherwise, weights are positive). Thresholds are equal to 1 for all rules (the result is 1 if the threshold is reached, and 0 otherwise). I restrict the possible values of facts to -1, 0, or 1. However, for b_i's, I will also apply the following function (which carries out the mapping M regarding $\Diamond$) to the link between b_i and c:

$$f_j(b_j) = \begin{cases} 1 & \text{if } b_j = 1 \\ 1 & \text{if } b_j = 0 \text{ and } n_j \neq \neg \\ -1 & \text{if } b_j = 0 \text{ and } n_j = \neg \\ -1 & \text{if } b_j = -1 \end{cases}$$

I will call this function the *elevation* function because it turns all 0's into 1's or -1's. We can view an elevation function as a part of the weight of the corresponding node, that is, $w'_j *' b_j = w_j * f_j(b_j)$, where w'_j is the combined weight and $*'$ is the abstract multiplication operator. There is no need for such functions for any a_i, since the weighted-sum thresholding computation is sufficient for implementing the mapping for (and the semantics of) $\square$.

Now it is easy to verify that a rule in FEL with this specific weighting scheme and threshold is equivalent to a corresponding formula in causal theory: suppose that there is the following formula in CT:

$$\square a \, \square b \, \Diamond c \, \Diamond d \rightarrow \square e$$

It can be translated into FEL as follows:

$$a\,b\,c'\,d' \rightarrow e \qquad (w_1 \; w_2 \; w_3 \; w_4)$$

where $c' = f_c(c)$ and $d' = f_d(d)$ and $\Sigma_i w_i = 1$, and the threshold is equal to 1 for the rule. Let us look into it case by case:

- If a, b, c, and d are known to be true (or, in FEL, "$a = 1$," "$b = 1$," "$c = 1$," and "$d = 1$"), then according to CT, e can be proved (because $\square e$ can be proved; see the Appendix). The same happens in FEL: $a = 1$, $b = 1$, $c' = 1$, $d' = 1$, and $w_1 * 1 + w_2 * 1 + w_3 * 1 + w_4 * 1 = 1$, so we conclude that "$e = 1$" (which satisfies the mapping M).

- If a and b are known to be true (or, in FEL, "$a = 1$" and "$b = 1$"), and c and d are unknown (or, in FEL, "$c = 0$" and "$d = 0$"), then according to CT, e can be proved. The same happens in FEL: $a = 1$, $b = 1$, $c' = 1$, $d' = 1$, and $w_1 * 1 + w_2 * 1 + w_3 * 1 + w_4 * 1 = 1$, so we conclude that "$e = 1$" (which satisfies the mapping M).

- If a and b are known to be true (or in FEL "$a = 1$" and "$b = 1$"), and c and d are known to be false (or in FEL "$c = -1$" and "$d = -1$"), then according to CT, e cannot be proved. The same happens in FEL: $a = 1$, $b = 1$, $c' = -1$, $d' = -1$, and $w_1 * 1 + w_2 * 1 + w_3 * -1 + w_4 * -1 < 1$, so we cannot conclude that "$e = 1$" (thus "$e = 0$").

- If a and b are known to be false (or in FEL "$a = -1$" and "$b = -1$"), and c and d are unknown, then according to CT, e cannot be proved.

The same happens in FEL: $a = -1$, $b = -1$, $c' = 1$, $d' = 1$, and $w_1 * -1 + w_2 * -1 + w_3 * 1 + w_4 * 1 = 1$, so we cannot conclude that "$e = 1$" (thus "$e = 0$").

Other cases can be analyzed the same way. A generic proof of the implementation can easily be constructed and is thus omitted.

To find a full correspondence between FEL and causal theory, we also need a proof procedure that enables the derivation of all the correct results (theorems in the form of atomic formulas in any CT) from a theory. Although in Shoham's causal theory, inferences are defined in terms of minimal models in a model-theoretic way. I will use a proof procedure instead, to facilitate the correspondence with FEL:

Given a causal theory CT and a set of initial conditions (initially true atomic formulas) I:

—For all $a \in I$, infer a, $\Box a$, and $\Diamond a$.
—Repeat:
  for $\wedge_i \Box n_i a_i \wedge_j \Diamond n_j b_j \to \Box c$ where $n_i a_i$'s are inferred, and $\neg n_j b_j$'s are noninferable,[9]
  infer c, $\Box c$, and $\Diamond c$.

It is easy to see the correctness of this procedure:

Theorem 5.2   The proof procedure above is sound and complete for causal theory as defined above.

We can have a similar proof procedure for FEL: Given a FEL theory, and a set of initial conditions (true facts) I:

—For all $(a, v_a) \in I$,[10] infer $a = v_a$.
—Repeat:
  for $\wedge_i n_i a_i \to c$ where each $n_i a_i$ is inferred with a certain value, or is noninferable (and therefore a value zero is assumed),[11]
  infer $c = v_c$, where v_c is calculated according to the weighting scheme used.

---

[9]They are not in I and not in the RHS of any rule, except the RHS of a rule that has a necessary condition in its LHS that is not inferable. Since CT is hierarchical (Shoham 1987), this is easy to detect. I can preconstruct a "dependency graph" that depicts the inferability relation.
[10]For simulating CT, $v_a = 1$.
[11]According to the weighting scheme used in simulating CT, if a fact is inferred, it must be inferred with a value 1; if a fact is noninferable, its value is 0. When other weighting schemes are used, the results can be different.

It is easy to see the correctness of this procedure for FEL, and the mapping between the two proof procedures (see the Appendix for the proof):

Theorem 5.3   The proof procedure above is sound and complete for hierarchical FEL.

Theorem 5.4   The proof procedure for FEL carries out exactly the proof procedure for causal theory when causal theory is implemented in FEL in the aforementioned way.

Therefore,

Theorem 5.5   For every hierarchical, nontemporal causal theory, there is a FEL such that CT: $I \vdash a$ iff FEL: $I' \vdash a = 1$, where I is the initial condition (a set of initially true propositions) for causal theory CT, I' is the initial condition for FEL mapped over from I in CT, and $\vdash$ denotes logical derivations.

It follows directly from the analysis above. In terms of the complexity of the procedure, I have the following theorem:

Theorem 5.6   The problem of deciding if the value of a fact is a certain given number (or deriving that number), given a hierarchical FEL and a set of initial facts and their values, is polynomial.

To keep our perspective, there are some issues to be noted regarding the correspondence between rules and connectionist models. One is that there are also other ways to establish correspondence between rules and connectionist models. For example, in the work of Oden and Jenison (1990), a fuzzy logic formalism is transformed into a connectionist model with logistic activation functions. In the work of Pinkas (1992), a type of logic is transformed into symmetric neural networks, for finding satisfying models. The preceding discussion adds another way of linking rules (logics) with connectionist models, especially the most commonly used one—the weighted-sum model.

Another issue is that the correspondence between FEL and CONSYDERR is not perfect when the proof procedure is taken into consideration. For one thing, in the CD level, which has a distributed overlapping representation, the proof procedure above cannot be carried out as it is, because of the parallel nature of the network and the interaction that the parallelism creates (see Chapter 6 for a detailed discussion of this topic). On the other hand, since in CL there is no overlapping in representation, parallelism will not cause any problem as long as the FEL theory in question is consistent, where *consistency* is defined as that the same fact cannot be inferred with two (or more) values of opposite signs. To see this, notice that the proof procedure above is actually performing a search (with the rules as "operators"), but the procedure itself does not specify a particular order (such as breadth-first or depth-first) used in search. What happens in CL (according to the equations specified in Chapter 3) amounts to a parallel breadth-first search.[12] For a consistent theory, a parallel search works perfectly.

To summarize, a new logical formalism FEL has been proposed to account for commonsense causal reasoning, which corresponds to the CONSYDERR architecture. The relationships between this formalism and some existing ones—Horn clause logic and Shoham's logic—have been explored to demonstrate the representational capability of FEL.

5.5 ACCOUNTING FOR COMMONSENSE CAUSAL REASONING

Cause and effect, means and ends, seed and fruit, cannot be severed;
for the effect already blooms in the cause, the end pre-exists in the
means, the fruit in the seed.
—R. W. Emerson, ESSAYS, FIRST SERIES: COMPENSATION

Based on the review of previous causal theories, the analysis of problems associated with them, especially with Shoham's formalism, and the introduction of FEL, I am now ready to explain how FEL can extend Shoham's formalism to remedy the problems mentioned previously. (The following discussion refers to FEL_2 only.) CONSYDERR will be shown to be a proper framework for representing commonsense causal knowledge.

5.5.1 Extending the Causal Theory

Now I are ready to extend Shoham's causal theory, to solve the problems identified earlier. Since I have already showed that FEL can implement Shoham's causal theory, I can now extend that implementation (instead of the original version), because FEL offers a more general framework that allows greater flexibility.

To extend the FEL version of Shoham's causal theory, I first notice that the causes need not be known with absolute certainty; that is, we should allow a confidence measure being associated with each *necessary* fact (i.e., the one with □), because of the uncertainty and fuzziness of commonsense knowledge. By the same token, the conclusions need not be binary either, so that uncertain causes can generate uncertain effects. Moreover, even facts (causes) of absolute certainty may not guarantee the expected effects (i.e., the idea of uncertain causality; Suppes 1970). Therefore, I will associate a confidence measure with each of the causes (i.e., the facts in LHS of a rule,

---

[12]It is parallel in the sense that all steps that can be explored at a given time are explored together at the same time. The equivalence, however, is approximate; see Chapter 6 for more explanations.

to use the FEL terminology) between -1 and 1, and a confidence measure also with the effect (i.e., the fact in RHS of a rule, to use the FEL terminology). Weights can be used to create a mapping between confidence measures of causes (i.e., values of the corresponding facts) and confidence measures of effects (i.e., values of the corresponding facts), so from a set of causes and their confidence measures (i.e., a set of facts and their values in the LHS) a confidence measure can be inferred for an effect (or a value for a fact in RHS). Moreover, the set of weights associated with facts in LHS of a rule should reflect their relative importance: more important causes should have a larger weight associated with them, and since the total weights sum to 1, the value of a weight for a particular fact (condition) reflects its relative importance against a background of all other conditions.

Another issue to consider is how to handle *possible condition* facts (i.e., those with $\Diamond$). As explained before, there are special functions associated with them, which elevate 0 to 1 or -1 (according to whether positive or negative forms appear in the causal rule). Since I now extend the binary (or bipolar) space for truth values into a graded, continuous space, there is no more need for elevation functions. It follows from the fact that when a *possible condition* fact is unknown (i.e., its value is 0), the conclusion can still be reached, albeit with a smaller value (in confidence level). Now that a binary (or bipolar) outcome is no longer required, it is fine to have a smaller value for a conclusion when some enabling conditions are unknown. When one of these enabling conditions become known, the value will become higher; that is, one will have more confidence in the conclusion. Normally, the weights associated with those enabling conditions will be relatively small anyway, because they are nonessential. So it is advantageous to remove elevation functions in the FEL version of Shoham's causal theory and assign proper weights instead.

An alternative way of viewing the extension is that of "fuzzifying" the necessity function (the mapping from $\Box a$ to its values in FEL) and the possibility function (the mapping from $\Diamond a$ to its values in FEL). Instead of having a necessity function as depicted in Figure 5.1, I can have a fuzzified necessity function as in Figure 5.2, for the purpose of accounting for the inexact nature of real-world situations and knowledge. Similarly, instead of having a possibility function as depicted in Figure 5.3, I can have a fuzzified possibility function as in Figure 5.4. Once fuzzified, these new functions wind up to be identity functions (as if no function at all).[13] Therefore, combining the two perspectives above, *causes* are those conditions that have *high* weights, and *enabling conditions* are those conditions that have *low* weights. There is no clear-cut boundary and thus there is no qualitative difference between them.

---

[13]Other ways of fuzzifying them are also possible; I adopt this particular way for its simplicity. If a certain domain requires more complex ways of fuzzifying these functions, this approach can be extended in a straightforward way.

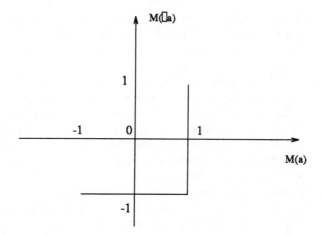

Figure 5.1. *Necessity function. (M is a mapping function).*

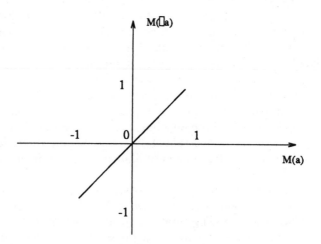

Figure 5.2. *Fuzzified necessity function. (M is a mapping function).*

I map the causal terminology into the FEL terminology as follows:

- **Events** *are facts in FEL.*
- **Causal statements** *are rules in FEL.*
- **Causes** *are those conditions of a rule that have high weights associated with them according to some weighting scheme.*
- **Enabling conditions** *are those conditions of a rule that have low weights associated with them according to some weighting scheme.*
- **Effects** *are facts in the RHS of a rule.*

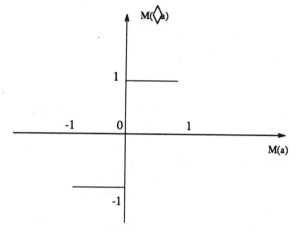

Figure 5.3. *Possibility function. (M is a mapping function).*

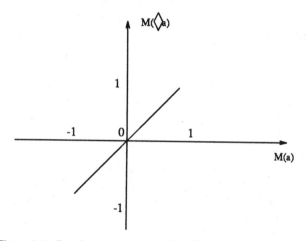

Figure 5.4. *Fuzzified possibility function. (M is a mapping function).*

5.5.2 Dealing with the Problems

I can now go back to the issues identified earlier and demonstrate that FEL (with the extended definition of causality) can better handle the issues identified in Section 5.3:

- Gradedness is readily taken care of in FEL, by confidence values associated with facts.
- Because of the introduction of gradedness and uncertain causal rules (i.e., rules with the total weight less than 1), the confidence in a

conclusion will weaken along the way in a chaining. For example, here is a FEL rule stating that if one is alive at time *t*, one will be alive at time *t* + 1:

$$alive(t) \rightarrow alive(t + 1)$$

Suppose that the weight is equal to 0.99. If given *alive(0) = 1*, we will have *alive(1) = 0.99*, *alive(2) = 0.98*, *alive(3) = 0.97*, and so on.

- The explanation for the distinction between causes and enabling conditions is simple (as mentioned before): causes (necessary conditions) are the ones that have high weights, and enabling conditions (possible conditions) are those that have low weights. Thus, the clear-cut boundary between the two in Shoham's theory is found to be an (over)idealization, in that the graded difference in the real world is (unnecessarily) turned into the all-or-nothing distinction (which can only be justified by the logical approach itself).

- The need to tell exactly which condition is necessary (a cause) and which condition is possible (an enabling condition) is no longer existent: they are all graded and the difference is only quantitative (see Section 5.6 regarding weights).

- The need to list all conditions (the total number of which might be infinite) is no longer existent: as long as I leave room in the weight distribution (i.e., keeping total weights less than 1) for unspecified conditions, I need list only those conditions that I care about, and the sum of weights will then be less than 1, accommodating possible roles of other (unlisted) conditions in determining the causal outcome.

- The indeterminate or probabilistic nature of causality is readily captured in the weighting scheme: the sum of the weights do not have to be 1 (it could be less), and not all the conditions have to be known for certain to deduce a plausible conclusion.

5.5.3   Two Principles

Let me further explicate what is implicit in the definitions of FEL concerning how causality is handled. Causality is handled in the FEL framework uniformly based on the following two basic principles:

Minimality Principle   Nothing should be assumed unless given or explicitly derived (making minimal assumptions about the world). If something is unknown and cannot be derived, assume neutrality regarding its truth (i.e., assume values to be zero in case of FEL_2).

Weighting Principle   In deriving an effect based on a causal statement, calculate the highest possible value of the effect based on the values of the conditions of the causal statement (with the weighted-sum computation), without violating the minimality principle.

In the shooting example above, instead of having two separate causal statements in CT:

$$\square \; shoot(t, t) \; \wedge \; \lozenge \neg \; wearing\text{-}bulletproof\text{-}vest(t, t) \ldots \to \square \; dead(t + 1, t + 1)$$

and

$$\square \neg \; wearing\text{-}bulletproof\text{-}vest(t, t) \; \wedge \; \lozenge shoot(t, t) \ldots \to \square \; dead(t + 1, t + 1)$$

I use one single causal statement in FEL for all the situations:

$$\neg \; wearing\text{-}bulletproof\text{-}vest \; \wedge \; shoot \ldots \to dead \quad weights = (w_1, w_2, \ldots)$$

The minimality principle and the weighting principle (or in other words, the previously defined FEL inference procedure can thus be applied); that is, assume that the values of the unknown facts are zero and calculate the value of the conclusion by inner products of the weights and the values of the facts in the LHS of the rule. So each fact in a LHS can be a cause when the rest of the LHS is obvious in a certain context or is unknown for lack of information. When the rest of the LHS is known for certain in a given context (such as in "His failure to wear the bulletproof vest caused his death"), the value of the conclusion is high; when the rest of the LHS is simply unknown, the value of the conclusion is lower, representing a weaker causal connection.

5.5.4 Causality in CONSYDERR

In the CONSYDERR architecture, causal events are represented by nodes (including causes, enabling conditions, and effects), and causal statements are represented by the links between a node representing a cause and a node representing an effect (recall also the mapping between causal terminology and FEL). The minimality principle is carried out by setting node activations to zero initially and keeping them at zero when there is no input. The weighting principle is carried out by the weighted-sum computation (with MAX) in each node that represents an effect.

In the systems discussed in Chapter 4, there are many instances of causal statements. For instance, in the Florida protocol, we have the following rule:

big-area warm-area flat-area freshwater $\to$ *rice-growing*

which specifies the causal connection between being a warm, big, and flat area with a freshwater supply and being a rice-growing area. In another instance, we have the knowledge that the Brazil rainforest area is a rubber-producing area (i.e., *Brazil* $\to$ *rubber-producing*), and the features of that area include "tropical," "high-precipitation," "rainforest," "rugged," and so on. The causal knowledge is captured by the links in CD (for replicating the CL link diffusely) that connect these features to the nodes representing "rubber-producing-area," which amounts to a causal statement (although it is not explicitly known):

$$tropical\ high\text{-}precipitation\ rainforest\ rugged\ \rightarrow\ rubber\text{-}producing$$

Therefore, causal knowledge is captured in two different forms: one form is explicit causal rules in CL, such as the first instance, and the other is a set of links in CD between features of different concepts (diffusely replicating original noncasual rules in CL).

Reasoning can either follow strict causal statements (rules), to find the corresponding causal effects, or can utilize similar, related, but not directly applicable causal statements, for example, in case of analogy. In CONSY-DERR, such analogy is achieved through similarity in the CD representation. Through this lower-level similarity, one concept finds a related (similar) concept that can help in continuing the reasoning with its associated causal statements that are not available to the original concept. This capability extends the meaning of causality, and can produce parsimonious representation, by specifying only prototypical causal connections.[14]

5.5.5   Rules and Causality Revisited

After tearing apart existing accounts of causality and proposing a new approach in their stead, it is now the time to face the following question: What is left of causality? Is it just a set of generic rules (in the sense of a determinate relation or a semideterminate relation; apart from "analogy"), or does it have something unique to it, meriting special attention? My answer is that causality and generic rule-based reasoning have (1) conceptual distinction, and (2) mechanistic indistinction. The conceptual distinction is intuitively clear, although no approach (including connectionist approaches) is able to characterize it satisfactorily. The mechanistic indistinction is also quite evident, in this as well as in other formulations of causality: none of the existing mechanisms for modeling causality can capture all causal reasoning forms but exclude all noncausal reasoning forms (not even for Shoham's logic). I suspect that there is no distinction in terms of computational mechanisms involved, simply for the sake of uniformity and thus cognitive economy (which might be favored by evolution and natural selection). An additional reason might be the need to intermix causal and noncausal inferences in commonsense reasoning.

---

[14]This "analogy-based causality" might also be explained by probabilistic approaches, though maybe not very elegantly.

To summarize, FEL provides an elegant and justified way of extending Shoham's causal theory, and constitutes a step toward capturing the graded and inexact nature of real-world commonsense causal knowledge. The CONSYDERR architecture with dual-representation implements FEL and provides a set of primitives for representing and reasoning with causal rules.[15]

5.6 DETERMINING WEIGHTS

One last question is how we should interpret (and/or determine) weights in FEL rules. I will look briefly into this question.

Before we can possibly determine the nature of the weights used in calculating values assicated with facts, we must first explain those values. Those values can be viewed, alternatively, as grades of membership in a fuzzy set (Zadeh 1965), as probabilities, as possibilities (Zadeh 1978), or as all of the above combined, and so on. In fact, fuzziness, probability, and other inexactness are often mixed together and cannot really be separated and dealt with in isolation. For example, in the sentence "John is probably very angry by now", there is uncertainty (probability), as represented by the word "probably", and fuzziness, since "very angry" is not something with clear-cut boundaries. In order to be able to handle all of these in one framework, we must either (1) adopt a more generic measure that encompasses all of them, or (2) use more than one measure to cover them all. In the second approach, this situation is handled by having two (or more) measures, one for uncertainty and another for fuzziness, and so on (Collins and Michalski 1989). This approach will work but seems to me *unnecessary*, because one parameter is sufficient to measure the degree of *fit* of a situation to a description (i.e., the "distance" between them), which is all we need to know. So I shall adopt the first approach, using one generic measure.[16]

---

[15]Clearly, I do not deal with *all* aspects of causality as discussed in numerous philosophical and psychological literatures, for example, the principle of temporal contiguity, the principle of space contiguity, and or the principle of antecedence (Anderson 1990, Salmon 1984).

[16]It can be determined by a *generalized characteristic function* over the domain of all possible objects. Note that in classical logic theory, for any predicate, there is a set of objects (from the universe of discourse) that make the predicate true, and we can define a characteristic function that maps each object in this set to 1 and all the other objects to 0; similarly, for a predicate in fuzzy logic (Zadeh 1988), there can be a set of objects that make it true to a certain extent (but not necessarily to its full extent); the degree of the truth (fuzziness) of a particular object with regard to that predicate is determined by a fuzzy characteristic function defined based on the particular predicate. Since in FEL I am dealing with more than just fuzziness, I use a more generic measure—a measure of the confidence that we have in that predicate considering fuzziness, probability, and other factors with respect to the object and the context, which is thus a generalized characteristic function and can take a value between -1 and 1 (or between 0 and 1) for each object in the universe.

Several different interpretations of weights relate FEL to existing frameworks. Here I concentrate on FEL_1.[17] First there is the **fuzzy interpretation**. Suppose that we have fuzzy sets $A_1, A_2, \ldots, A_n$, and B, and a fuzzy rule $A_1 A_2 \ldots A_n \rightarrow B$. As explained in Chapter 8, when given fuzzy sets $A'_1, A'_2, \ldots, A'_n$, we can derive B' by

$$m_{B'}(y) = \max_{x_1, x_2, \ldots, x_n} \min\left(\min\left(m_{A'_1}(x_1), m_{A'_2}(x_2), \ldots, m_{A'_n}(x_n)\right),\right.$$
$$\left.\min\left(1, \left(1 - \min\left(m_{A_1}(x_1), m_{A_2}(x_2), \ldots, m_{A_n}(x_n)\right)\right) + m_B(y)\right)\right)$$

where m is the grade of membership with respective fuzzy sets.

However, the MIN/MAX operation above is not the only possible operation, uniquely determined by empirical desiderata or by mathematical necessity; as a matter of fact, many different formulations have been proposed (cf. Dubois and Prade 1988). According to the arguments presented in Section 5.3, I can justifiably replace the formula above with weighted sums. To do this, instead of using one confidence measure as above for a rule, I will use a vector of measures (a set of weights), with its dimension equal to the number of conditions in a rule and its values corresponding to the relative importance of each of the conditions; instead of using MIN/MAX (which does not accumulate evidence), I use $+$ for the accumulation of evidence and $*$ for the weighing of pieces of evidence; that is,

$$w_1 * m_{A_1}(x_1) + w_2 * m_{A_2}(x_2) + \cdots + w_n * m_{A_n}(x_n)$$

where the w_i's are elements in the vector of confidence measures associated with rules, the x_i's are elements from fuzzy sets A_i's, respectively, and m's are grades of membership for respective fuzzy sets. This interpretation shows that FEL is just another version of fuzzy logic, with some different operators.

The second interpretation is the **probabilistic interpretation**: suppose that $A_1, A_2, \ldots, A_n$, and B are probabilistic events. A rule such as $A_1 A_2 \cdots A_n \rightarrow B$ can be readily interpreted as computation of $p(B)$ from $p(A_1)$, $p(A_2), \ldots, p(A_n)$, that is,

$$p(B) = p(B|A_1 A_2 \cdots A_n) p(A_1 A_2 \cdots A_n)$$

When A_i's are pairwise independent and exhaustive, the formula above can be rewritten as

$$p(B) = p(B|A_1) p(A_1) + p(B|A_2) p(A_2) + \cdots + p(B|A_n) p(A_n)$$

Comparing it with the weighted-sum formula, we immediately notice the similarity: $p(A_i)$'s are values of the conditions, $p(B)$ is the value for the

---

[17]Note that the two different formalisms FEL_1 and FEL_2 can be transformed into one another.

conclusion, and $p(B|A_i) = w_i$ are the weights. So we have an interpretation of weights in FEL rules as conditional probabilities (given the assumption of the independence of evidence). The advantage of this approach versus full-fledged probabilistic approaches is discussed in Chapter 8.

Since probability and fuzziness can be, and in most cases are, mixed together, giving rise to a single measure of confidence, a way to obtain weights based on such measures is to use some learning algorithms (connectionist or nonconnectionist), so that weights can develop from the data presented, taking into account all kinds of inexactness. A learning algorithm adopted serves as an **operational definition** or **operational interpretation** for weights in FEL. From the vast array of available learning algorithms, those that guarantee that each of the weights for a group of links reflects the relative importance of the corresponding link and the total weights for a group of links sum to be equal to or less than 1 (or those that can be modified to fit this criterion) are suitable for this purpose. Many algorithms are thus applicable in this regard, such as the competitive learning algorithm (Rumelhart et al. 1986) or ART (Grossberg 1987).

5.7 SUMMARY

To explain and justify the way rules are encoded in CONSYDERR, this chapter turns to theories of causality and logic formalisms that purports to explain and express causality. Let me summarize succinctly the conclusions that can be drawn based on the discussions of this chapter:

- FEL is a suitable way for representing rules and performing commonsense reasoning.
- Connectionist models are, therefore, fully capable of representing rules —syntactically there is little difference between connectionist models and rules in general.
- Causality plays an important role in commonsense reasoning and representation, and the power of FEL, and that of CONSYDERR, derives (in part at least) from its ability to represent commonsense causal knowledge of various sorts.

To a large extent, this chapter has been devoted to showing that there is a direct correspondence between weighted-sum connectionist models and rules (or logics), notably without complicated transformations and intermediate steps (such as in the proof of Turing equivalence of connectionist models). In Chapter 6, I discuss another set of questions regarding CONSYDERR that complements the discussion in this chapter, showing the unique characteristics of this architecture, different both from traditional rule-based reasoning and from conventional connectionist models.

5.8 APPENDIX: PROOFS FOR THEOREMS

Theorem There is an isomorphic one-to-one mapping between FEL and CL.

Proof FEL is defined to be a 6-tuple $\langle A, R, W, T, I, C \rangle$. A particular FEL theory is a 4-tuple $\langle A, R, W, T \rangle$. CL is defined to be $\langle N, C \rangle$. I will show a mapping from CL to FEL; the inverse mapping can be done the same way. Let $A = N$. For each $n \in N$, do the following: find all links that have the form (m, n); among them find all links that rest on the same site (forming a group), that is, $(m_1, n), (m_2, n), \ldots, (m_l, n)$, and make a corresponding rule in R (i.e., $m_1, m_2, \ldots, m_l \to n$); do the same for all sites. The weights in all the node activation functions make up W in FEL. T is the same set of thresholds as in the node activation functions of CL. Q.E.D.

Theorem The binary FEL is sound and complete with respect to Horn clause logic.

Proof Assume that FEL_2 is used here. The inference rule for FEL can be defined as a variant of forward chaining (in accordance with the definition of *conclusion*). Let K be a set of FEL facts and their values, in the form of pairs (f, v), where f is a fact and v is its value (i.e., "$f = v$"). Assume that all facts are uniquely represented in K (though their confidence values may be zero). The inference rule will simply add FEL facts to K until no new ones can be added:

(1) Given the FEL rule: $a_1 \cdots a_r \to b$ with $(w_1, \ldots, w_r)$. If $(a_1, v_1), \ldots, (a_r, v_r)$ are in K, let $v' = w_1 * v_1 + \cdots + w_r * v_r$ and assume (b, v) to be in K. If $|v'| \geq \theta$ and $|v'| > |v|$, replace (b, v) by (b, v').

(2) Given the FEL fact: $(b, 1)$ (the known fact), we simply replace (b, v) in K by $(b, 1)$.

In case of binary FEL, the threshold $\theta = 1$. Also, if we know that the value of b is 1, we know that the value of $\neg b$ is -1, and vice versa.

Given a Horn clause theory H, one can produce a corresponding binary FEL theory F as follows: each Horn clause $a_1, \ldots, a_r \to b$ is transformed into a FEL rule by associating a weight w_i with each fact a_i, in such a way that $w_i > 0$ and their sum is 1. Conversely, given a binary FEL theory F, one can also produce a corresponding Horn clause theory H as follows: each FEL rule $a_1, \ldots, a_r \to b$ $(w_1, w_2, \ldots, w_r)$ is transformed into a Horn rule directly, by ignoring weights w_i's, since according to the definition of binary FEL, we always have $w_i > 0$ and their sum is 1.

Assume that all facts in K initially have values 0. Then $(b, 1)$ is a FEL conclusion of F iff b is a logical consequence of H. To see this, observe that a

FEL fact $(b, 1)$ is added to K if and only if all of the facts in the LHS of the rule have values 1. Thus, $(b, 1)$ is introduced to K if and only if there exist facts $(a_1, 1), \ldots, (a_r, 1)$ in K. It follows that the FEL inference rule behaves exactly like the forward chaining operator for Horn clause logic when we restrict our attention to facts of value 1. b can be inferred by forward chaining in H iff $(b, 1)$ can be inferred by the FEL inference rule. Therefore, because the Horn clause forward-chaining inference rule is sound and complete, binary FEL is sound and complete with respect to Horn clause logic. Q.E.D.

A **weighting scheme** that can equate FEL to causal theory:

$$M(f) = \begin{cases} 1 & \text{if } f = \text{true} \\ -1 & \text{if } f = \text{false} \\ 0 & \text{if } f \text{ is unknown} \end{cases}$$

$$M(\neg f) = \begin{cases} 1 & \text{if } f = \text{false} \\ -1 & \text{if } f = \text{true} \\ 0 & \text{if } f \text{ is unknown} \end{cases}$$

$$M(\Diamond f) = \begin{cases} 1 & \text{if } M(f) = 0, 1 \\ -1 & \text{if } M(f) = -1 \end{cases}$$

$$M(\Box f) = \begin{cases} 1 & \text{if } M(f) = 1 \\ -1 & \text{if } M(f) = 0, -1 \end{cases}$$

$$M(f_1 \wedge f_2) = \begin{cases} 1 & \text{if } M(f_1) = 1 \text{ and } M(f_2) = 1 \\ -1 & \text{if } M(f_1) = 0 \text{ or } M(f_2) = 0 \\ 0 & \text{otherwise} \end{cases}$$

$$M(f_1 \rightarrow f_2) = \begin{cases} 1 & \text{if } M(f_1) = M(f_2) = 1 \text{ or } M(f_1) = -1 \\ -1 & \text{if } M(f_1) = 1 \text{ and } M(f_2) = 0 \\ 0 & \text{otherwise} \end{cases}$$

This mapping amounts to a S5 system (Creswell and Hughes 1968). The axioms for S5 are

$$\Box(a \rightarrow b) \rightarrow (\Box a \rightarrow \Box b)$$
$$\Box a \rightarrow \Box \Box a$$
$$\neg \Box a \rightarrow \Box \neg \Box a$$
$$\Box a \rightarrow a$$

It is easy to verify that the aforementioned mapping satisfies all the axioms, and thus it is a S5 system. I can also make the mapping a K45 (or weak S5) system by mapping $\Box a$ into $1 - \varepsilon$ instead of 1 (and making other related changes). Note that a K45 system has all the axioms as a S5 system except the last one, and it is easy to verify that this new mapping no longer satisfies the last axiom in the S5 system.

As mentioned in the chapter, if nodes representing $\Diamond a$ and $\Diamond \neg a$, for all atom a, are added, then there is no need for the elevation function f on links. Instead, some extra nodes $\Diamond a$ and $\Diamond \neg a$ are created, which have incoming links (with weights equal to 1) from their corresponding node a and have thresholds 0. For $\Diamond a$,

$$\Diamond a = \begin{cases} 1 & \text{if } w * i >= 0 \\ -1 & \text{otherwise} \end{cases}$$

For $\Diamond \neg a$,

$$\Diamond \neg a = \begin{cases} -1 & \text{if } w * i >= 0 \\ 1 & \text{otherwise} \end{cases}$$

It can easily be shown that this accomplishes the same as the elevation function.

Theorem   The problem of deciding if the value of a fact is a certain given number (or deriving that number), given a hierarchical FEL, a set of initial facts, and their values, is polynomial.

Proof   I will use the proof procedure defined in Section 5.4. Obviously, the first step takes polynomial time (for checking all initially true facts). In the second step, the REPEAT loop takes a number of iterations up to the number of rules, by using a dependency graph as a data structure. In each iteration, time taken is proportional to the number of facts in the LHS, which is bounded to be less than or equal to the total number of facts in the particular FEL (in R or I). So the total amount of time taken is polynomial with respect to the number of facts and the number of rules (i.e., the sizes of R and I).   Q.E.D.

Theorem   The proof procedure for FEL carries out exactly the proof procedure for causal theory when causal theory is implemented in FEL in the aforementioned way (the two systems are sound and complete for each other).

Proof   Let us look at each step of the procedure.

Step 1:

For implementing CT, the initial conditions are given with value 1. So inferring that $a = 1$ in FEL is equivalent to inferring a, $\Box a$, and $\Diamond a$ in CT.

Step 2:

Inferability is dealt with in the same way in FEL and CT. When a rule is chosen in FEL, we infer the conclusion $c = v_c$ according to the particular weighting scheme. With the particular weighting scheme for implementing CT, v_c has to be 1, which means that all the conditions of the rule used are true: with the mapping M, it is easy to see that in CT all the corresponding conditions are true; so we can infer c, $\square c$, and $\diamondsuit c$. Conversely, if we infer c, $\square c$, and $\diamondsuit c$ in CT, we can also infer $c = 1$ in FEL, based on the mapping between conditions in CT and the corresponding conditions in FEL and the weighting scheme used. Q.E.D.

CHAPTER 6 _____

More on the Architecture: Beyond Logic

Logic is one thing and commonsense another.
  —Elbert Hubbard, THE NOTEBOOK

6.1 OVERVIEW

A few other topics regarding CONSYDERR are covered in this chapter. I will concentrate on three different issues: inheritance, representational interaction, and knowledge acquisition for CONSYDERR. The discussion of all these issues together shows the *difference* between rules in traditional "symbolic" systems and rules in connectionist models. The difference is, first and foremost, the difference between isolated, context-free inferences and complex, interacting processes.

In the first section I explore further the issue of inheritance. I analyze how a complete inheritance hierarchy can be implemented, and discuss the issues of cancellation, multiple inheritance, and generation of new concepts. In the second section I explore interaction in representation. In the third section I touch briefly on the problem of learning and knowledge acquisition. Since these topics per se are beyond the main focus of this work, I will not talk too much about the basics. For those not interested in details, a summary is provided for each section.

6.2 FURTHER ANALYSIS OF INHERITANCE

In Chapter 3, I discussed several important but isolated cases of inheritance as part of the requirements and constraints utilized in developing CONSYDERR. To clarify this topic further, in this section a complete analysis of inheritance reasoning in CONSYDERR is presented (see also Sun 1993a). To put this analysis into perspective, some background regarding inheritance is first discussed. Then the solution in CONSYDERR is thoroughly analyzed.

6.2.1 Background

Inheritance is one of the central problems in artificial intelligence, and it has been receiving a lot of attention. Many different variations of the inheritance problem have been studied and many different solutions have been proposed. Most knowledge representation systems nowadays embody some kinds of inheritance mechanisms; various implementations exist, ranging from simple ones to highly complex parallel spreading activation systems. The intensity of activities in this area signifies its importance—inheritance is an essential part of commonsense reasoning.

In a nutshell, inheritance is the derivation of information for one concept (class) based on known information associated with another concept (class) in a hierarchically structured knowledge base. Hierarchical structuring of knowledge allows economical representation, by minimizing the redundancy of information stored, and allows efficient reasoning, by directing inference in a predetermined way. Intelligent reasoning systems rely on inheritance to enable certain useful and frequently made inferences (i.e., inheritance of property values) to be made. The research in this area centers on developing sound mechanisms that can handle various inheritance situations correctly and efficiently.

Among all the work in this area, Touretzky's (1985) is by far the most comprehensive study of inheritance. In his work, inheritance networks are construed to be *lattice* structures, enabling a full mathematical analysis of them, and a clear semantics is developed for the problem. The analysis leads to the rule of *the shortest inferential distances* for deducing correct results; various kinds of inheritance scenarios are analyzed in his work to show how each can be handled correctly by the rule.

Instead of dealing only with top-down inheritance (inheritance from a superclass to a subclass), Shastri (1988) presents an evidential framework for the inheritance problem in both top-down and bottom-up directions and a connectionist implementation of the evidential formulation. His treatment of inheritance is extensional, based on counting the numbers of objects with different property values, and the conclusion is reached with information maximization based on the counts. The connectionist implementation is localist and makes use of several specially designed node types for evidential combination.

Yager (1989), on the other hand, presents a *possibilistic* treatment of the inheritance problem based on the fuzzy set theory (Zadeh 1965, 1975). Basically, results of inheritance are rated with a possibilistic measure and the highest rated result is adopted; other devices are also needed, one of which is the ordering of facts from the most specific to the most general. The idea of a fuzzy solution to the inheritance problem is very interesting, but the particular solution seems somewhat ad hoc. Mili and Rada's work (1990) represents a different approach in applying the fuzzy set theory to inheritance and deals with inheritance as *generalized fuzzy regularity*; that is, hierarchical relationships between concepts are to reflect relationships between the properties of these concepts, and vice versa. It treats both top-down and bottom-up inheritance in one framework. It is a mathematically motivated treatment, not a cognitively motivated one.

In this section I advocate the view that inheritance is better dealt with intensionally instead of extensionally. Briefly, as discussed before, *extension* is the class of objects that fits a concept, and *intension* is the "meaning" of a concept (and of the class it describes), or more precisely it is a set of *features* of a concept. Extensional approaches thus deal only with the classes (of objects) per se, while intensional approaches can take into account meanings of classes. This distinction can be likened to that of syntax vs. semantics, in that extensional approaches deal only with syntactic relations while intensional approaches also deal with semantic content of concepts. Specifically, the problems with the existing purely extensional approaches are the following:

- The complexity and often ad hoc-ness of mechanisms for handling various cancellation scenarios (Yager 1989, Shastri 1988, Besnard 1989)
- The difficulty in finding correct solutions to various situations, such as multiple inheritance (Thomason 1990, Shastri 1988)
- The computational inefficiency resulting from the complex mechanisms employed

I believe that inferences in an inheritance system should be based on intensions (features, semantics, etc.) of concepts involved, at least to a certain extent, rather than based solely on syntactic, extensional relations (such as *is-a*); for intensional approaches represent a deeper and more fundamental (meaning-oriented) understanding of relationships between concepts. Intensional approaches provide a way of remedying the aforementioned problems:

- It provides a computationally efficient (constant time) solution for a theoretically and practically important problem.

- With this solution, the inheritance problem is reduced to the more general problem of rules and similarities. The solution is provided as a part of the solution to problems of much broader scope and thus is not an ad hoc trick (not even a specialized mechanism).

Next, a treatment of inheritance in CONSYDERR is presented, based on the idea of two-level dual representation (as in the CONSYDERR architecture).

6.2.2   Analysis of Inheritance in CONSYDERR

Two Types of Links   First, some clarifications are made regarding the basic notations used in formulating the inheritance problem. Touretzky (1985) describes inheritance as inheritance between classes (concepts), with only *is-a* links used to connect various classes (concepts). In my discussion, however, a slightly different formulation of the problem is used: instead of all *is-a* links, I will use two types of links: *is-a* and *has-property-value*; *is-a* is used here to denote relations between a subclass and a superclass; *has-property-value* is used to denote a property value of a class. Although, mathematically, through some transformation one type can be turned into another, the resulting representation is unnatural.[1] These two types of relations are fundamentally different.

For example, the elephant example can be expressed in Touretzky's formalism as

elephant *is-a* gray-thing

royal-elephant *is-a* white-thing

royal-elephant *is-a* elephant

Here "gray-thing" or "white-thing" are not natural categories, although one can always make up such categories if so desired. In my formalism, the

---

[1] Let p represent a particular property, v its value, and c a class. I can make a class out of all classes that have a certain value for a certain property, that is,

$$c = c_1 \cup c_2 \cup \cdots \cup c_n$$

such that

$$p(c_i) = v \qquad i = 1, 2, \ldots, n$$

and

$$p(x) \neq v \qquad \text{if } x \neq c_i$$

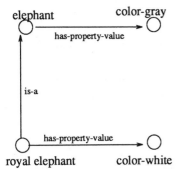

elephant   color-gray

royal elephant   color-white   **Figure 6.1.** *Inheritance graph.*

example can be expressed, more naturally, as

> elephant *color* gray
> royal-elephant *color* white
> royal-elephant *is-a* elephant

Or equivalently,

> elephant *has-property-value* color-gray[2]
> royal-elephant *has-property-value* color-white
> royal-elephant *is-a* elephant

Here I treat a property-value pair (e.g., color-gray) as a single concept. See Figure 6.1

This formulation of inheritance can be described by *rules* and *similarities*. The elephant example can be translated into the following rules for expressing property values:

$$elephant \rightarrow color\text{-}gray$$
$$royal\text{-}elephant \rightarrow color\text{-}white$$

and similarities between royal elephants and elephants (for *is-a* or subclass/ superclass relations):

$$elephant \sim royal\text{-}elephant$$

That is, *is-a* (the subclass/superclass relation) is handled here as a special case of similarity. Similarity in general can be attributed to the overlap in the meanings of two concepts: when we decompose "meanings" into features, similarity amounts to the overlap of the feature sets of the two concepts.

---

[2]It means that elephant has a property *color* whose value is *gray*. The same applies below.

Therefore, in this sense, a superclass and a subclass are similar to each other, as a special case of the general similarity, because the feature set of a superclass is the subset of that of a subclass and therefore one is contained in another (a special case of feature overlap).

In general, as in the example above, it is a rule of thumb that in CONSYDERR, *is-a* links are implemented implicitly through CD representations and *has-property-value* links are implemented explicitly with rules in CL (and diffusely replicated in CD).

Chaining of is-a Links   Now I will analyze how inheritance *hierarchies* can be formed with rules and similarities in CONSYDERR. An inheritance hierarchy is an acyclic structure with nodes representing either a concept (a class of objects) or a particular property-value pair (e.g., color-gray), connected by two types of links. The chaining of *is-a* links forms the backbone of an inheritance hierarchy (see Figure 6.2). The chaining of *is-a* links is handled in CONSYDERR, the same was as before, by utilizing overlapping feature representations (see Figure 6.3). The question now is how property values of a concept can be inherited correctly along this chain upward or downward. In the following analysis, for the sake of clarity, I will assume that weights on all links connecting concepts and their property values are all 1's.

Let us look at top-down inheritance first. By "top-down" I mean that the property values of a class are inherited by its subclasses. It seems easy to accomplish this task: based on the similarity between the superclass and the subclass in their corresponding feature representations (one is contained in the other), the subclass can easily inherit the property values. So can the subclass of the subclass, the subclass of the subclass, and so on. Troubles arise when there are one or more cancellations of the property values somewhere along the chain. In such cases we have to make sure that correct values are inherited.

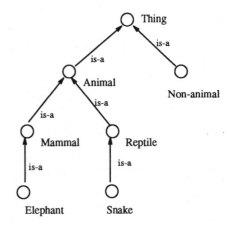

Figure 6.2. *Inheritance graph with long chains of is-a links.*

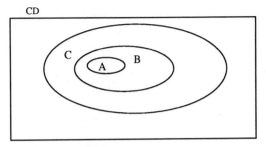

Figure 6.3. *Implementing chains of is-a links: C is-a B and B is-a A ($A \supset B \supset C$ and $F_A \subset F_B \subset F_C$).*

Suppose in an inheritance graph that A is a class and B is its closest superclass that has a value for a property that we want; that is, $A \subset B$ and $p(B) \neq \varnothing$, and there is no C such that $A \subset C, C \subset B$, and $p(C) \neq \varnothing$, where $p(x)$ stands for the value of property p for class x. See Figure 6.4. To simplify the discussion, I assume that there is no bottom-up inheritance. I want to have, regardless of other superclasses of A,

$$p(A) = p(B)$$

The question is: How can I accomplish this? The only situation I have to look into is that there is D such that $A \subset B \subset D$ and $p(D) \neq \varnothing$. If $p(D) = p(B)$, there is no difficulty at all accomplishing the goal. If $p(D) \neq p(B)$, A has to inherit $p(B)$, not $p(D)$; in other words, the node representing $p(B)$ has to fire more strongly than the node representing $p(D)$. This is exactly what CONSYDERR will do, given the feature representation in CD. Intuitively, since we have $F_A \supset F_B \supset F_D$, the feature set of A is closer to the feature set of B than to the feature set of D; therefore, A will inherit B's property values instead of D's. Mathematically, suppose that $p(B)$ and $p(D)$ are

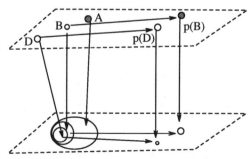

Figure 6.4. *Inheritance case 1. $A \subset B \subset D$. $F_A \supset F_B \supset F_D$. $p(x)$ denotes a property value of x. Arrows in CD represent pairwise links across two sets.*

represented in CD by one feature node each, according to the formulas specified before,

$$ACT_{p(B)} = \sum_{F_B} \frac{ACT_A}{f(|F_B|)}$$

$$= |F_B| \frac{ACT_A}{f(|F_B|)}$$

and

$$ACT_{p(D)} = \sum_{f_D} \frac{ACT_A}{f(|F_D|)}$$

$$= |F_D| \frac{ACT_A}{f(|F_D|)}$$

where ACT_x represents the activation of x, and ACT_A represents the initial activation of A. Since $F_D \subset F_B$, and f is a monotonic increasing function (slower than linear), it follows that $ACT_{p(B)} > ACT_{p(D)}$.

Let us now look into bottom-up inheritance. By bottom-up I mean that the property values of a class are "inherited" by (or percolate up to) its superclasses. Based on the similarity between the superclass and the subclass (one feature set is contained in the other), the superclass can easily activate the same property values. This inheritance can occur farther and farther along the *is-a* chain. When there is a cancellation along the chain, however, I have to make sure that correct values are inherited. Since this case is symmetrical to the top-down case, it is easy to see why CONSYDERR will work. In an inheritance graph, suppose that A is a class and B is its closest subclass that has a value for a property that we want; that is, $A \supset B$ and $p(B) \neq \varnothing$, and there is no C such that $A \supset C \supset B$ and $p(C) \neq \varnothing$, where $p(x)$ stands for the value of property p for class x. See Figure 6.5. To simplify the discussion, I assume for the time being that there is no top-down inheritance. I want to have, regardless of whether or not there are other subclasses of A,

$$p(A) = p(B)$$

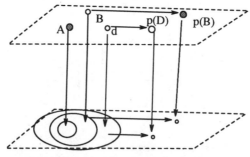

Figure 6.5. *Inheritance case 2.* $A \supset B \supset D$. $F_A \subset F_B \subset F_D$.

Suppose that there is D such that $A \supset B \supset D$ and $p(D) \neq \emptyset$. If $p(D) = p(B)$, there is no difficulty at all. If $p(D) \neq p(B)$, A has to inherit $p(B)$, not $p(D)$; in other words, the node representing $p(B)$ has to fire more strongly than the node representing $p(D)$. Mathematically, suppose that $p(B)$ and $p(D)$ are represented in CD by one feature node each, according to the formulas specified before,

$$ACT_{p(B)} = \sum_{F_A} \frac{ACT_A}{f(|F_B|)}$$

$$= |F_A| \frac{ACT_A}{f(|F_B|)}$$

and

$$ACT_{p(D)} = \sum_{F_A} \frac{ACT_A}{f(|F_D|)}$$

$$= |F_A| \frac{ACT_A}{f(|F_D|)}$$

where ACT_A represents the initial activation of A. Since $F_D \supset F_B$, and f is a monotonic increasing function (slower than linear), it follows that $ACT_{p(B)} > ACT_{p(D)}$.

When there are both top-down inheritance and bottom-up inheritance, there are some complications that have to be analyzed. Suppose that A is a class and B is its closest superclass that has a value for a property that we want and C is the closest subclass that has a value for the property; that is, on one hand, $A \subset B$ and $p(B) \neq \emptyset$, and there is no D such that $A \subset D$, $D \subset B$, and $p(D) \neq \emptyset$; on the other hand, $C \subset A$ and $p(C) \neq \emptyset$, and there is no D such that $D \subset A$, $C \subset D$, and $p(D) \neq \emptyset$. If $p(C) = p(B)$, there is no difficulty at all in having the correct property value inherited. If $p(C) \neq p(B)$, we have to make sure that the right property value is inherited. Mathematically, suppose that $p(C)$ and $p(B)$ are represented in CD by one node each, according to the formulas specified before,

$$ACT_{p(C)} = \sum_{F_A} \frac{ACT_A}{f(|F_C|)}$$

$$= |F_A| \frac{ACT_A}{f(|F_C|)}$$

and

$$ACT_{p(B)} = \sum_{f_B} \frac{ACT_A}{f(|F_B|)}$$

$$= |F_B| \frac{ACT_A}{f(|F_B|)}$$

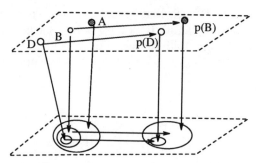

Figure 6.6. *Inheritance case 3.* $A \subset B \subset D.$ $F_A \supset F_B \supset F_D.$ $p(B) \subset p(D).$ $F_{p(B)} \supset F_{p(D)}.$

Since $F_C \supset F_A \supset F_B$ and f is a monotonic increasing but slower-than-linear function, it follows that the result can go either way. This ambiguity is the direct result of the ambiguity in the knowledge given originally in the problem specification; I can resolve it once all the feature sets are known. For example, I will have $ACT_{p(B)} > ACT_{p(C)}$, if and only if $|F_B|/f(|F_B|) > |F_A|/f(|F_C|)$; or intuitively, to inherit from top-down, the feature set of the superclass C should be as close to the feature set of A as possible. By the same token, to inherit from bottom-up, the feature set of the subclass B should be as close to the feature set of A as possible.

In the discussion above, I assume that each property value is represented by one node in CD. What if those property values form a hierarchy, too? In case of top-down inheritance, suppose that $A \subset B \subset D$, and $p(B)$ and $p(D)$ are represented in CD by the corresponding feature sets with $F_{p(B)} \supset F_{p(D)}.$[3] When A is activated,[4]

$$ACT_{p(B)} = \sum_{F_{p(B)}} \frac{\Sigma_{F_B}[ACT_A/f(|F_B|)]}{g(|F_{p(B)}|)}$$

and

$$ACT_{p(D)} = \sum_{F_{p(D)}} \frac{\Sigma_{F_B}[ACT_A/f(|F_B|)]}{g(|F_{p(D)}|)}$$

Since $F_D \subset F_B$ and $F_{p(D)} \subset F_{p(B)}$ and g is a monotonic increasing function (slower than linear), it follows that $ACT_{p(B)} > ACT_{p(D)}$. So the result is correct. See Figure 6.6.

In case of bottom-up inheritance, suppose that $A \supset B \supset D$, and $p(B)$ and $p(D)$ are represented in CD by the corresponding feature sets with $F_{p(B)} \subset$

---

[3]It cannot be otherwise. See Touertzky (1985). The same applies below.
[4]In this case, those nodes in $F_{p(D)}$ receive inputs from two different rules: $B \rightarrow p(B)$ and $D \rightarrow p(D)$, and the former is stronger than the latter. We use MAX in combining results from different rules. The same applies below.

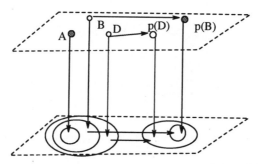

Figure 6.7. *Inheritance case 4.* $A \supset B \supset D$. $F_A \subset F_B \subset F_D$. $p(B) \supset p(D)$. $F_{p(B)} \subset F_{p(D)}$.

$F_{p(D)}$. When A is activated, we have

$$ACT_{p(B)} = \sum_{F_{p(B)}} \frac{\Sigma_{F_A}[ACT_A/f(|F_B|)]}{g(|F_{p(B)}|)}$$

and

$$ACT_{p(D)} = \sum_{F_{p(B)}} \frac{\Sigma_{F_A}[ACT_A/f(|F_B|)]}{g(|F_{p(D)}|)} + \sum_{F_{p(D)}-F_{p(B)}} \frac{\Sigma_{F_A}[ACT_A/f(|F_D|)]}{g(|F_{p(D)}|)}$$

Since $F_D \subset F_B$ and $F_{p(D)} \subset F_{p(B)}$ and f and g are monotonic increasing functions (slower than linear), we have $ACT_{p(B)} > ACT_{p(D)}$. So the correct result is obtained. See Figure 6.7.

Having analyzed these cases, it is now certain that CONSYDERR captures accurately inheritance in hierarchies. CONSYDERR provides an "implementation" of inheritance which is not exactly an implementation of explicitly *path-based* inheritance, but merely rules and similarities intermixed.

This analysis also shows that CONSYDERR provides a computationally efficient solution to inheritance: even in face of a huge hierarchy with long *is-a* chains, it can accomplish inheritance within constant time. All inferences are done in parallel and within one cycle, and there is no need to trace long chains since they are represented implicitly.

Multiple Inheritance Multiple inheritance is a difficult problem for all inheritance reasoners. When different answers are obtained from inheritance through different paths, an inheritance reasoner is in an ambiguous situation. CONSYDERR has a way of resolving ambiguity in multiple inheritance based on feature similarities; that is, CONSYDERR decides which inheritance path has the strongest strength, depending on which superclass (or subclass) is closer in feature representation to the focal concept. (In case that graded rules are allowed, both the similarities of feature sets and the strengths of rules need to be taken into account.)

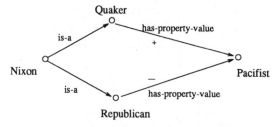

Figure 6.8. *The Nixon diamond: A typical multiple inheritance problem.*

A typical example of multiple inheritance is the Nixon diamond (see Figure 6.8), which can be stated as follows (I treat *Nixon*, which is an instance, as a class of one element):

Nixon is a Quaker. Nixon is a Republican. Republicans are nonpacifists. Quakers are pacifists. Is Nixon a pacifist or a nonpacifist?

The problem can be represented as follows:

$$Nixon \subset Republican$$

$$Nixon \subset Quaker$$

$$Quaker \rightarrow Pacifist$$

$$Republican \rightarrow Nonpacifist$$

The general principle is: the property value of a class are to be inherited from a class that is the closest to it in terms of feature representation, when all rules connecting classes to their property values have equal strengths.[5]

Generally speaking, suppose that $A \supset C$ and $B \supset C$, and $A \rightarrow E$ and $B \rightarrow F$ (A and B are both superclasses of C, and each has a different property value E or F). Then in CD, $F_A \subset F_C$ and $F_B \subset F_C$. Assume that all links have the same weight. Assume that E and F are each represented by one single feature node in CD. Let me further assume that $|F_A| > |F_B|$. Since $|F_C| > |F_A|$ and $|F_C| > |F_B|$, A is closer to C in feature representation. Now if C is activated, after a cycle we have

$$ACT_E = \sum_{F_A} \frac{ACT_C}{f(|F_A|)}$$

[5]If we deal with nonbinary cases, we also need to take into consideration how strong each tendency is (a Quaker being a pacifist or a Republican being a nonpacifist) and then combine the scores to reach the final conclusion.

and

$$ACT_F = \sum_{F_B} \frac{ACT_C}{f(|F_B|)}$$

where f is a monotonic increasing function (slower than linear). So under the assumption that $|F_A| > |F_B|$, E is activated more strongly than F.

Emergent Concepts For most inheritance reasoners, only concepts explicitly structured into an inheritance hierarchy can be brought out. However, for many AI applications, some sort of a generative capability is very useful or even crucial (cf. Pustejovsky 1993); new concepts and classes need to be formed and generated dynamically when the need for them arises.

For example,

If carrying cargo, buy utility vehicles. If carrying passengers, buy passenger vehicles. If carrying both cargo and passengers, what shall one buy?

What we want is to have a reasoner to come up with a solution such as "van," which is both a passenger vehicle and a utility vehicle, without the need for a rule to take care of the particular situation (in case the rule base is incomplete or inconsistent for various reasons, as often seen in reality). In CONSYDERR, certain new concepts can be generated dynamically through interaction in representation. An informal description is as follows (see the next section for a formal analysis): different types of vehicles are represented as nodes in CL and as features in CD; rules (*carrying-cargo* → *utility-vehicle* and *carrying-passengers* → *passenger-vehicle*) are represented as links; in response to the question, two concepts, *carrying-cargo* and *carrying-passengers*, are both activated, and their corresponding feature sets are activated in CD (after the top-down phase); then the two rules are activated (in the settling phase), so all the features corresponding to both utility and passenger vehicles are activated in CD; all of this activation goes up to CL (in the bottom-up phase). Concepts corresponding to the intersection of utility and passenger vehicles will be activated strongly, because they have all the activated features. So finally, something like "van" will result in CL. This is possibly only when an intensional approach is taken. It shows further that CONSYDERR is not just a straight "implementation" of existing inheritance theory.

6.2.3 Discussion

Touretzky (1985), Shastri (1988), and Thomason (1990) all describe path-based solutions; that is, to inherit from a concept, a path has to be found that connects the concept to inherit from and the concept to inherit to. This approach requires a fixed, static hierarchy and a mechanism for tracing the path. First, a path-based approach entails the necessity of tracing paths step by step in performing inheritance; thus the time complexity is proportional to the length of the longest path, to say the least. In contrast, a feature-based scheme takes only constant time for all kinds of inheritance scenarios as shown above. This computational efficiency matches human commonsense reasoning well. Second, a static hierarchy can be unwieldy in many respects. For instance, it is difficult to take context effects into consideration when using a static hierarchy, because of its fixed topology. On the other hand, a feature-based approach such as CONSYDERR can easily adopt itself by dynamically modifying connections between concept nodes and feature nodes, as connectionist models customarily do (see Section 4.5).

Most of the existing inheritance systems are extensional. For example, the system of Shastri (1988) counts the numbers of instances in each class, and then by evidential combination, calculates the plausibility of a particular property value for a particular class; his system will conclude with the property value with the highest score. In contrast, my approach is intensional; that is, the intensions (or semantics) of concepts are explored, and inheritance is performed based on the semantic closeness (i.e., feature overlap) of concepts. The intensional approach can result in better accuracy, because it can take account of meaning and semantics as well as syntactic, extensional relations. For example, one may see a lot more chickens that do not fly than birds that do fly (imagining living in a chicken farm). Still, one will conclude that birds usually fly, because it is an essential feature of birds. It is also my contention that the intensional approach represents a deeper and more fundamental understanding of the concepts involved and thus is better for any task that is suitable for the approach. Only when one does not or cannot understand the nature of things, does one take the extensional approach as a way out (and thus the extensional approach is complementary to the intensional approach).

Recent work on skeptical inheritance (Stein 1990; Horty et al. 1987, 1990; etc.) aims at deriving sound conclusions despite the existence of ambiguity. Roughly speaking, skeptical inheritance reaches a single set of unambiguous conclusions from an inheritance hierarchy, by eliminating all ambiguous paths in some way; an ideally skeptical system reaches those and only those conclusions that are justified by every possible inheritance scenarios ("credulous extensions"). Although this is an important goal for some purposes, it is different from my goal of commonsensical evidential reasoning. I am more interested in the question of how sensible (but fallible) conclusions can be reached efficiently in a cognitively plausible way.

Although most connectionist models use optimization as a means for reaching the most plausible conclusion (see, e.g., Hopfield 1982, Thagard 1989), CONSYDERR adopts a different method for inheritance reasoning, in which rule-based spreading activation and massively parallel feature comparisons (implemented in a connectionist network) do the job of finding plausible conclusions; there is no overall energy function to minimize in this architecture. One of the advantages of this approach is that it avoids a host of problems associated with energy-minimizing network models: for example, long settling time, local minima, and global interaction (cf. Rumelhart et al. 1986).

In summary, in this section I have further analyzed how inheritance can be dealt with in CONSYDERR, in terms of implementing a complete hierarchy (for either top-down inheritance or bottom-up inheritance, or both), dealing with multiple inheritance, and forming new concepts. The results indicate that CONSYDERR is well equipped to handle this aspect of commonsense reasoning.

6.3 ANALYSIS OF INTERACTION OF REPRESENTATION

In this section I examine the problem of *representational interaction*, which is defined to be the interaction between different concepts and rules due to the overlapping representations in CONSYDERR. First, some background is presented, and then various kinds of representational interaction in CONSY-DERR are analyzed.

The analysis shows that in CONSYDERR, rules are no longer context-free pieces of knowledge; instead, all the rules together form a complex, interacting process. Interaction in representation can result in the generation of new concepts during reasoning processes, which is useful in filling knowledge gaps that a reasoner may have.

6.3.1 Background

Many researchers point out that there are severe problems associated with purely rule (logic)-based models of reasoning[6]:

- Israel (1987), in his discussion of what is wrong with default logic, argues that real inferences are made through belief revision and fixation, not just rules of purely syntactic manipulation. As he puts it: "[It is not] the case that if one is justified in believing that p and justified in believing that if p then q, is then one justified in believing that q. Unless, of course, one has no other relevant beliefs. But one always does."
- Perlis (1986) continues the same theme. He distinguishes the two different approaches: one is to seek a specification of formal rules, and the other is to seek to identify the process of drawing conclusions. (In his original discussion, he refers only to default reasoning, but clearly the same idea applies to all kinds of reasoning.)
- Johannessen (1990), in his discussion of rule-following behavior, points out: "There must be a non-interpretive way of grasping a rule. On the

---

[6]Here the word *rule* is used to refer to *forms* rather than *contents*.

basic level, rules are simply followed. That is the point of saying that practices, the established ways of believing, giving words their meaning. Hence rules get their identity from the practices in which they are embedded. To understand a rule is to master the corresponding practices in which it is 'inscribed'. The established practices are not isolated monads; they are essentially interrelated."

There are some attempts in AI at dealing with the problem of context-freedom of rules and the resulting inconsistency/incompleteness. A cursory survey shows a number of efforts. For example, Wilkins and Tan (1989) deal with inconsistent, incomplete, and incorrect rules in a rule base through using learning methods to amend the rule base; Duval and Kodratoff (1986) deal with inconsistent databases through introducing *modulation*, a type of quantifiers, in rules.

In this section I deal with the inconsistency and incompleteness through representational interaction, that is, treating reasoning as a process, not just applications of isolated rules. I analyze the issue of interaction and attempt to answer the following questions:

- How is interaction made possible?
- How should the results from interaction be combined?
- How may the interaction help to deal with inconsistency and incompleteness in rules?

Cases of interaction include those among conditions in a rule, between conditions and conclusions in a rule, among different rules leading to the same conclusion, and among different conclusions reached by different rules.

6.3.2 How Is Interaction Possible?

Two Sources of Representational Interaction Representational interaction is made possible, first, by the massively parallel nature of the CONSYDERR architecture, and second, by the overlapping feature representations in CD, both of which differ from the typical symbolic counterparts of CONSYDERR.

In order to explain the implication of the massively parallel nature of the connectionist architecture, I review below some more traditional ways of conducting reasoning. In traditional rule-based systems (or production systems; see, e.g., Klahr et al. 1989, Posner 1989, Anderson 1983), a *control structure* is usually devised so that a system can decide which rules are eligible to fire, how rules are picked for actual firing, and in which order they are to fire. Usually, conditions of rules are matched against data in a working memory; those rules having conditions matching the working memory data are eligible to fire. Conflicts are resolved by ordering rules and firing the rule that comes first in the order. Other policies are also used in various systems, for example, the policy of refractoriness for avoiding a high-priority rule being executed repeatedly with the same data, or the policy of giving preference to rules that match the data most recently created, or the policy of giving preference to rules with stronger conditions, and so on. In more recent systems, *goal symbols* are used to control the order and to focus on relevant rules. A goal symbol is a symbol that can be created by a rule, and thereafter only rules that have that goal symbol in their conditions are allowed to fire, until new goal symbols are created. In this way attention is focused on rules that are most relevant to a particular situation, and an order in which rules are picked to fire can be created dynamically.

The main problem with this traditional rule-based approach is that by restricting a system to fire one rule at a time (even in parallel systems, only rules that are not in conflict with each other are allowed to fire at the same time), we miss out on the opportunity to combine results from different rules to fill in knowledge gaps that may exist in a system; in other words, the interaction between rules, which can enable the generation of new concepts, cannot be utilized.

Interaction can be made possible, in part, by allowing conflicting (and nonconflicting) rules to fire simultaneously and then obtaining the combined results from their interaction. In CONSYDERR, inference is not carried out one rule at a time as in typical production systems, or by other symbolic strategies such as those used in mathematical logic (e.g., various resolution methods; cf. Chang and Lee 1973). Inference in CONSYDERR amounts to a parallel process as described by the following equations (from Chapter 3):

In the top level,

$$ACT_C = \sum_i r_i * ACT_{A_i}$$

and in the bottom level,

$$ACT_y = \sum_j lw_j * ACT_{x_j}$$

where r's and lw's are link weights.

As is evident from the earlier description of CONSYDERR, reasoning in this architecture is performed mainly during this settling phase, which is highly parallel: all steps that can be explored at a given time are explored together at the same time. According to the equations above, activations are propagated from an activated node toward all postlink nodes in parallel and then toward subsequent nodes, and so on. Since links represent rules, the activation propagation is equivalent to applying rules in chains. Moreover, this activation propagation is similar to a parallel breadth-first search. With this highly parallel process, different rules interact with each other.

Overlapping similarity-based feature representation in CD introduces another kind of interaction. Concepts (in their feature representations) are activated if a concept similar to them is activated, due to their overlapping representations. This results in a simple kind of generativity (actually, a form of generalization): based on similarity matching, the CD representation (the feature set) of a concept can be partially invoked (and thus the concept can be generated, if it is not already there) because another concept similar to it is activated (from rule application or some other means). Moreover, more complex kinds of generativity can also occur; feature sets (the CD representations) of different concepts may overlap and interact with each other and thus, if activated at the same time, may cause the formation of new feature sets corresponding to new concepts. The resulting CD activations will then go up to CL during the bottom-up phase. The results of this entire process of interaction, as will be analyzed, are the generation of new concepts that are some kinds of logical (or illogical) combinations of the concepts participating in interaction. This characteristic makes CONSYDERR even more different from traditional rule-based reasoning: it is not mere syntactic transformation, but meaning-oriented (intensional) reasoning. It is because of the features used for representing a concept, which form a finer-grained representation.

Relationship between CL and CD   To understand better the issue of interaction, we need to look into the relationship between the corresponding CL and CD representations, given the foregoing specification of representational interaction in CONSYDERR.

First, the relation between a CL node (a concept) and its corresponding CD representation (the feature set, the meaning, or the intension) is not necessarily that of necessary and sufficient conditions. According to traditional logic theories (see, e.g., Leonard 1967), the set of features of a concept that is common and jointly peculiar to the concept, termed *total contingent intension*, is sufficient to determine the concept (by definition); however, such an intension is most likely infinite in number and hard to come by. Subsets of it, if consisting only of *necessary* members (excluding *merely contingent* ones; see also discussions in Brachman 1985) of the total contingent intension, are termed *total strict intension*. The smallest subset of a total strict intension from which all other features can be deduced is termed *definitive intension* or simply *definition* (members of which are, naturally, *definitive* features), and it is exactly the necessary and sufficient condition which we are seeking for the feature representation needed in CD. In such a case (with definitive intensions, or total strict intensions), the superclass/subclass relation is a special case of similarity (feature overlapping): the feature set of the superclass is always contained in that of the subclass, as described by *the principle of reverse containment*.

Unfortunately, a feature set that corresponds exactly to a definitive intension (or total strict intension) sometimes may not exist, especially for natural language concepts and notions in commonsense reasoning (see Leonard 1967 and Lakoff 1986 for detailed discussions). So, what does it mean in such cases to have a set of features in CD as a representation of a concept? Most features, like concepts themselves, are fuzzy, uncertain, and evidential, so the relationship between a concept and its features are likewise inexact and evidential; that is, a concept is *likely* to have certain features, and a certain set of features is *likely* to determine a concept. Therefore, instead of dividing members of a feature set into the three classes: merely contingent, necessary, and definitive, as in aforementioned logic theories. We view features as *indeterministically definitive*, lending evidential support for invoking a certain concept, and vice versa. This conception can lead to various useful ideas, such as (1) giving different weights to different members of a feature set, to correspond to their relative strengths of evidential support, or (2) a concept having multiple feature sets, to allow for complex disjunctive concepts, and so on.

When similarity matching is involved, that is, when a feature set of a concept is activated and it shares some features with other concepts, these other concepts (affected by similarities) have only a part of their feature sets actually activated. Thus conclusions regarding these concepts are highly uncertain, because the relation between a concept and a subset of its feature set is even more indeterminate. This is, in a way, analogous to an *indexical intension* (Leonard 1967), which is a set of features that does not define a concept but merely provides some clue to its presence. Clearly, interaction in CD produces uncertain but plausible conclusions, which, when lacking better evidence, can be useful, although they are never foolproof; this is exactly what commonsense reasoning is like.

In the following subsections, I first analyze various cases of representational interaction in an abstract way, and then I show, by examples, how interaction can lead to the generative capability and how it can help to deal with the problem of inconsistent/incomplete knowledge.

6.3.3   Interaction among Conditions

Various concepts that are conditions in a rule can interact with each other; the interaction can produce effects that neither of these conditions alone can produce. Suppose that there are two conditions in the same rule (such as $A\ B \rightarrow C$), each of which has a corresponding representation in CD. Several different types of interaction may occur; these different types are shown in Figure 6.9.

According to this table, depending on the relationship between, and the way of combining, the two feature sets associated with the two concepts, different kinds of concepts can emerge from the interaction, which can be the logical OR, the logical AND, or some other logical combination of the two original concepts (provided that feature sets involved form total strict inten-

No.	Type	Description	Logical Equivalence
1	overlapping	$F_A \cap F_B$	$\supset A \cup B$
2	additive	$F_A \cup F_B$	$A \cap B$
3	subtractive	$(F_A - F_B) \cup (F_B - F_A)$	no simple equivalence
4	subtractive	$F_A - F_B$	no simple equivalence
5	subtractive	$F_B - F_A$	no simple equivalence

Figure 6.9. *Different types of interaction in CD between two conditions. (A and B represent classes; F_A and F_B represent their corresponding feature sets.)*

sions):

- The first case is the overlapping interaction, depicted in Figure 6.10, in which the new concept has a feature set that is the intersection of the two original feature sets; because the new concept has some features from both of the two original concepts, it is a superclass of both, and therefore it is a superclass of the union of the two.
- The second case is the additive interaction, depicted in Figure 6.11, in which the new concept has a feature set that is the union of the feature

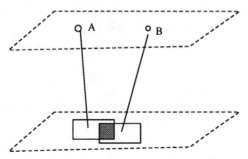

Figure 6.10. *First type of interaction: overlapping. (Shaded areas represent new concepts.)*

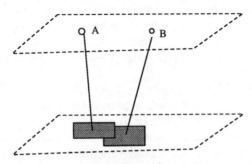

Figure 6.11. *Second type of interaction: additive. (Shaded areas represent new concepts.)*

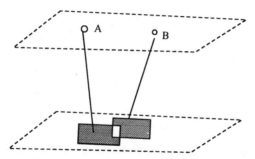

Figure 6.12. *Third type of interaction: subtractive. (Shaded areas represent new concepts.)*

sets of the original concepts; because the new concept has all the features of both original concepts, it represents the intersection of the two classes represented by the two original concepts.

- The third case is a subtractive interaction, depicted in Figure 6.12, in which the new concept has a feature set that results from the union of the feature sets of the two original concepts minus their differences (both ways); there is no simple logical equivalence for this case.
- The fourth case is another subtractive interaction, depicted in Figure 6.13, in which the new concept has a feature set that is the difference of the feature sets of the two original concepts; there is no simple logical equivalence for this case either.
- The fifth case is yet another subtractive interaction, depicted in Figure 6.14, in which the new concept has a feature set that is the difference (the other way around) of the feature sets of the two original concepts; there is again no simple logical equivalence.

On the other hand, looking at the issue from a different perspective, for different set operations combining two concepts (classes), we can also find the corresponding feature set combinations, as shown in Figure 6.15. For the

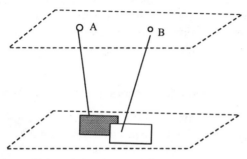

Figure 6.13. *Fourth type of interaction: subtractive. (Shaded areas represent new concepts.)*

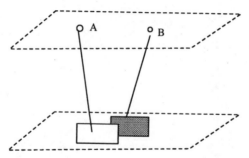

Figure 6.14. *Fifth type of interaction: subtractive. (Shaded areas represent new concepts.)*

No.	Operation on Classes	Expression	Feature Set
1	Intersection	$A \cap B$	$F_A \cup F_B$
2	Union	$A \cup B$	$F_A \vee F_B$
3	Difference	$A - B$	$F_A \cup \neg F_B$
4	Difference	$B - A$	$F_B \cup \neg F_A$

Figure 6.15. *Logical combinations and corresponding feature sets.*

intersection of the two classes (i.e., $A \cap B$), the corresponding feature set is
the union of the feature sets of the two original concepts. For the union of
the two classes (i.e., $A \cup B$), the corresponding feature set is the logical OR
of the combined bottom-up activations of the two feature sets, which is
carried out by the MAX operation across two sites of a node each of which
connects to one feature set. For the difference of the two classes (i.e., $A - B$
or $B - A$), the corresponding feature set is the union of the first feature set
and the negation of the second feature set. Here *negation* means having
negative weights on all the interlevel links between the concept and the
features in that feature set. The absolute value of any weight on an interlevel
link is the same as specified before in the CONSYDERR equations. It can be
easily verified that in all of the cases above, the new concept (class) node has
activation 1 if and only if its corresponding feature set (as specified in the
table) has the right activation (1 for positive feature and -1 for negative
features), when all the weights are set appropriately.

6.3.4   Interaction between Conditions and Conclusions

Now let us look into the interaction between the condition and the conclusion of a rule. There are two basic types of interaction between the condition
and the conclusion of the same rule: the additive interaction and the
subtractive interaction. Figure 6.16 shows the two cases.

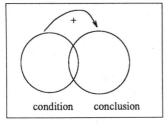

(1) Positive interaction

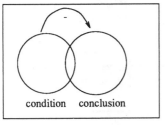

(2) Negative interaction

Figure 6.16. *Two types of interaction in CD between conditions and conclusions. Two feature sets in CD are depicted. One arrow in drawn in place of pairwise connections.*

In the case of additive interaction, the condition and the conclusion have overlapping CD representations (i.e., they share some features), and the condition has a positive influence on the conclusion (i.e., the link weight is positive). Thus, in CD, there could be positive self-loop; such a loop can lead to saturation at the highest possible value for these nodes that are in the intersection of the two feature sets. We can avoid this by eliminating all the self-loops in a network. As a general policy, I shall not allow any self-loop, or link originating and terminating at the same node, to be added during the construction of a network. In this way, the nodes in the intersection maintain the same activation levels as before the rule application (or as without the rule).

In the case of subtractive interaction, the condition has a negative influence on the conclusion, and the condition and the conclusion have overlapping CD representations. As before, to avoid negative self-loops, I shall eliminate all links from and to the same nodes. The nodes in the intersection of two feature sets will maintain the same activation levels.

6.3.5 Interaction among Conclusions for Different Rules

The interaction among conclusions reached from different rules is another interesting phenomenon. There is always the possibility that the same conclusions can be reached with different activation (confidence) values from different rules, and thus interaction of these different values can occur. For example, suppose that there are two rules: $A\ B \rightarrow G$ and $C\ D\ E \rightarrow G$. If both rules are activated to some degree, based on the activations of the

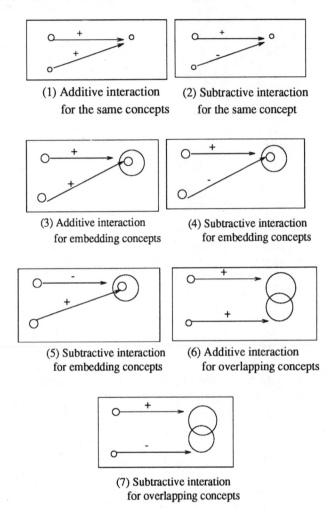

Figure 6.17. *Interaction in CD between conclusions from different rules. In each diagram, feature sets in CD are shown. Circles represent feature sets. For rules, one arrow is drawn in place of pairwise connections.*

conditions (A, B, C, D, and E) and the weight vectors of the rules, the conclusion G will be reached with two different values. For such a situation, seven distinct cases can be established, as in Figure 6.17. There is a need to combine different values reached from different rules, as these values will be reached simultaneously due to the massive parallel nature of CONSY-DERR.

Now the question is how we should go about combining them. There are different ways of accomplishing this. For example, all of the following operations are possible: ADD, MAX, CAM (i.e., combined ADD/MAX), HR (i.e., Heckerman's rule; Heckerman 1985) and many others. The results shown in Figure 6.17 are activations of nodes in the intersection of two CD representations. Among these different combination operators, MAX and ADD simply perform the corresponding operations on the two values; CAM obtains the maximum of the two values when they are of the same sign (representing the confidence when given two pieces of evidence leading to the same conclusion) and adds them whey they are of opposite signs (representing the reduced confidence when confronted with contradictory evidence); HR is a modified version of the MYCIN combination rule, which calculates the sum of the two values divided by 1 plus their product: $H(a, b) = (a + b)/(1 + ab)$ (it is considered by Shultz et al. 1989 to be the best among all the methods tested). The outcomes for all seven types of interaction are tabulated (see Figure 6.18) in order to compare them and find out which one is most reasonable.

Let us analyze each combination operation in turn. ADD will produce incorrect results: the results may well exceed the upper limit 1 in case of the additive interaction. MAX works fine with the additive interaction, but in case of the subtractive interaction, it has some problems. When the two values are of opposite signs but their absolute values are the same, the result is indeterminate, which results in a random decision with mean equal to 0 (statistically, half the results are positive and half are negative). This is fine until we look into the situation where the two values are of opposite signs and their absolute values are very close but not the same, in which case the result will be the same as one of the values, as if the other value did not exist, whereas the semantics of the problem requires that the result be close to zero. In all these cases, HR gives proper results, but there is one problem: it will prevent inheritance from being carried out correctly in CONSYDERR.

From this analysis it is evident why CAM is preferred over the others. In implementation, the CAM operation can be carried out in a node by a node activation function when combining results from multiple sites. I should point

Type	MAX	ADD	CAM	HR
additive, the same concept	max	sum	max	stronger
subtractive, the same concept	max	0	0	0
additive, embedding concepts	max	sum	max	stronger
subtractive, embedding concepts	max	0	0	0
subtractive, embedding concepts	max	0	0	0
additive, overlapping concepts	max	sum	max	stronger
subtractive, overlapping concepts	max	0	0	0

Figure 6.18. *Different operations for dealing with interaction between conclusions from different rules. (Each entry indicates the resulting activation of a CD node in the intersection.)*

out, however, that if rules and facts are *consistent*,[7] the MAX operation will be sufficient; this is because the situation where two values of the same conclusion are of different signs will never occur if a theory is consistent. In that case, MAX is equivalent to CAM. This is why in the previous specification of CONSYDERR, MAX is used for combining results from different sites. By now I have answered another of the lingering questions, concerning node activations in CONSYDERR.

Different conclusions reached from different rules at the same time can also interact. It is similar to the interaction among different conditions of a rule; the same sort of analysis as in Section 6.3.3 regarding logical equivalences of the resulting concepts can also be performed: the concept that emerges from the interaction can be the logical AND, the logical OR, or some other more complex logical combination of the two original concepts involved in the interaction; readers are referred to Figure 6.9. When there are more than two concepts involved in interaction, the situation can be much more complicated, and logical equivalences can be more difficult to identify. Nevertheless, the basic approach taken here is still applicable.

6.3.6 The Generative Capability

The foregoing analysis of representational interaction in CONSYDERR leads naturally to an interesting result: the generative capability of the CONSYDERR architecture (including generalization based on similarity matching). As hinted before, representation in this architecture is capable of generating new concepts dynamically. In other words, what it can do is not limited to what have been stored there explicitly and is not limited to the logical closure of its explicit representations. To help to demonstrate this, let us look again into the earlier example:

> If carrying cargo, buy utility vehicles. If carrying passengers, buy passenger vehicles. If carrying both cargo and passengers, what shall one buy?

For this example, the additive interaction of two different concepts in CONSYDERR as analyzed in Section 6.3.3 can be utilized to come up with a new conclusion that is different from either of the two original conclusions (utility vehicles and passenger vehicles). In the system, there are two rules in accordance with the background knowledge of the reasoner:

$$carrying\text{-}cargo \ \rightarrow \ utility\text{-}vehicles$$

$$carrying\text{-}passenger \ \rightarrow \ passenger\text{-}vehicles$$

Different types of vehicles are represented as individual concepts in CL and

---

[7]*Consistency* is defined the same as before: the same fact cannot be inferred with two (or more) values of opposite signs, through either rule application or similarity matching.

as sets of features in CD. As explained before, in CONSYDERR, when the two rules above are both activated (in response to the question), all the features corresponding to either utility or passenger vehicles (or both) will be activated in CD. All of this information will go up to CL, and the concepts that have all the features (corresponding to the intersection of utility and passenger vehicles) will be activated strongly, due to the additive interaction. Thus concepts in CL representing "combined-utility/passenger-vehicle" (or "van") will result, although there is no explicit rule regarding it. Other related concepts may also be activated from rule application and/or similarity matching.

With the CONSYDERR equations (specified in Chapter 3), the activation can be determined as follows:

$$ACT_{combined\text{-}utility\text{-}passenger}$$

$$= \sum_{i \in F_{passenger\text{-}vehicle} \cup F_{utility\text{-}vehicle}} \frac{ACT_i}{g(F_{passenger\text{-}vehicle} \cup F_{utility\text{-}vehicle})}$$

where

$$ACT_i = \sum_{F_{carrying\text{-}passenger}} \frac{lw_1}{f(F_{carrying\text{-}passenger})} ACT_{carrying\text{-}passenger}$$

if $i \in F_{passenger\text{-}vehicle}$; or

$$ACT_i = \sum_{F_{carrying\text{-}cargo}} \frac{lw_2}{f(F_{carrying\text{-}cargo})} ACT_{carrying\text{-}cargo}$$

if $i \in F_{utility\text{-}vehicle}$; or

$$ACT_i = \max\left(\sum_{F_{carrying\text{-}passenger}} \frac{lw_1}{f(F_{carrying\text{-}passenger})} ACT_{carrying\text{-}passenger}, \right.$$

$$\left. \sum_{F_{carrying\text{-}cargo}} \frac{lw_2}{f(F_{carrying\text{-}cargo})} ACT_{carrying\text{-}cargo} \right)$$

if $i \in F_{passenger\text{-}vehicle} \cap F_{utility\text{-}vehicle}$ (see Section 6.3.5).

If we assume that $ACT_{carrying\text{-}passenger}$ and $ACT_{carrying\text{-}cargo}$ are equal to 1 and $lw_1 = lw_2 = 1$, then

$$ACT_{combined\text{-}utility\text{-}passenger} \approx 1$$

A similar example involves the subtractive interaction. It can be stated as follows:

A particular automobile assembly plant produces all kinds of passenger vehicles, but none of utility vehicles.

In this example, there are two rules:

$$plant\text{-}production \rightarrow passenger\text{-}vehicles$$
$$plant\text{-}production \rightarrow \neg utility\text{-}vehicles$$

In CL, each concept involved is represented by an individual node; in CD, each concept is represented by a set of features. The dynamics of CONSYDERR is as follows: when the node "plant-production" is activated, through the application of the two rules above, "passenger-vehicles" is positively activated and "utility-vehicles" is negatively activated. In CD, their corresponding feature representations are also activated accordingly. So, with the subtractive interaction (see Section 6.3.3), during the bottom-up phase, concepts representing "pure-passenger-vehicles" are positively activated; concepts representing "pure-utility-vehicles" are negatively activated; and all the concepts representing vehicles that are both passenger and utility vehicles (and thus they have both types of features in their CD representations) have zero (or near zero) activations, because those features that are related to passenger vehicles send positive activations up and those features that are related to utility vehicles send negative activations up.

With the CONSYDERR equations, the activation of "pure-passenger-vehicle" can be determined as follows:

$$ACT_{pure\text{-}passenger\text{-}vehicle}$$

$$= \sum_{i \in F_{passenger\text{-}vehicle} \cup F_{utility\text{-}vehicle}} \frac{ACT_i}{g\left(F_{passenger\text{-}vehicle} \cup F_{utility\text{-}vehicle}\right)}$$

where

$$ACT_i = \sum_{F_{plant\text{-}production}} \frac{lw_1}{f\left(F_{plant\text{-}production}\right)} ACT_{plant\text{-}production}$$

if $i \in F_{passenger\text{-}vehicle}$; or

$$ACT_i = - \sum_{F_{plant\text{-}production}} \frac{lw_2}{f\left(F_{plant\text{-}production}\right)} ACT_{plant\text{-}production}$$

if $i \in F_{vehicle\text{-}production}$; on the other hand, if

$$i \in F_{passenger\text{-}vehicle} \cap F_{vehicle\text{-}production}$$

then ACT_i will be one of the above two, depending on which one is greater in absolute values. (See Section 6.3.5 for the discussion of this type of interaction.)

If we assume that $ACT_{plant-production} = 1$ and $lw_1 = -lw_2 = 1$, then

$$ACT_{pure-passenger-vehicle} \approx 1$$

Viewing the two examples above as describing interaction within an inheritance hierarchy, we see that (at least) one new concept is generated in each case, based on the interaction of concepts at a certain level of a hierarchy: "combined-passenger/utility-vehicle" (including "van") in the first example and "pure-passenger-vehicle" in the second example. "Combined-passenger/utility-vehicle" is the intersection of the two sets, "passenger-vehicle" and "utility-vehicle," and it is generated automatically based on the interaction, that is, through dynamically forming a new feature set that includes all the features of passenger vehicles and utility vehicles; formally, $F_{combined-utility-passenger} = F_{passenger-vehicle} \cup F_{utility-vehicle}$. "Pure-passenger-vehicle" in the second example is the difference between the two sets, "passenger-vehicle" and "utility-vehicle," and it is generated based on the emergence of a feature set that includes all the features of "passenger-vehicle" plus the negation of the features of "utility-vehicle" (by having negative weights for the interlevel links from the concept to these features); that is, $F_{pure-passenger-vehicle} = F_{passenger-vehicle} \cup \neg(F_{utility-vehicle})$. However, in general, a concept generated in CD may not have a corresponding node in CL already; in such a case, a *recruitment learning* algorithm (Feldman and Ballard 1982) may be used to establish such a node representation in CL.

It can be seen from this analysis that in CONSYDERR, there is no more *fixed* inheritance hierarchy (see also Section 6.2). An actual hierarchy can change dynamically, through the similarity-based feature representation in CD and through the interaction among concepts and among rules. As demonstrated by the examples above and the analyses summarized in Figure 6.9, new concepts can be generated at various places in a hierarchy, from interaction of feature sets of several concepts at a certain level of a hierarchy. In addition to interaction among concepts at the same level of the hierarchy, two concepts at different levels can also interact and generate new concepts, although their final positions in the hierarchy are dependent on many factors and thus difficult to determine.

As pointed out before, interaction can be utilized to deal with incomplete and inconsistent knowledge bases, as well as to provide a compact and flexible representation. The examples show how inconsistent and incomplete knowledge bases can produce correct results; interaction helps to generate consistent and complete conclusions out of inconsistent and incomplete rules:

- In the utility/passenger vehicle buying example, the knowledge of the reasoner is incomplete: it lacks rules for handling the combination of utility vehicles and passenger vehicles. When such a combination is encountered, in order to handle it, a reasoner has to choose one of several possible options: (1) applying one of the applicable rules and giving the (partial) answer derived from that rule (e.g., suggesting buying trucks based solely on the requirement of carrying cargo); (2) acknowledging the inability for handling the combination and requesting more information (including possibly new rules specifically for the situation); (3) utilizing the interaction between the two feature sets through top-down/bottom-up flow and coming up with a combined (correct) answer (i.e., suggesting a vehicle that is both a passenger vehicle and a utility vehicle). The first option is adopted in most existing knowledge-based systems, the second option is adopted in some research work, especially in machine learning, and the third option is what is employed in CONSYDERR. The advantage of the third option is obvious: it reduces the possibility of giving out partial and thus potentially wrong answers, and it can come up with answers taking into account all the relevant knowledge in store; moreover, it does not require additional information. What it needs is a new way of structuring knowledge (such as the CONSYDERR architecture).

- The assembly plant example is a case of inconsistent knowledge bases: the vehicles that are both a passenger vehicle and a utility vehicle receive both positive and negative activations; thus the knowledge is inconsistent in this case, because the two existing rules are contradictory regarding this situation. Again, a reasoner has the same three options as before for handling the situation, and again only the third option is an acceptable way of dealing with this situation. Through interaction of existing knowledge, a consistent answer is formed out of inconsistent pieces.

In some way, in CONSYDERR, reasoning is not accomplished through merely applying isolated rules. Statically, it is in part made of individual rules (along with distributed feature representations). But dynamically, it is a complex, interacting process, with activation flows through various types of nodes, producing conclusions reached with different values from different sources and generating overlapping, additive, and subtractive types of interaction. Rules do not operate in isolation: related rules can fire at the same time if their respective conditions are satisfied at the same time and they interact with each other. Reasoning is accomplished by a complex interacting process arising in a tangled web of a vast number of rules.

To conclude, this section has showed that various kinds of interaction can occur in representation, which produce some useful generative capability. In CONSYDERR, although knowledge can be partially described by isolated rules, the reasoning process should be viewed as a complex process instead of strict rule-following as in the oversimplistic traditional picture of common-sense reasoning.

6.4   KNOWLEDGE ACQUISITION, LEARNING, AND ADAPTATION

One of the major practical problems in building intelligent systems is how to acquire all the necessary knowledge for a system. The difficulty lies in the fact that in order to build systems that can scale up, the method of acquiring knowledge must somehow be systematic and preferably automatic, and moreover, the acquired knowledge has to be organized in such a way that it can be revised and updated easily. This difficulty is currently insurmountable with existing approaches or methodologies.

There are nevertheless many ways for ameliorating the situation, by using some partially successful techniques, coupled with some clever software engineering. Below I look into some of these techniques, from a practical point of view, and briefly discuss their relevance to CONSYDERR.

Knowledge acquisition research produces techniques and software tools that help with the usually tedious and sometimes painful process of obtaining knowledge manually. Marcus (1989) presents a bird's eye view of this field. Potentially, many of the techniques developed in this field can be useful in setting up connectionist knowledge-based systems based on CONSYDERR.

Learning serves us another alternative for system building. With automated processes, learning enables intelligent systems to be developed with minimal human intervention. Learning algorithms typically extract knowledge from input/output data, or through interacting with the external world. Some of these algorithms are undoubtedly useful for building systems based on the CONSYDERR architecture. For example, Neal (1990) presents statistical learning techniques for developing feedforward multilayer connectionist networks. Although designed for different purposes, the algorithm can be adapted to CONSYDERR for setting up rules. Another algorithm is the IARL algorithm proposed by Sun and Waltz (1991).

Examining connectionist learning algorithms, one of the most famous is *back-propagation* (Rumelhart et al. 1986), which, despite the fact that there is no explicit rule in networks, can learn rulelike behavior (to a certain extent at least). But it is excruciatingly slow, and therefore it is not very likely to scale up well. Gallant (1988) presents the *pocket learning* algorithm, a generalized *perceptron learning* algorithm, for developing connectionist networks from data presentations. One obvious advantage of it is that one can extract rules from a developed network and therefore make representation more systematic and explicit. Towell et al. (1990) present another technique for structuring initially approximate rules into networks and extracting them after rectified by training.

Evolution or adaptation algorithms can be used to improve system performance on the fly. For example, Holland et al. (1986) present the best known of these techniques, *the genetic algorithm*, for creating new rules and eliminating old ones. These algorithms can potentially be useful, if adapted to CONSYDERR, for updating, fine-tuning, and revising rules. Another kind of adaptation that can be performed in CONSYDERR involves transformations that turn similarity matching into separate, specialized rules: if we keep deriving the same result based on indirect means, we can then establish a rule specifically for the particular inference to facilitate future performance.

With this brief overview in mind, now let me explain how CONSYDERR actually acquires knowledge currently. Basically, I try to do it the simplest way possible. There are basically two questions that need to be answered for CONSYDERR:

- How are rules obtained?
- How are similarity-based representations obtained?

These two questions can be, although not necessarily, dealt with separately.

Rules can generally be obtained from domain experts, textbooks, manuals/instructions, or by using learning algorithms (e.g., back-propagation type gradient-descent algorithms). There is no universally applicable way to do this; in other words, it is domain-specific. In GIRO, rules are obtained by going through geographical sourcebooks, picking out the relevant information, and integrating it into the network with the CFRDN procedure (see the Appendix to Chapter 7). The rules being put into the system include *western-Texas is cattle-country*, and others.

Similarity-matching measures can be obtained by an indirect means. One way is to identify all the relevant features for all the concepts involved, and then clearly the amount of feature overlap determines the similarity between two concepts. To come up with detailed feature representations, I preestablish a set of feature nodes and then go through sourcebooks, establishing links between a concept in CL and its features in CD, based on what is obtained from the sourcebooks. The features in GIRO include altitude, rainfall, vegetation, population, temperature, terrain, and many others, with various ranges. Another possible way of obtaining similarity-matching measures is to conduct a test, asking a group of subjects to rate the similarities of the concepts involved and then calculating the similarity-matching measures based on the collected test scores with the STSIS procedure (see the Appendix to Chapter 4). It is also possible to obtain feature representations by asking subjects to identify features of each concepts. Some combinations of sourcebook information extraction and psychological experiments are promising avenues to be explored. Yet another way is to make the system to develop its own feature representations through interaction with the external world, by using back-propagation or other connectionist learning algorithms (see Dyer 1990 for this type of experiments). The feature representation developed this way may not be interpretable as in GIRO, but may be better at capturing realistically the natural similarities among concepts.[8]

---

[8] In general, features should not be required to be interpretable, since the idea is that CD represents low-level, subconceptual reasoning.

It should be emphasized that knowledge acquisition in GIRO is accomplished with a rather mechanical process. There is no hand-tuning and there is no ad hoc trick, in contrast to typical expert systems or some of the early connectionist models. Because the architecture is modular, the process can be incremental: new nodes can be added and the existing ones can be deleted at either level and the effect is localized, without changing the global structure.

6.5 SUMMARY

In this chapter I have addressed the issues of inheritance, representational interaction (and the generative capability), and knowledge acquisition. Regarding inheritance, I have shown that CONSYDERR is capable of implementing a complete hierarchy (for either top-down inheritance or bottom-up inheritance, or both), dealing with cancellation, multiple inheritance, and formation of new concepts. Regarding interaction, I have shown that in CONSYDERR, various kinds of interaction can occur in representation, which produce some useful generative capability, and that reasoning is tantamount to a complex process. Various methods for knowledge acquisition have been surveyed. Many possible ways of knowledge acquisition for CONSYDERR have been discussed and the methods currently used have been explained. Overall, this chapter has touched on those aspects of CONSYDERR that make it different from traditional rule-based or logical approaches; these differences stem from the dynamics, not the statics, of the CONSYDERR architecture.

CHAPTER 7 _____

An Extension: Variables and Bindings

But strictly held by none, is loosely bound
By countless silken ties. . . .
                    —Robert Frost

7.1 OVERVIEW

In the previous discussion of CONSYDERR, to simplify the discussion I intentionally omitted issues related to variables and variable binding. In the same vein, I avoided mentioning predicates and arguments when discussing the logic FEL, so only the propositional version of it is examined. However, variables are important, or even essential, for connectionist models, as indicated by many leading researchers (see Feldman and Ballard 1982, Pinker and Prince 1988, Fodor and Pylyshyn 1988). The problem of incorporating variable binding into connectionist models is considered to be a difficult problem.

In this chapter I try to solve this problem, by extending the definitions of FEL and CONSYDERR as described earlier. Specifically, I have the following goals:

- Developing a first-order version of FEL, which will add more expressive power to this formalism.
- Developing mechanisms for variables and variable binding in CON-SYDERR.

- Developing a better understanding of the correspondence between logics and connectionist models (or more precisely, between FEL and CONSYDERR).

The plan for this chapter is as follows: in the first section I explain in detail the variable binding problem in connectionist models. In the second section I extend the definition of FEL to the first-order case. In the third section I deal with issues involved in adding variables into the CONSYDERR architecture. In the fourth section I introduce some formal accounts of activation functions and assembly structures for variable binding in CONSYDERR. In the fifth section I discuss the compilation of FEL rules into networks. Finally, in the sixth section I discuss the logical correctness of compiled connectionist networks. The Appendix contains some technical details left out in the general discussion.

7.2 THE VARIABLE BINDING PROBLEM

In this section I discuss in general the problem of variable binding, a problem that was once considered to be a major shortcoming or even a serious handicap for connectionist models.

Why are variables important in connectionist models? As in the work of Feldman and Ballard (1982), the following example demonstrates the necessity of having variables: suppose that there are a red circle and a black square; we have to have a way to associate red with circle and black with square, such as *COLOR(obj, red) and SHAPE(obj, circle)*. Moreover, this binding has to occur and cease dynamically when reasoning with (visual) input data. Variable binding is essential in creating dynamic structures in connectionist networks. (A similar example is Grossberg's (1987) turkey/lover dilemma, although it was presented in a narrower context in relation to classical conditioning.)

In the same vein, based on linguistic data, Pinker and Prince (1988) point out that rules, modular structures, and variables are essential for the human language faculty and are thus important to be taken into account in connectionist models of linguistic processes and the like. The lack of variable binding is considered by them to be a major shortcoming of early connectionist models.

Variables and variable binding mechanisms are also needed to achieve greater computational power in connectionist models. Early research in high-level connectionist models avoids the variable binding problem by reasoning with one object at a time or by using multiple instantiations, such as in the works of Gallant (1988), Shastri (1988), Kosko (1986), and Blelloch (1986). This approach limits the processing power of the respective systems and increases their computational complexities. That is, to deal with multiple objects, many instances of a rule have to be deployed: instead of

$$inflation\ (x)\ \rightarrow\ high\text{-}interest\text{-}rate(x)$$

we have to have

$$inflation_{US}\ \rightarrow\ high\text{-}interest\text{-}rate_{US}$$
$$inflation_{Japan}\ \rightarrow\ high\text{-}interest\text{-}rate_{Japan}$$

and so on.

So, in order to enhance the representational and computational capability of CONSYDERR, I need to have variables, and I thus need variable binding mechanisms in CONSYDERR. It is important to solve the variable binding problem.

The difficulty of variable binding stems from the simplicity of connectionist models, in which each node performs very simple processing—usually just weighted sums or similar numerical calculations, and structurally these models are uniform—usually using simple processing elements of the same type with regular connection patterns.[1] Therefore, it is extremely difficult to impose any particular dynamic symbolic structures onto them because of the uniformity; in comparison, to store, retrieve, or modify a symbolic structure in conventional computers, one has to go through a sequence of operations with the help of central processing units and other components, which are not readily available to connectionist models. The problem of introducing variables into connectionist models amounts to the question of how to incorporate particular structures into networks without losing too much of that characteristic uniformity and how to enhance the processing power of each processing element to a degree sufficient for symbolic processing while maintaining its simplicity. Different existing solutions (e.g., Touretzky and Hinton 1985, Barnden 1988, Sun 1989, Lange and Dyer 1989, Ajjanagadde and Shastri 1989) can be viewed as different ways of achieving the balance between these conflicting demands.

Touretzky and Hinton (1985) were the first to confront the variable binding problem directly. Their system is made up of several modules. With distributed representation in each module, it is able to match variables against data in the working memory by winner-take-all. The system has very complex structures and is costly in terms of computational resources, but it uses only very simple node functions. It serves as an "existence proof" of solutions to the problems of introducing rules, variable binding, and other symbol-processing capabilities into connectionist models. Another piece of early work is by Smolensky (1987), who uses tensor products for variable binding, with either local or distributed representation. Basically each combination of variables and values is represented by a single node (or a group of

---

[1]There are, of course, many exceptions to this description.

them), which detects dynamically if the right binding is present. It utilizes simple node functions but highly complex networks.

Ajjanagadde and Shastri (1989) and Ajjanagadde (1990) have presented systems that perform backward-chaining inference with variable binding handled by temporal spike trains of two different types. The later version works basically this way: a node representing a variable produces a spike train with a specific phase that is synchronized with the spike train representing a particular binding, when inputs are received which indicate that the node should produce that binding. This scheme has relatively simple network structures but needs complex node functions (with temporal properties). See Chapter 8 for some analyses of existing work.

Having examined the past efforts, in the following sections I develop a better scheme for solving this problem in CONSYDERR. My aim here is, first, to devise a network structure as uniform as possible and to keep node functions well-defined and relatively simple, but at the same time to be able to create dynamic symbolic structures. Second, I am concerned with developing a generic, domain-independent framework, not tied to (and limited to) particular applications, so generality and descriptive precision are the main considerations. Finally, besides the basic capability of variable binding, in order to enable a connectionist reasoner to incorporate logic rules and to possess reasoning power comparable to a sequential symbolic system, there are in fact many more difficult problems to be solved; most of these issues are not addressed adequately by the existing solutions to the variable binding problem; therefore, I will provide some treatments of these more intricate issues. All of this discussion is in relation to the CONSYDERR architecture.

7.3 FIRST-ORDER FEL

In this section I look into the question of how to add variables to FEL, that is, extending FEL from a propositional logic to a first-order logic. The purpose of this exercise is to understand more the nature of variables and to explore the consequence of including them in a logic like FEL, so that I will be better prepared when variable binding is added into the CONSYDERR architecture, since CONSYDERR is, in a way, an "implementation" of FEL.

Like any other propositional logic, FEL has arguments hidden in propositions. For example, "Chaco is cattle country" can be expressed in propositional FEL as

$$Chaco \rightarrow cattle\text{-}country$$

This can be easily extended into a predicate version:

$$Chaco(x) \rightarrow cattle\text{-}country(x)$$

which means that if x, which is an argument to be bound to something, is Chaco, then x is a cattle country. Other rules and facts presented before can all be turned into a corresponding predicate version in exactly the same way.

Besides this simple single-argument case, multiple arguments in one predicate for expressing n-ary relations can be dealt with in a similar way. For example, to express "if one locale is north to another, that locale may be colder than the other," the following predicate rule is used:

$$north\text{-}to(x, y) \rightarrow colder\text{-}than(x, y)$$

Of course, each of these predicate rules should have weights associated with them according to the definition of FEL.

Based on these examples, it seems straightforward to turn the propositional FEL into the first-order FEL. Let me describe formally the predicate version of FEL:

Definition 7.1 A **fact** is an atom or its negation, represented by a letter (with or without a negation symbol $\neg$), with a fixed ordered set of arguments and having a value between l and u (e.g., $l = -1$ and $u = 1$). The value of an atom is related to the value of its negation by a specific method, so that knowing the value of an atom results in immediately knowing the value of its negation, and vice versa.

For example, $a(x)$, $\neg a(u, v)$, x, and $u(y)$ are facts.

Definition 7.2 A **rule** is a structure composed of two parts: a left-hand side (LHS), which consists of one or more facts, and a right-hand side (RHS), which consists of one fact. When facts in LHS get assigned values, the fact in RHS can be assigned a value according to a weighting scheme. Any binding associated with an argument in LHS will be assigned to the arguments with the same name in RHS.

Definition 7.3 A **conclusion** in FEL is a value associated with a fact, calculated from rules and facts by doing the following:

(1) For each rule having that conclusion in its RHS, obtain conclusions of all facts in its LHS, or assume their values to be whatever value represents an unknown if they are unobtainable; then calculate the value of the conclusion according to the weighting scheme.

(2) Take the MAX of all these values associated with that conclusion calculated from different rules or given in initial input.

(3) For each argument in the fact, assign a correct binding, if it exists, from the corresponding argument in the LHS of the winning rule (i.e., the one producing the MAX value).

Now the predicate version of FEL can be defined as follows:

Definition 7.4 A **fuzzy evidential logic** (FEL) is a 6-tuple: $\langle A, R, W, T, I, C \rangle$, where A is a set of atoms, R is a set of rules, W is a weighting scheme for R, T is a set of thresholds each of which is for one rule, I is a set of elements of the form (f, v) (where f is a fact with arguments and v is the value of f), and C is any particular procedure for deriving conclusions.

We can use the same proof procedure C as before for this version of FEL, with the addition of binding propagation (which will be discussed in detail later). I can also differentiate the first-order FEL into two types: FEL_1 and FEL_2, just as with the propositional FEL.

7.4 REPRESENTING VARIABLES

In this section, the question of how variables are added to CONSYDERR is discussed in light of FEL, and some related issues are addressed. First, there is the question of how to represent individual variables. As suggested by Sun (1989), each variable in a predicate can be handled by one separate node. A variable can get bound by an application of a relevant rule that has in its RHS the predicate that contains the variable. Basically, a binding is a numerical value, which represents a particular constant (a domain object), being passed along a link (which represents the rule in question) to the node representing the variable, from a node representing a variable having the same name in the LHS of the rule applied. For example, suppose that a rule is: "If an area grows something, it is an agricultural area." It can be expressed as follows:

$$grow(x, y) \rightarrow agr(x)$$

Suppose that the input is $grow(a, b)$ (meaning "*area a* grows *b*"), where a and b are constants (e.g., $a = Florida$ and $b = orange$). The binding a is passed to the node representing x, and b to the one representing y in $grow(x, y)$. Then, by applying the rule, a is further passed from the node representing x in $grow(x, y)$ to the node representing x in $agr(x)$.

So with this representation, for each predicate we need an *assembly*, or a collection of nodes interconnected in some way, one of which is for computing and storing the (confidence) value of a predicate (I will call it the C node), and the rest are for variables (I will call them X nodes). Supposing that there are k variables in a predicate, an assembly then contains $k + 1$ nodes, each of which (except one C node) is for storing and passing along bindings of the variable that it represents. Among these nodes, the C node of an assembly basically receives inputs from C nodes in other assemblies that are conditions (LHS) of a rule that uses this assembly for its RHS and

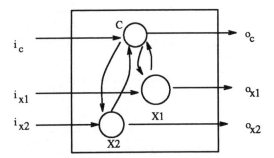

Figure 7.1. *An assembly.*

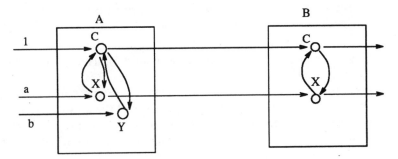

Figure 7.2. *Network for representing the rule: if grow(x, y), then agr(x).*

computes the value that represents the confidence one has on the predicate that the assembly represents based on the values of the conditions. Each variable (X) node receives inputs from variable (X) nodes in the same other assemblies as its corresponding C node, picks up its own binding, and passes it on. See Figure 7.1.[2] For the example above, $grow(x, y) \rightarrow agr(x)$, there are two assemblies: one for $grow(x, y)$ and the other for $agr(x)$. The first assembly has three nodes: C, X, and Y. The second assembly has two nodes: C and X. The C node in the first assembly is linked to the C node in the second assembly. The X node in the first assembly is also linked to the X node in the second assembly. See Figure 7.2. Variable binding is then taken care of by passing values along links. First the C node in the first assembly is activated, and the binding a is passed to the X node in $grow(x, y)$, and b to the Y node. Then by applying the rule (i.e., propagating activation along the link), the C node in the second assembly is activated, and a is passed from

---

[2] Each of the variable nodes in an assembly should also communicate with the C node to send its binding, so that the C node can check consistency and other matters, and should receive "instructions" from the C node, which are to tell a variable node whether or not to pass on a binding and which binding to take. These issues are addressed later in this chapter.

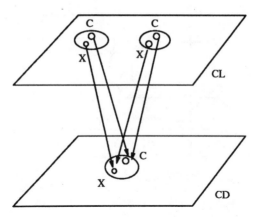

Figure 7.3. *Multiple bindings received during the top-down phase.*

the X node in $grow(x, y)$ to the X node in $agr(x)$. Thus a conclusion is reached: $agr(a)$.

The description above regarding CL is readily applicable to CD. From a computational standpoint, CD is the same as CL and the only difference is in the representational primitives: instead of concepts and propositions, features are used as basic elements in the CD representation. So whatever works for CL works for CD.

One issue I need to look into more deeply is the interlevel connection between CL and CD. The main question is how bindings are passed along when the top-down flow, or the bottom-up flow, is in effect. A simplistic answer is that we can pass appropriate bindings along with activations in the same way as in the intralevel case. One question that arises from this solution is how to deal with the situation, at the bottom-up phase, where different feature assemblies corresponding to the same CL assembly have different bindings associated with them (see Figure 7.3). One way to deal with this is to use the majority rule principle, choosing the binding that is associated with more features than any others. A related, but complementary problem at the top-down phase is how to decide on a proper binding when more than one binding is received at a CD assembly (representing a feature) from different CL assemblies (see Figure 7.4). This can occur when two assemblies representing two different facts with different arguments and bindings but sharing some features are activated at the same time. This problem can be solved by choosing the binding associated with the assembly that has the stronger activation (and hence stronger confidence). The solutions to the two problems above give the system a flavor of competition and winner-take-all.

In this section we have described rather informally how to add variables to the CONSYDERR architecture. A problem that emerges from the preceding discussion is exactly what functions are needed in a node in order to deal with variables. A formal treatment is necessary to qualify the problem clearly, and is presented next.

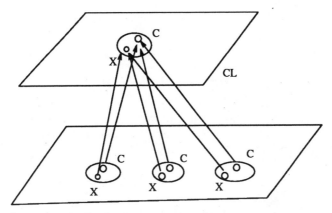

Figure 7.4. *Multiple bindings received during the bottom-up phase.*

7.5 A FORMAL TREATMENT

Based on the idea explained above, a formal treatment of variable binding in CONSYDERR is presented below, with a detailed example. Readers who are not interested in technical details can safely skip the rest of this chapter and go on to the next chapter.

7.5.1 The DN Model

One question that needs to be answered is exactly what functions should be included in a node in order to deal with variables. Some formal treatments are needed to qualify the problem clearly. I will use a very general formalism for connectionist models, the *discrete neuronal* (DN) *model* (see Sun 1991b, d). It can deal with variable binding and confidence value propagation at the same time, and it can be mapped back into conventional models, such as weighted-sum models. Thus the model forms a unifying framework for complex reasoning in connectionist models incorporating variables.

An automaton-theoretic description of a node in a DN model is (cf. Hopcroft and Ullman 1979)

$$N = \langle S, A, B, I, O, U, V \rangle$$

where S = the set of all the possible states of a node

O = the output-line vector

A = the set of all output symbols

I = the input-line vector

B = the set of all input symbols

U = the state transition function

V = the action function (the output function)

I think of a DN node as having a set of input lines and a set of output lines:

$$I = (I_1, I_2, \ldots, I_n)$$
$$O = (O_1, O_2, \ldots, O_m)$$

where each element of I, I_i, is in B, and each element of O, O_i, is in A. Therefore, the value of I is in $\Pi_n B$, and the value of O is in $\Pi_m A$. And the state transition and action functions are

$$U: S \times \Pi_n B \rightarrow S$$
$$V: S \times \Pi_n B \rightarrow \Pi_m A$$

A network of DN nodes is a graph with (multiple) directed links between pairs of nodes. An added constraint is if there is a directed link from node i to node j; then $A_i \subset B_j$.

The formalism has been kept general and complex because it is aimed for generality beyond this work (see Sun 1989 and 1991d). By no means am I claiming that this model is more biologically plausible, only that it can be a useful formalism. The *actual* mechanism for variable binding is simple. The formalism can also easily be mapped into conventional models, as will be seen below. Because of the generality, the DN model can emulate conventional connectionist models (see the Appendix of this chapter for details). Conversely, DN nodes can also be implemented with conventional models (see the Appendix). These two facts together further ensure the compatibility of this formalism with more conventional models. This formalism should thus be viewed as a descriptive tool and/or a notational convention for presenting and explaining complex (conventional) connectionist network structures as will be developed later.

7.5.2 Assemblies

I describe now how the DN formalism can be used to construct the CL level of CONSYDERR, given some first-order FEL rules with variables. The first-order FEL rules can be mapped to a CL network with variable binding as follows: a predicate is represented by an assembly of DN nodes, and rules are encoded in a network by the connections that an assembly has to the other assemblies. For example, Figure 7.5 shows how assemblies representing predicates are wired into a network. So CL is made up of assemblies that in turn are made up of DN nodes representing predicates and arguments, that is,

$$CL =_{\text{def}} (AS, L)$$

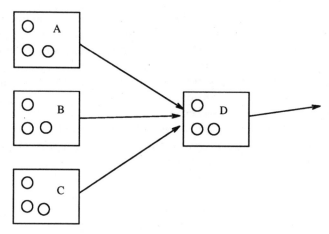

Figure 7.5. *Wiring of a network for representing the rule: if A(X) B(Y) C(Z), then D(W) (where X, Y, Z, and W are vectors of arguments).*

where

$$AS = \{(C, X_1, X_2, \ldots, X_k) | k \text{ is an arbitrary integer;}$$

$$C \text{ and } X\text{'s are a set of DN nodes as specified below}\}$$

$$L \subset \{(AS_1, AS_2, i, j) | AS_1, AS_2 \in AS,$$

$$i, j \text{ are integer labels denoting nodes within an assembly}\}$$

The connections among nodes are specified in L by labels indicating that a particular node in one assembly is connected to another particular node in another assembly. In each assembly, there are $k + 1$ nodes of the DN type: $C, X_1, X_2, \ldots, X_k$. The C node contains the (confidence) value of the predicate (representing the confidence one has in the concept) and is connected to other nodes (mainly C nodes) in other assemblies representing different predicates that are related to it by rules. The X nodes take care of variable bindings (for arguments to the predicate) for a total of k variables. There may also be connections from each X to C and from C to each X. The set of input/output symbols (A and B) in the variable nodes are values (numerical or symbolic) representing all possible bindings used in a task, the range of which is fixed a priori, but the meaning can be dynamically assigned. Each node in an assembly, C or X's, has a specific action function but does not need a state transition function for the present purpose. The action functions are as follows: For C,

$$O_C^1 = V_C^1\left(I_1, I_2, \ldots, I_l, O_{X_1}^2, \ldots, O_{X_k}^2\right) \in A_C$$

$$O_C^2 = V_C^2\left(I_1, I_2, \ldots, I_l, O_{X_1}^2, \ldots, O_{X_k}^2\right) \in A_C$$

Note. O_C^1 and O_C^2 denote the values of the corresponding output lines. Superscript 1 denotes the interassembly output and 2 the intraassembly output. Action function V_C^1 here is a weighted-sum function. V_C^2 produces a signal to the X nodes (see examples later). I_i's are outputs of other nodes (mainly C nodes but possibly X nodes) in other assemblies impinging on this node (here I_i denotes the value of the input line, not the line per se; the same below). The C node also receives inputs from X nodes in the same assembly, useful in certain situations, as will be explicated later. l is the total number of interassembly inputs, so the total number of inputs (intraassembly and interassembly) is $l + k$. A_C is the set of output symbols in the C node.

And for X_i: $i = 1, 2, \ldots, k$,

$$O_{X_i}^1 = V_{X_i}^1(I_1, I_2, \ldots, I_n, O_C^2) \in A_{X_i}$$
$$O_{X_i}^2 = V_{X_i}^2(I_1, I_2, \ldots, I_n) \in A_{X_i}$$

Note. $O_{X_i}^1$ and $O_{X_i}^2$ denote the values of the corresponding output lines. Action function $V_{X_i}^1$ here is a mapping specifying the output (the binding) of X_i based on I_i's, inputs from X nodes in other assemblies. O_C^2 is the signal from the C node in the same assembly. $V_{X_i}^2$ produces a signal to the C node (see examples later). A_{X_i} is the set of output symbols in the node X_i.

The formalism above reveals some subtle timing considerations that need to be addressed. Outputs of a node depend not only on inputs from other assemblies, but also on inputs from other nodes in the same assembly, and thus it is important to make sure that there is no mutual waiting (deadlock) situation. In this case, intraassembly communication from X to C does not depend on input from other nodes in the same assembly, only on input from other assemblies. So this intraassembly communication can finish first, and next the intraassembly communication from C to X is facilitated. Then outputs to other assemblies can be computed without further impediments. I refine I and O into two parts, respectively, as follows:

$$I = I^1 \circ I^2$$
$$O = O^1 \circ O^2$$

where the superscript 1 denotes interassembly input/output, the superscript 2 denotes intraassembly input/output, and "$\circ$" denotes vector concatenation. For action functions:

$$V = V^1 \cup V^2$$

where for X nodes

$$V^1: B^I \to A^{O^1}$$
$$V^2: B^{I^1} \to A^{O^2}$$

and for C nodes

$$V^1: B^I \rightarrow A^{O^1}$$
$$V^2: B^I \rightarrow A^{O^2}$$

V^2 is done during the first phase of a cycle, communicating within an assembly. V^1 is done during the second phase of a cycle, sending outputs to other assemblies downstream. Note that O^2 (intraassembly output) of X is I^2 (intraassembly input) of C and O^2 (intraassembly output) of C is I^2 (intraassembly input) of X.

7.5.3 An Example

As an illustration, I will use the DN formalism to describe the following reasoning process:

if one is human, one is mortal.
Socrates is human,
so Socrates is mortal.

The rule to be represented is

$$human(x) \rightarrow mortal(x)$$

First I set up a network for representing the rule. Applying the DN formalism, I build up two assemblies (see Figure 7.6). The first assembly represents "X is human" and the second assembly represents "X is mortal." The input j is the string "Socrates" or its numerical representation, and the input i is the value of the proposition "Socrates is human," which is 1 in this case. The output v in this case should be the string "Socrates" or its numerical representation, and the output u should be the value of the proposition "Socrates is mortal," which is also 1 in this case. (States and state transitions in the DN formalism are not needed here, so I will not be concerned with states in the following discussion.)

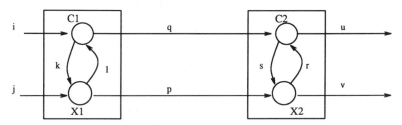

Figure 7.6. *Example network: Socrates. (See the text for explanations.)*

Let R stand for real numbers, and Σ stand for strings (or their numeric representation). For C_1,

$$I = (i, l)$$
$$O = (k, q)$$

where $B_i = R$, $B_l = \Sigma$, $A_k = R$, and $A_q = R$.

The signals from variable nodes to the C node are to inform it whether there is a proper binding present at each variable node: when there is no needed binding, the C node should not be activated. The signals from the C node to variable nodes are to tell them if they should pass on bindings: when the C node is not activated, the variable nodes need not work on the binding. This provides double insurance for practical purposes, although it is not necessary for logical purposes.

Now the action function for C_1 is

$$V: R \times \Sigma \to R^2$$

Expressing it in functional forms, we have

$$q = V_{C_1}^1(i, l) = i$$
$$k = V_{C_1}^2(i, l) = 1 \text{ if } i \neq 0, \perp \text{ otherwise}$$

where $\perp$ denotes no output, and q, k, i, and j denote the values of the corresponding input or output lines.

For X_1,

$$I = (j, k)$$
$$O = (l, p)$$

where $B_j = \Sigma$, $B_k = R$, $A_l = \Sigma$, and $A_p = \Sigma$. The action function is

$$V: \Sigma \times R \to \Sigma^2$$

Expressing it in functional forms, we have

$$p = V_{X_1}^1(j, k) = j \text{ if } k = 1, \perp \text{ otherwise}$$
$$l = V_{X_1}^2(j, k) = j$$

It is the same for C_2 and X_2. In the case of C_2:

$$u = V_{C_2}^1(q, r) = q * w$$
$$s = V_{C_2}^2(q, r) = 1 \text{ if } q \neq 0, \perp \text{ otherwise}$$

where w is the weight on the link from C_1 to C_2 (in this case we have $w = 1$). And for X_2:

$$v = V_{X_2}^1(p, s) = p \text{ if } s = 1, \perp \text{ otherwise}$$

$$r = V_{X_2}^2(p, s) = p$$

Simplifying the notations above, I come up with some simple assignment statements, so that they can be easily programmable. Let prime signs represent the next time period. For C_1,

$$q' = i$$
$$k' = 1 \text{ if } i \neq 0, \perp \text{ otherwise}$$

For X_1,

$$l' = j$$
$$p' = j \text{ if } k' = 1, \perp \text{ otherwise}$$

For C_2,

$$u' = q * w$$
$$s' = 1 \text{ if } q \neq 0, \perp \text{ otherwise}$$

For X_2,

$$r' = p$$
$$v' = p \text{ if } s' = 1, \perp \text{ otherwise}$$

After two time periods, the result can be described as follows:

$$u'' = q' * w$$

and

$$v'' = p' \text{ if } s'' = 1, \perp \text{ otherwise}$$

With the equations above for p', q', and s', by simple substitution we get

$$v'' = j \text{ if } i \neq 0, \perp \text{ otherwise}$$
$$u'' = i * w$$

where u'' is the output from the C node and v'' is the output from the variable node, all in the "mortal" assembly. In this case, the input i is 1, the input j is "Socrates," and the weight w is 1. So the output u'' is 1, and the output v'' is "Socrates," which together mean that "Socrates is mortal."

7.5.4 Discussion

Let me discuss some possible objections to the model presented above and explicate some implicit assumptions made along the way. One objection to the variable binding mechanism described above is that given a limited resolution in a node, it is impossible to represent all of the domain objects. However, I hold that for a cognitive agent, only a relatively small number of objects are involved in any particular reasoning task at a given time, and therefore a network with a reasonable resolution should be able to handle such a set. A simple calculation suffices: suppose that the value range is $[-1, 1]$ and the resolution is 0.001; then a total of 2000 objects can be handled at one time. A mechanism for dynamically assigning values to objects is necessary though (Shastri and Ajjanagadde 1990), to fully utilize an available value range. We can dynamically map all relevant visual or mental objects onto a set of values within a range; this can be accomplished by a connectionist network in the form of a simple counterlike circuit, which assigns to each incoming object the (distinct) current value to be used in reasoning and increments its own value by a small amount for the next object. This mechanism, which is concerned primarily with inputs for a reasoning system, need not be part of the reasoning system per se. Another technique for expanding ranges is to use a group of nodes (and a group of links attached to them) to represent the binding of one variable (which in this case is represented by a vector), and thus achieve much wider ranges than a single node. More nodes can be added to the group to reach any given resolution (see the Appendix for the details of this technique, which is used there for mapping DN nodes back into conventional nodes). To simplify the discussion, the two mechanisms above are not assumed in the following sections.

A related objection is that the mechanism discussed above violates a standard connectionist precept that only simple messages are allowed to pass along links (because activation values represent firing frequencies of neurons, etc.). The answer is threefold: (1) as shown in the Appendix, DN nodes can be mapped to a network of the standard type, so that complex computations and messages are not necessary; the DN formalism merely provides the convenience necessary for describing complex structures; (2) as indicated by many leading experts, the neural model with "activation values representing firing frequencies" is clearly too simplistic and probably wrongheaded; although the generic DN node is too powerful, its various instantiations used here are more plausible; (3) similar network models have been advocated and used by some leading researchers, and they have proven advantageous in certain respects.

Another objection questions the use of abstract formalisms. The reason for using the DN formalism here is simply that I need (1) a rigorous means of description in order to address some complex issues, (2) an abstraction that hides away some network details unnecessary for discussing the problem in hand, (3) a formal and meticulous model that can reveal subtle problems that might otherwise be overlooked, and (4) a conceptual tool and a guide for (hardware) implementation in the future. As emphasized earlier, basic elements of this formalism can readily be implemented in conventional connectionist models.

7.6 DEALING WITH DIFFICULT ISSUES

There are a number of important issues in variable binding beyond what was discussed above. These issues include binding generation, consistency checking, selection, multiple rules, functions, and unification. They were not adequately addressed in previous work but are crucial for achieving adequate symbolic processing capabilities. A detailed treatment of these issues is provided in this section.

7.6.1 Free Variables

First, a clarification needs to be made: X nodes do not necessarily contain a particular numerical value or symbol that represents a particular domain object (a constant); in other words, they can represent free variables. For example, if we have a rule

$$a(x) \rightarrow b(x)$$

given $a(z)$, where z is a variable, we can derive $b(z)$, by representing z with a special value in the X nodes of the assemblies for $a(x)$ and $b(x)$. In order to distinguish a constant (a real binding) from a free variable (*a pseudo-binding*), free variables are represented by values greater than a certain threshold θ, so a simple test (such as "if $x > \theta$") suffices to distinguish them.

7.6.2 Binding Generation

Instead of simply passing bindings on, an X node representing an argument of a predicate may need to generate bindings. The situation can be illustrated by the following example:

$$a(x_1) \rightarrow b(x_1, x_2, c)$$

Here the value for x_1 is simply passed from a to b, but two other values need to be generated in the b assembly to cover the last two arguments: x_2 and c (note that c is a constant but x_2 is a free variable). The issue of *binding generation* is taken care of implicitly in the inference engine in symbolic systems, but it has to be taken care of explicitly in connectionist models. There are two cases, both of which can be illustrated by this example: (1) the value generated for c is a genuine binding, and it should have been preset in the network, but (2) the value generated for x_2 simply denotes a free variable (i.e., a possible binding, or a *pseudo-binding*). In the same way as usually done in Horn clause logic, a universal quantifier is assumed over x_2. Just as performing resolution theorem proving for Horn clause logic (Chang and Lee 1973), we can assume that different rules have different variable names before being compiled into a network (so that there will be no conflict); then a unique value representing x_2 can also be preset in the network. Both cases can be taken care of in the assembly representing the RHS of the rule (the b assembly in this case):

- In the X node of the first type, if the input from the C node is not zero, then output a particular value c, otherwise output nothing ($\perp$).
- In the X node of the second type, if the input from the C node is not zero, then output a particular value p (where $p > \theta$), otherwise output nothing ($\perp$).

So the functions used for the C node in the b assembly are as follows:

$$O_C^1 = V_C^1(O_{C_a}^1, O_{X_1}^2, O_{X_2}^2, O_{X_3}^2)$$
$$= W * O_{C_a}^1 \text{ if } O_{X_1}^2 \neq \perp \text{ and } O_{X_2}^2 \neq \perp \text{ and } O_{X_3}^2 \neq \perp \text{ and } O_{C_a}^1 \neq \perp, \perp \text{ otherwise}$$

$$O_C^2 = V_C^2(O_{C_a}^1, O_{X_1}^2, O_{X_2}^2, O_{X_3}^2)$$
$$= 1 \text{ if } O_{X_1}^2 \neq \perp \text{ and } O_{X_2}^2 \neq \perp \text{ and } O_{X_3}^2 \neq \perp \text{ and } O_{C_a}^1 \neq \perp, \perp \text{ otherwise}$$

where $O_{C_a}^1$ is the input from the C node in a, and W is the weight between the C node in a and its counterpart in b. The functions for the three X nodes carry out the two kinds of generation listed above:

$$O_{X_1}^1 = V_{X_1}^1(O_{X1_a}^1, O_C^2) = O_{X1_a}^1 \text{ if } O_C^2 = 1, \perp \text{ otherwise}$$
$$O_{X_1}^2 = V_{X_1}^2(O_{X1_a}^1) = O_{X1_a}^1$$
$$O_{X_2}^1 = V_{X_2}^1(O_C^2) = p > \theta \text{ if } O_C^2 = 1, \perp \text{ otherwise}$$
$$O_{X_2}^2 = 1$$
$$O_{X_3}^1 = V_{X_3}^1(O_C^2) = c \text{ if } O_C^2 = 1, \perp \text{ otherwise}$$
$$O_{X_3}^2 = 1$$

where $O_{X1_a}^1$ is the input from the X node in a; the three nodes perform binding as described before. As will be shown later, these functions can be set up systematically when compiling a rule set into a network.

Note that pseudo-bindings will not cause a problem downstream, because they will be treated as variables with (implicit) universal quantifiers and can be unified in just the same way as any other variables (as will become clearer later).

7.6.3 Consistency Checking

There is also the issue of *consistency checking*. We may need to check the consistency of bindings in case certain constraints are imposed regarding values of possible bindings for different arguments. For example, suppose that we have the following rule:

$$a(x_1, x_2)\ b(x_2, x_3) \rightarrow c(x_1)$$

where the constraint is that the x_2 in a is to be bound to the same value as the x_2 in b. Another example is

$$a(x_1, x_2)\ x_1 \neq x_2 \rightarrow c(x_1, x_2)$$

where we have to make sure that the inequality holds. To check input consistency, all X nodes have to pass on their inputs to a central location, the C node, for comparison. The C node in the c assembly then checks for equality or inequality. Given the DN formalism, the checking can be easily formalized. With the first example, the functions used for X in the c assembly are

$$O_X^1 = V_X^1\left(O_{X1_a}^1, O_C^2\right) = O_{X1_a}^1 \text{ if } O_C^2 = 1,\ \perp \text{ otherwise}$$
$$O_X^2 = V_X^2\left(O_{X1_a}^1\right) = O_{X1_a}^1$$

where $O_{X1_a}^1$ is the input from X_1 in the a assembly; and the function forms for C are

$$O_C^1 = V_C^1\left(O_{C_a}^1, O_{C_b}^1, O_X^2, O_{X2_a}^1, O_{X2_b}^1\right)$$
$$O_C^2 = V_C^2\left(O_{C_a}^1, O_{C_b}^1, O_X^2, O_{X2_a}^1, O_{X2_b}^1\right)$$

where $O_{X2_a}^1$ and $O_{X2_b}^1$ are inputs from X_2 nodes in assemblies a and b, and $O_{C_a}^1$ and $O_{C_b}^1$ are inputs from C nodes in a and b, respectively; the functions for the C node in the c assembly perform the following mappings (where $I_1 = O_{C_a}^1$ and $I_2 = O_{C_b}^1$):

	O_C^1	O_C^2
$O_{X2_a}^1 = O_{X2_b}^1,\ I_1 \neq \perp\ I_2 \neq \perp$	$\Sigma W_i I_i$	1
otherwise	$\perp$	$\perp$

These mappings take care of consistency checking for this example. The other example above can be dealt with in a similar fashion.

7.6.4 Unification

An extension of the issue of consistency checking is that of *unification*, a much restricted version of the unification problem in first-order logic (because I perform only unifications of variable/variable and variable/constant).

Suppose that there is a rule

$$a(x,n) \rightarrow b(x)$$

When given an input, say, $a(z, y)$, we have to make sure that y is unifiable with n; that is:

If $y = n$ or y is a variable, then they are unifiable.

This can be done in the X_2 node in the a assembly[3]:

$$O^1_{X_2} = V^1_{X_2}(y, O^2_C) = n \text{ if } O^2_C = 1, \perp \text{ otherwise}$$
$$O^2_{X_2} = V^2_{X_2}(y) = n \text{ if } y = n \text{ or } y > 0, \perp \text{ otherwise}$$

A mapping table for $O^2_{X_2}$ is as follows ($O^1_{X_2}$ is too simple to tabulate):

y	$O^2_{X_2}$
$y = n$	n
$y > 0$	n
otherwise	$\perp$

Other functions (for C and X_1) remain the same.

What is especially difficult is the situation in which unification has to be done across predicates, as illustrated by the following rule:

$$a(x_1, x_2) \; b(x_2, x_3) \rightarrow c(x_1)$$

Suppose that the following conditions are given:

$$a(m, n)$$
$$b(x_4, p)$$

where m, n, and p are constants. Now we are in the following state:

$$a(m, n) \; b(x_4, p) \rightarrow c(x_1)$$

I should unify x_4 with n (and I have to make sure that x_4 is indeed unifiable with n), and bind x_1 to m. The unification can be done within the C node in

---

[3]Note that for each predicate appearing in a rule with a different set of arguments (ignoring the difference in variable names), there is a unique assembly specifically for it. See Section 7.7 for details.

the c assembly as follows:

If x_2 (of a) = x_2 (of b), or if x_2 (of a) > θ, or if x_2 (of b) > θ, then they are unifiable.

When the unification is done, a message is sent to the X node in the c assembly to enable it to accept input from the X_1 node in the a assembly; otherwise, inputs are deemed inconsistent with the rule and further activations are blocked. With the same equations as in the case of consistency checking, the C node performs the following mappings for unification (which carries out the test above):

$I_1 = O_{C_a}^1$	$I_2 = O_{C_b}^1$	O_X^2	$O_{X2_a}^1$	$O_{X2_a}^1$	O_C^1	O_C^2
not $\perp$	not $\perp$	not $\perp$	$< \theta, = O_{X2_b}^1$	$< \theta, = O_{X2_a}^1$	$\Sigma W_i I_i$	1
not $\perp$	not $\perp$	not $\perp$	$\geq \theta$	not $\perp$	$\Sigma W_i I_i$	1
not $\perp$	not $\perp$	not $\perp$	not $\perp$	$\geq \theta$	$\Sigma W_i I_i$	1
		otherwise			$\perp$	$\perp$

Note that there is no sequential search involved in performing unification here. Note also that in cases there are multiple occurrences of variables and constants within and/or across predicates, the same approach applies, but the mappings will be more complicated. For the sake of space, such cases will not be discussed here.

7.6.5 Multiple Rules

A question here is how we should deal with the situation in which *multiple rules* having the same conclusion (but different conditions) reach their conclusions with different values; that is, how we combine conclusions from different rules. For example:

$$a(m, x)b(n, x) \rightarrow c(m, n)$$

$$a(m, x)d(x, n) \rightarrow c(m, n)$$

If both rules are activated, there are two conclusions: for example, $c(m, n)$ with a confidence value of 0.9, and $c(m, n)$ with a confidence value of 0.8. The question is how we should combine them (or choose one of them). I want to choose the one with the maximum activation value (i.e., with the highest confidence value). This seems to be a reasonable choice; it is actually the *best* choice when considering the rule interaction issue (see Chapter 6). Nevertheless, we lose completeness by doing that (see Section 7.8).

7.6.6 Selection

Given the answer to the question posed above, the issue of *selection* arises; that is, how do I choose and pass on the right binding when multiple sets of bindings are available? With the DN model, I do the following: (1) the C node (in the assembly representing the conclusion) will receive inputs from different rules, MAX them, and output k if its kth input is the maximum; (2) then the corresponding X nodes will pass on the kth interassembly input if the input from the C node (the intraassembly input) is k. This simple two-step procedure basically takes care of the issue; the mappings for the C node in the c assembly can easily be set up as follows:

$$O_C^1 = V_C^1\left(O_{C_a}^1, O_{C_b}^1, O_{C_d}^1, O_{X_1}^2, O_{X_2}^2\right)$$

$$= \begin{cases} \max\left(W_1^1 O_{C_a}^1 + W_2^1 O_{C_b}^1, W_1^2 O_{C_a}^1 + W_2^2 O_{C_d}^1\right) & \text{if } O_{X_1}^2 \neq \perp \text{ and } O_{X_2}^2 \neq \perp, \\ & \text{and the maximum is not } \perp \\ \perp \text{ otherwise} \end{cases}$$

$$O_C^2 = V_C^2\left(O_{C_a}^1, O_{C_b}^1, O_{C_d}^1, O_{X_1}^2, O_{X_2}^2\right)$$

$$= \begin{cases} 1 \text{ if } W_1^1 O_{C_a}^1 + W_1^1 O_{C_b}^1 \geq W_1^1 O_{C_a}^1 + W_1^1 O_{C_d}^1 \\ 2 \text{ if } W_1^1 O_{C_a}^1 + W_1^1 O_{C_b}^1 < W_1^1 O_{C_a}^1 + W_1^1 O_{C_d}^1 \\ \perp \text{ otherwise} \end{cases}$$

where $O_{C_a}^1$, $O_{C_b}^1$, and $O_{C_d}^1$ are inputs from C nodes in the a, b, and d assemblies, respectively. If one of the inputs is $\perp$, the weighted sum is $\perp$. If both weighted-sums are $\perp$, the result is $\perp$. (These two functions can easily be put into table forms as before.) For X_1 and X_2,

$$O_{X_1}^1 = V_{X_1}^1\left(O_{X1_a}^1, O_C^1\right)$$

$$= O_{X1_a}^1 \text{ if } O_C^1 = 1 \text{ or } O_C^1 = 2, \perp \text{ otherwise}$$

$$O_{X_1}^2 = V_{X_1}^2\left(O_{X1_a}^1\right)$$

$$= 1 \text{ if } O_{X1_a}^1 \neq \perp, \perp \text{ otherwise}$$

$$O_{X_2}^1 = V_{X_2}^1\left(O_{X1_b}^1, O_{X2_d}^1, O_C^1\right)$$

$$= O_{X1_b}^1 \text{ if } O_C^1 = 1, O_{X2_d}^1 \text{ if } O_C^1 = 2, \perp \text{ otherwise}$$

$$O_{X_2}^2 = V_{X_2}^2\left(O_{X1_b}^1, O_{X2_d}^1\right)$$

$$= 1 \text{ if } O_{X1_b}^1 \neq \perp \text{ or } O_{X2_d}^1 \neq \perp, \perp \text{ otherwise}$$

where $O_{X1_a}^1$, $O_{X1_b}^1$, $O_{X2_b}^1$, and $O_{X2_d}^1$ are inputs from X_1 or X_2 nodes in assemblies a, b, or d, respectively.

7.6.7 Functions

Yet another issue is how to extend variable binding to include *functions* such as in *living-in*(*father*(*john*), *boston*, *mass*), or even *second-order predicates*. The basic idea for solving this problem is: instead of one node for one argument, I can use a set of nodes, or a *subassembly*, for an argument. By doing this, a function, with all its parameters, can readily be assigned to a subassembly, in ways similar to assigning a predicate and its arguments to an assembly; in a subassembly, one node represents the function symbol and the other nodes represent parameters of the function. Since a parameter of a function can be a function itself, the structure can be arbitrarily long. However, in any implementation, a subassembly can contain only a limited number of nodes, and this creates a dilemma. I would like to have as many nodes as possible, but want to limit the computational resources used. In practice, I can always choose a reasonable number of nodes for a subassembly, taking into consideration the characteristics of the domain.

In the following discussion, to simplify the matter, I only deal with one level of function, that is, only functions of constants and variables. To wire up rules that can contain one level of functional terms, I can set up assemblies for all predicates involved just as before, but in place of each X node, there is now an X subassembly, which consists of an F node (for a function symbol) and a number of Y nodes (for function parameters). Revising the original definition in Section 7.5 regarding assemblies:

$$AS =_{\text{def}} \{(C, X_1, X_2, \ldots, X_k)| \ k \text{ is an arbitrary integer; } C \text{ is a node,}$$

$$\text{and } X\text{'s are subassemblies}\}$$

where

$$X_i =_{\text{def}} (F, Y_1, Y_2, \ldots, Y_t)$$

The connectivity pattern in an assembly basically remains the same, and all Y nodes (corresponding to X nodes in the original definition) will send messages (their inputs) to the C node as before. Each F node sends its input to the C node, too. Then the C node can perform consistency checking, unification, and other tasks. t is the maximum number of parameters for a function. A special case is that when the binding of a whole subassembly is just one constant or one variable, only one of the nodes (F) is used. To distinguish such a case, the C node has to be able to distinguish a functional term, a constant, and a variable. This can be accomplished by the following test (extended from the test used before):

Suppose that two thresholds are θ_1 and θ_2; if $I_i < \theta_1$, then I_i is a constant; if $I_i > \theta_2$, then I_i is a variable; if $I_i < \theta_2$ and $I_i > \theta_1$, then it is a function symbol.

Based on this, I can specify the mappings used in the C, F, and Y nodes as an extension of the mappings specified previously. As a simplified example, suppose that

$$AS =_{\text{def}} \{(C, X)\}$$

where

$$X =_{\text{def}} (F, Y_1, Y_2)$$

that is, I only allow functions of up to two parameters in this example (other cases are similar). Suppose that I want to set up a network connection for the rule

$$a(x) \rightarrow b(x)$$

Let us look into the assembly for b. In the assembly, I first determine the function forms for C:

$$O_C^1 = V_C^1\left(O_{C_a}^1, O_F^2, O_{Y_1}^2, O_{Y_2}^2\right)$$

$$O_C^2 = V_C^2\left(O_{C_a}^1, O_F^2, O_{Y_1}^2, O_{Y_2}^2\right)$$

where $O_{C_a}^1$ is the output from the C node in the a assembly. Next, the functions for F are determined:

$$O_F^1 = V_F^1\left(O_{F_a}^1, O_C^2\right) = O_{F_a}^1 \text{ if } O_C^2 = 1, \perp \text{ otherwise}$$

$$O_F^2 = V_F^2\left(O_{F_a}^1\right) = O_{F_a}^1$$

where $O_{F_a}^1$ is the input from the F node in the a assembly; the functions for Y_1 are

$$O_{Y_1}^1 = V_{Y_1}^1\left(O_{Y1_a}^1, O_C^2\right) = O_{Y1_a}^1 \text{ if } O_C^2 = 1, \perp \text{ otherwise}$$

$$O_{Y_1}^2 = V_{Y_1}^2\left(O_{Y1_a}^1\right) = O_{Y1_a}^1$$

where $O_{Y1_a}^1$ is the input from the Y_1 node in the a assembly; the functions for Y_2 are similar and thus omitted. Now the detailed mapping for C can be determined, which basically distinguishes three different cases (a constant, a variable, or a function):

$O_{C_a}^1$	O_F^2	$O_{Y_1}^2$	$O_{Y_2}^2$	O_C^1	O_C^1
not $\perp$	$\geq \theta_1, < \theta_2$	any	any	$W * O_{C_a}^1$	1
not $\perp$	$\geq \theta_2$	$\perp$	$\perp$	$W * O_{C_a}^1$	1
not $\perp$	$< \theta_1$	$\perp$	$\perp$	$W * O_{C_a}^1$	1
	otherwise			$\perp$	$\perp$

Given a functional term, say $a(f(m))$ or $a(g(m, n))$, as input to the a assembly, the functions above can handle properly the propagation of bindings.

To investigate the issue further, look at a variation of the example above:

$$a(x) \rightarrow b(f(x, m))$$

In this case, the functions for F in the b assembly have to generate the binding (recall the earlier discussion of binding generation):

$$O_F^1 = f \text{ if } O_C^2 = 1, \perp \text{ otherwise}$$
$$O_F^2 = f$$

The functions for Y_1 in the b assembly are

$$O_{Y_1}^1 = O_{F_a}^1 \text{ if } O_C^2 = 1, \perp \text{ otherwise}$$
$$O_{Y_1}^2 = O_{F_a}^1$$

where $O_{F_a}^1$ is the input from the F node in the a assembly. The functions for Y_2 in the b assembly also have to generate a binding:

$$O_{Y_2}^1 = m \text{ if } O_C^2 = 1, \perp \text{ otherwise}$$
$$O_{Y_1}^2 = m$$

The functions for C remain the same. The three nodes (F, Y_1, and Y_2) give their respective outputs, when given permission by the C node (through O_C^2). Note that in more complex cases, the mappings will also have to take into account the other issues discussed above (see the Appendix).

The approach above is not limited to one level only as the example seems to suggest. However, when multilevel embedding of functional terms is allowed, the complexity will be greatly increased, since many more nodes have to be allocated for each assembly. In the end, a limit has to be imposed on how complex a formula can get. This special problem in implementing functional terms in connectionist networks stems from the fact that function symbols introduce structures whose size is indeterminate at the time of constructing the network (at "compile time") and can only be decided when the actual binding is formed (at "run time"), whereas the other elements of rules and logics have predeterminable size and structure. It may not be unreasonable to impose an artificial limit. As a comparison, in human reasoning, no structural embedding of infinite depth can occur. For example, despite the theoretical possibility of doing so with transformational grammars, no human being can actually produce and comprehend a very long spoken sentence beyond a certain length and complexity limit. Additional techniques, such as dynamic recruitment of nodes into assemblies, can be explored to circumvent the difficulty for practical purposes.

7.7   COMPILATION

The examples are small and isolated. For a large rule set, it is not easy to hand-wire a network. When given a set of rules with weights, we need a systematic procedure for building up a network. CFELDNN (*Compilation of Fuzzy Evidential Logic into DN Networks*) is such a procedure.

I use three different types of assemblies in this procedure (see Figure 7.7)

- *Ordinary Assemblies:* computing weighted sums of inputs and passing along bindings for the variables.
- *OR Assemblies:* computing the maximum of inputs and selecting one set of bindings associated with the winner (the maximum).
- *Complex Assemblies:* the same as ordinary assemblies, except performing constraint checking and/or unification, and also binding generation when necessary. (It does not perform OR functions, because I do not want to make complex assemblies too complex and unmanageable.)

Assume that each node has a set of intraassembly inputs and a set of interassembly inputs; similarly, each node has a set of intraassembly outputs and a set of interassembly outputs; assume that there is no recursion in the rule set (i.e., the rule set is hierarchical); assume that rules come with weights attached. The main procedure is as follows:

```
SET-UP-RULE-NET:
Initialize the rule set to include all the rules to be
   implemented.
Repeat until the set is empty:
   Choose a rule P₁(X₁) P₂(X₂)......Pₙ(Xₙ)  →  Q(X) (w₁,
      w₂,...,wₙ) to work on, if there is no rule in the
```

set that has P_i as the conclusion.
Identify all the existing assemblies for P_i, i =
   1,2,....,n; if there is none (with the same binding
   requirement), make one.
Identify all the existing assemblies for Q,
   if there is none (with the same binding
   requirement), make one.
If there is only one assembly for each P_i and there
   is no in-link to Q, link each P_i to Q, assign
   weights to each link.
If there are in-links to Q, link P_i's to an intermediate assembly, then or-link this assembly with the
   existing Q to a new Q assembly which assumes all
   the out-links of Q, and assign weights as appropriate.
If there are multiple assemblies for P_i, or-link all
   assemblies for the P_i to an intermediate assembly,
   and then link that intermediate assembly to Q, and
   assign weights as appropriate.
Delete from the set the rule implemented.

Note that if we deal only with hierarchical rule sets, the relations between the LHSs and RHSs of various rules impose a partial ordering among rules; what the algorithm does is to choose a full ordering out of the partial ordering. Note also that I do not use any nodes with multiple sites in this procedure (Feldman and Ballard 1982); this is because I simply eliminate the need by introducing multiple nodes, each of which replaces one site, for the sake of clarity. Since I always put a set of related nodes together in an assembly, this means that instead of one assembly with nodes having multiple sites, now I simply have multiple assemblies consisting of nodes with only a single site. Note that in the algorithm, "with the same binding requirement" refers to consistency checking, binding generation, and other internal mechanisms that have to be individualized for each particular instance. When such requirements exist for a predicate (in the LHS or RHS of a rule), I have to make a separate assembly for that predicate in that particular rule.

All the basic ideas concerning this compilation procedure have been discussed before; therefore, I leave to the Appendix all the details of subprocedures for setting up assemblies, including C and X nodes, for linking together assemblies in various ways, and for dealing with issues identified earlier, such as consistency checking, selection, and unification.

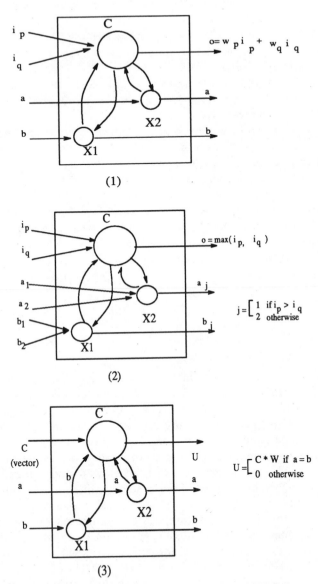

Figure 7.7. *The three types of assemblies: (1) an ordinary assembly, (2) an OR assembly, and (3) a complex assembly (for equality checking and other tasks).*

7.8 CORRECTNESS

Let us look into the logical correctness of the CONSYDERR architecture.

Theorem 7.1   Assume that there is no recursion in FEL (i.e., with a hierarchical rule set) and that there is no functional term. Then the implementation of FEL in CONSYDERR with DN is complete and sound with respect to FEL.[4]

Sketch of Proof. Since the FEL rule set in question is hierarchical, I can order them into levels. Then an inductive proof on the number of levels will do. From all of the previous discussions regarding the issues, I can prove the base case and carry out the induction.

Note that the completeness (i.e., whatever can be inferred in FEL can be inferred in the implementation) comes under the assumption that we replicate and rename a predicate (and all rules involving that predicate) throughout the entire rule set if it appears more than once with different kinds of arguments in the RHSs of different rules (note that this is possible only when the rule set is hierarchical). Otherwise, the different outcomes (with different bindings) from these different rules will be MAXed, and therefore the implemented system loses its completeness. For example,

$$a(m, x)\ b(n, x) \rightarrow c(x, n)$$

$$a(m, x)\ d(x, l) \rightarrow c(x, l)$$

If both rules are activated, there are two conclusions—but only one will be sustained because the MAX operation is combining the results. If I reach $c(m, n)$ with a confidence value of 0.9 and $c(m, l)$ with a confidence value of 0.8, only the first conclusion will remain. What I can do to avoid this is to replicate c:

$$a(m, x)\ b(n, x) \rightarrow c(x, n)$$

$$a(m, x)\ d(x, l) \rightarrow c'(x, l)$$

and also replicate all the rules that have c in their LHSs: suppose that originally I have the rule

$$c(x, y) \rightarrow e(x, y)$$

---

[4]Here *soundness* means that whatever can be inferred in the implementation can be inferred in FEL; *completeness* means that whatever can be inferred in FEL can be inferred in the implementation.

Then I will have the following duplicated rules:

$$c(x, y) \rightarrow e(x, y)$$
$$c'(x, y) \rightarrow e'(x, y)$$

and this process continues recursively until I exhaust all such rules.

With recursive rules, either direct or indirect, the logic will lose its completeness if implemented with cyclic connections. However, I am mainly interested in hierarchical FEL (as a comparison, note that human reasoning is mainly forward-chaining and does not involve circular inferences; Posner 1989). Besides, there are also a number of ways that I can circumvent recursive structures. One way is to replicate a recursive structure a number of times in the network, up to the maximum expected depth of the recursion, provided that I have that information a priori. Another possible way is to use an external stack, which stores and pops out multiple bindings when necessary.

Corollary 7.1   Assume that there is no recursion and there is no function symbol; then the implementation of FEL is sound and complete in the binary case with respect to the first-order Horn clause logic.

Sketch of Proof. Observe the fact that the theorem in Chapter 5 relating binary FEL to Horn clause logic can be extended to the first-order case; so binary first-order FEL is sound and complete with respect to first-order Horn clause logic. The corollary follows directly, from this fact and the theorem above.

It should be noted that the foregoing theorems do not imply that rule sets used in CONSYDERR *must* be hierarchical; rather, they show only that in such special cases where the rule sets are indeed hierarchical, the implementation in CONSYDERR can carry out some logics precisely. In fact, human reasoning in general can hardly be characterized as being very logical; nevertheless, it can be precise on some occasions, and these theorems abstractly demonstrate this possibility.

It is also interesting to note the following:

Theorem 7.2   In case of propositional FEL, no matter whether or not it is hierarchical, the implementation of FEL as described before is always sound and complete with respect to propositional FEL.

Sketch of Proof. An inductive proof on the number of steps (rules applied) will do. The base case is concerned with all the rules that are directly applicable given the initial input. Then with an inductive hypothesis, induction can be carried out by examining all the rules that can be applied given the current state. Note that this can be done because there is no multiple binding problem at all for propositional logics.

7.9 SUMMARY

In this chapter I have discussed the problem of variable binding in connectionist networks, in the context of the CONSYDERR architecture. To help with this discussion, a predicate version of the logic FEL has been defined. A thorough and rigorous solution to the variable binding problem has been presented, and formal definitions have been introduced to clarify subtle details that were overlooked before. I have analyzed the solution to see how it can deal with the intricate issues involved in variable binding and have demonstrated its logical capabilities. A procedure has been developed to transform a set of FEL rules into a DN network systematically. This solution to the variable binding problem aims for structural simplicity while maintaining well-definedness and simplicity of individual nodes.

7.10 APPENDIX

7.10.1 Compatibility of the DN Model

To see how a DN model emulates other connectionist models, let us look into various connectionist (neural network) models. In general, connectionist models can be divided into four classes:

- Continuous input/discrete activation models (e.g., the linear threshold model in Rumelhart et al. 1986)
- Discrete input/discrete activation models (e.g., Feldman and Ballard 1982)
- Continuous input/continuous activation models (e.g., the interactive activation and competition model; Rumelhart et al. 1986)
- Discrete input/continuous activation models (as another possibility)

All of them can be handled easily by DN. To simulate a continuous input/discrete activation model (e.g., the weighted-sum threshold model), let a DN model be

$$\langle S, A, B, I, O, U, V \rangle$$

where $B = \{0, 1\}$

   $A = \{0, 1\}$

   $S = \{ \ \}$

   V = the original weighted-sum thresholding activation function

   U is not needed

This model can emulate the original model and produce the same output: 0 if the weighted sum of inputs is less than the threshold and 1 if the weighted sum of inputs is greater than the threshold. The model can carry out the computation exactly as do its conventional counterparts.

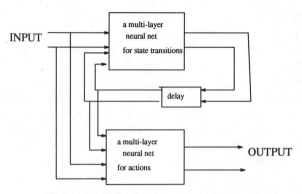

Figure 7.8. *Implementing a finite-state automaton in weighted-sum threshold networks.*

Conversely, DN nodes can also be implemented with the conventional weighted-sum threshold model or the sigmoid activation model. The question here is how to implement the state variable and the state transition function of a DN node. It has been shown that a modular multilayer network can do the job: a layer represents the current state and each input/output value is represented by a group of nodes and is sent through a group of links associated with these nodes. The output is fed back into the input layer to help decide, together with current inputs, which state to enter next and what to output (see Sun 1992c, 1993b). See Figure 7.8.

If, for certain applications, the state is not needed, the top half of the diagram (concerning state transitions and delays) can be removed.

7.10.2 Compilation Procedures

The procedure for setting up each individual assembly is as follows:

SET-UP-ASSEMBLY (for Ordinary Assemblies)

```
Set-Up-C
Set-Up-X
```

SET-UP-C (for Ordinary Assemblies)

```
(I = (I1, I2,.....In) is the input from other
   assemblies)
(I' =(I1', I2',...) are the inputs from Xs in the
   same assembly)
output to other Cs: W*I, if I' is not empty and I is
                       not empty
                    nothing, otherwise
output to Xs: 1 if I' is not empty and I is not empty
              nothing, otherwise
```

The output to Xs are to inform them if they should pass on bindings. I′ is used to determine if there is right binding present at variable nodes; "not empty" means that none of the components of the vector involved is empty ($\perp$).

SET-UP-X (for Ordinary Assemblies)

```
        (I is the input from Xs in other assemblies)
        (I' is the input from C)
output to C: I if I is not empty
             nothing, otherwise
output to Xs in other assemblies: I if I' = 1
                                  nothing, otherwise
```

OR-LINK-ASSEMBLY (for OR Assemblies)

```
For C node:
      (I is the input from other assemblies. k denotes
      the group)
      (each group is a vector by itself)
  output to other Cs: W(k)*I(k) = max(W(j)*I(j)) if not
                          empty
                      nothing, otherwise
  output to Xs: k if I(k) is not empty
                nothing, otherwise
For X nodes:
        (I is the input from other assemblies)
        (Each element of I is a scalar)
        (I' is the input from C)
  output to C: 1 if I is not empty
               nothing, otherwise
  output to Xs in other assemblies: Ik, if I' = k
                                    nothing, if I' is
                                    empty
```

GENERATE-ARGUMENT (for Complex Assemblies)

```
For C node:
  (the same as for ordinary assembly)
For X:
output to Xs: p if I' = 1
              nothing, otherwise
(the same as before otherwise)
```

CONSTRAIN-ARGUMENT (for Complex Assemblies)

```
For C node:
  if constraints are satisfied, then outputs are
    the same as above
  nothing, otherwise
```

UNIFY-ARGUMENT (for Complex Assemblies)

```
For C node:
      (I is the input from Cs in other assemblies)
      (I' is the input from Xs)
   output to Xs: 1 if I' can be unified and I is not
                     empty
                   nothing, otherwise
   (the same as above otherwise)
For X node:
      (I is the input from Xs in other assemblies)
      (I' is the input from C)
   output to C: I if I can be locally unified and I is
                    not empty
                  nothing, otherwise
   output to Xs in other assemblies: the unified I, if
                              I' = 1
                     nothing, otherwise
```

7.10.3 Implementation of Assemblies

Let us see how the basic assembly types used in the network constructed by CFELDNN can be implemented in conventional connectionist networks (and thus a whole network of DN nodes can be implemented in conventional connectionist networks):

- For ordinary assemblies, the C node receives messages from X nodes, computes weighted sums of inputs, and sends a simple message to X nodes; its functionality can be fully determined by the mappings specified before, which can be used to train a three-layer backpropagation network. The X nodes pass along bindings when receiving proper messages from the C node, and their implementation in conventional models are straightforward by doing back-propagation training of a three-layer network (mapping strings to numerical values and $\perp$ to 0, etc.).

- For OR assemblies, the C node computes the maximum of inputs, and the computation can be done by a three-layer back-propagation network. Each X node chooses one binding out of many based on which set is the winner (having the maximum activation for the C node); this can easily be carried out by a three-layer back-propagation network, too. Intraassembly communications can be taken care of along with the basic functionalities above.

- Complex assemblies perform constraint checking and/or unification (and other operations, except OR), and from the discussion in Section 7.6 it is clear that they can be implemented in conventional networks based on the mappings specified in table forms (which can be used to set up and train back-propagation networks).

Clearly distributed representation is used in this implementation. But contrary to Touretzky and Hinton (1985), who use globally distributed representation (i.e., the same representational space for all symbols), I use modularly distributed representation, in which each variable has its own separate representational space. We can avoid a lot of interferences and crosstalk in this way.

CHAPTER 8 _____

Reviews and Comparisons

Comparisons do ofttime great grievance.
   —John Lydgate, BOCHAS

8.1 OVERVIEW

By now I have presented all the justifications for and the technical details of a connectionist architecture for commonsense reasoning. In order to identify precisely a place for CONSYDERR in the mental space of ideas, approaches, and paradigms, I will perform a comparative study in relation to other existing work.

In this study, I emphasize the following points:

- How good is each of these ideas in dealing with the kind of common-sense reasoning that I am interested in? Do they have the potential for generating robust commonsense reasoning?
- How are these different ideas related to each other? Particularly, how are they related to connectionist models?
- How can some of these diverse ideas, each of which excels at certain aspects, be synthesized so that better, more integrated models for commonsense reasoning can be formed?
- How does each of these various ideas fare compared with CONSYDERR?

I look into three different paradigms: rule-based reasoning, case-based reasoning, and connectionism. I reiterate two of my basic beliefs: the *inadequacy of rule-based reasoning thesis* and the *inadequacy of simple connectionism thesis*.

8.2   RULE-BASED REASONING

In this section I review rule-based accounts of commonsense reasoning and some attempts at solving the brittleness problem associated with them.

8.2.1   Rules in General

Among the paradigms used in modeling commonsense reasoning, the rule-based paradigm is by far the most successful. In this paradigm, generally some generic, common syntactic forms that consist of *antecedents* and *consequents* (or conditions and conclusions) are used as basic representational means (Newell and Simon 1972, Klahr et al. 1989). Since rule-based reasoning is the most popular paradigm in "symbolic" AI to date, there are numerous variants and implementations, for example, the OPS family of languages (Klahr et al. 1989), the ACT family of production system models of cognition and development (Anderson 1983) and the whole area of expert systems (Hayes-Roth et al. 1983).

However, this type of model is not free from problems, the most acute of which is the *brittleness* (or rigidity) problem. To be able to handle all kinds of situations, every possible combination of conditions and conclusions in a domain has to be well analyzed beforehand and structured into a system, which is not always possible, especially for large systems. This brittleness problem makes rule-based reasoning unwieldy in accounting for more realistic reasoning tasks and in building more intelligent machines, as alluded to before. A number of researchers from various backgrounds (as mentioned in Chapter 1) pointed out early on that a purely rationalistic research agenda as embodied in the traditional rule-based reasoning paradigm is incomplete. They argued for the incorporation of intuitive, reactive, or subconceptual processes in AI systems. The work by Agre (1988) represents such an approach. With an amazingly simple system, he demonstrated that simple reactive routines can be used to accomplish tasks that are very difficult for traditional AI systems in terms of computational complexity and other matters.

To alleviate brittleness, it is also important to deal with uncertainty, approximity, and adaptivity. One attempt worth mentioning is the *genetic algorithm* (Holland et al. 1986), which has a natural rule-based implementation (i.e., the *classifier* system). It tackles the problems of approximate match, credit assignment, and adaptivity (forming new rules by "mutation" and other methods). These capabilities are not what one usually associates with rule-based systems. The genetic algorithm is a unique combination of reasoning and learning models, aimed at amending the brittleness problem of rule-based systems. Its capabilities stem in part from its representation, which is capable of being rigorous and being flexible at the same time. The rigorous side of it includes precise specifications of conditions and conclusions, exact bit patterns of messages posted, and actions being carried out in exact fashion. The flexible side of it includes allowing approximate match of conditions and forming plausible but not exactly correct new rules. Thus it avoids *some* of the brittleness problem while retaining the precision and systematicity of rule-based reasoning.

It is evident from psychological and psychobiological research (Davidson and Davidson 1980) that intelligent systems (including human mind/brain) must be composed of complex structures: some parts have to be able to handle rules and analytical knowledge, and some other parts to handle intuitions, reactive routines, and associations (distinct from rules and analytical knowledge). There is clearly a need to structure these components so that they fit together, forming a functioning intelligent system. An attempt at this kind of structuring, even in its most rudimentary form, will provide valuable insight into the matter. But before we discuss such structuring any further, let us examine some existing components first.

8.2.2 Formal Logics

Let us look into formal logics, which are predominant in rule-based reasoning. As explained in Chapter 1, formal logics are simple, formally defined languages, capable of expressing rules in a rigorous way. According to the advocates for formal logics, the purpose of formal logics is to formalize in symbolic terms reasoning processes, in mathematics and in daily life. However, they have only limited successes toward this grandiose goal of accounting for all kinds of reasoning. Formal logics are too restrictive to account for a variety of human commonsense reasoning, for the following reasons: it has to have all preconditions precisely specified in order to perform one step of inference; it does not take into account gradedness of concepts, propositions, and rules; and there is no built-in device for similarity-based reasoning or reasoning with incomplete and approximate information. For example, in FEL a rule can be as follows:

$$A B C \to D$$

with weights equal to $(0.3, 0.3, 0.3)$. When only A (with a confidence value 1) and B (with a confidence value 1) are known, we can infer a conclusion D with a confidence value 0.6. When A is known instead with a confidence value 0.6, the confidence value of D is 0.48. But in classical formal logics there is no natural way that this type of reasoning can be performed. Similarly, neither can classical formal logics deal with nonmonotonic reasoning (reasoning with partial information), that is, drawing tentative conclusions from partial, inexact information.

There are some recent extensions to formal logics, which try to remedy some of the aforementioned problems. Those extensions include autoepistemic logic, default logic, and circumscription, among many others. *Autoepistemic logic* (Moore 1985) is an improvement of the *nonmonotonic logic* of McDermott and Doyle (1980) and McDermott (1982). It aims to model a rational agent's belief of its own knowledge. Formally, a modal operator L is introduced to denote *belief*, and formulas are defined as in standard logics except that L is allowed to appear in front of propositions. An autoepistemic theory (which describes the beliefs of a rational agent) satisfies the following conditions (where T is the closure of an agent's beliefs):

1. If $P_1 P_2 \cdots P_n \in T$ and $P_1 P_2 \cdots P_n \to Q$, then $Q \in T$.
2. If $P \in T$, then $LP \in T$.
3. If $P \notin T$, then $\neg LP \in T$.

which basically mean that if a fact is known to be true, an agent will believe it, and if a fact is not known to be true, an agent must not believe that it is true. This logic is nonmonotonic, allowing an agent to draw tentative conclusions based on the lack of information, in which case a tentative conclusion is drawn until more information becomes available. For example, the statement "if I do not believe P, then Q is true" can be expressed as

$$\neg LP \to Q$$

So if P is not in a theory T (the set of beliefs of an agent) and cannot be derived from it, then $\neg LP$ is in T. In this case, the agent can derive Q. However, if P becomes known to be true, Q is no longer derivable.

Shoham's *logic of chronological ignorance* (i.e., the *causal theory* discussed before) can more or less be viewed as a subset of Moore's logic, with efficient inference algorithms derived based on semantics (model theory). The restriction is mostly in the form of formulas allowed, which are basically limited to implications in Shoham's logic. However, this logic is intended to model causal reasoning, and thus, different from Moore's logic, the modal operator L (i.e., $\Box$) is interpreted as *necessity* and M (i.e., $\Diamond$, or $\neg L \neg$) as *possibility*. According to Shoham, there are two types of conditions. In reasoning, as long as we know that the *necessary conditions* are true and that there is no information that the *possible conditions* are false, we can draw the conclusion. This definition makes the theory nonmonotonic, because if later one of these possible conditions becomes known to be false, the reasoning has to be retracted.

Variable precision logic, proposed by Michalski and Winston (1986), is actually similar in spirit to Shoham's formalism. The general format for rules in this logic is

IF *condition*

THEN *conclusion*

UNLESS *censor*

or equivalently,[1]

$$condition \; \neg \, censor \rightarrow conclusion$$

However, *censors* play a different role in inference than ordinary conditions. For example, an unlimited amount of effort is put into showing that conditions are true, but only a limited amount of effort is used for censors, because the truth values of censors are usually more salient. Comparing this logic with Shoham's logic, conditions in the former logic are, roughly speaking, *necessary* conditions in the latter, and censors are the negated *possible* conditions, although in Shoham's logic, possible conditions are required not to be provably false based on current information, which is not the case with Michalski and Winston (1986). The basic idea behind both, "not all conditions are equal," is the same, and it has also been extended into the idea of weighting schemes in FEL.

In terms of nonmonotonic reasoning, *default logic*, proposed by Reiter (1980), is for modeling one particular type of it: when no exact conclusions may be reached because of incomplete (partial) information, people customarily make assumptions that are consistent with their current knowledge of the world but may be changed later. These assumptions are *defaults*, which can be expressed as

$$\frac{A(x) : MB_1(x) \cdots MB_n(x)}{C(x)}$$

This formula means that if $A(x)$ is believed and there is nothing to contradict $B_1(x), B_2(x), \ldots, B_n(x)$, then conclude the default $C(x)$.

Circumscription (McCarthy 1980) is also an attempt at capturing conjectural reasoning, especially regarding properties of some objects: assume that the objects that one can determine to have a property are the only objects that do. The general form of circumscription is as follows: the circumscription of P with regard to A is

$$A(\Phi) \wedge \forall X(\Phi(X) \rightarrow P(X)) \rightarrow \forall X(P(X) \rightarrow \Phi(X))$$

where $A(\Phi)$ is the result of replacing all occurrence of P in A with formula Φ. It means that only those X that satisfy P are those that do, given A. Circumscription are rules of conjecture, to be used along with rules of inference as in standard logics. It is also nonmonotonic, in that when new information becomes available, previous conclusions may be revised.

Although these logics are fine as *normative* models of knowledge, belief, and reasoning, they have some fundamental shortcomings from the stand-

---

[1]Actually, there is another interpretation of *censors* as exclusive-or conditions, which gets more attention in the original paper.

point of modeling commonsense reasoning. These shortcomings include the lack of capabilities for dealing with approximate information, partial match, inconsistency, and most of all, reasoning as a complex, interacting process (cf. Perlis 1986, Israel 1987).

8.2.3 Probabilistic Approaches

Probabilistic approaches for modeling reasoning (including commonsense reasoning) treat beliefs about facts as probabilistic events and utilize probabilistic laws for belief combination. It deals with inexact information, among other things.

The basic probabilistic law for predicting an event based on other known events is

$$p(B) = p(B|A_1)p(A_1) + p(B|A_2)p(A_2) + \cdots + p(B|A_n)p(A_n)$$

Assume that A's are independent from each other and are exhaustive. Notice the striking similarity between this and the weighted-sum formula in connectionist models: the calculation according to a FEL rule, $A_1 A_2 \cdots A_n \to B$ with weights $(w_1, w_2, \ldots, w_n)$, is

$$ACT_B = \sum_i ACT_{A_i} * w_i$$

where ACT_{A_i} can be viewed as $p(A_i)$ in the former formula, ACT_B can be viewed as $p(B)$, and w_i can be viewed as $p(B|A_i)$.

For updating probability based on evidence received, as explained in Chapter 1, the Bayesian rule can be used:

$$p(B|A) = \frac{p(A|B)p(B)}{p(A)}$$

Pearl (1988) investigates network implementations of Bayesian reasoning. With certain restrictions, some Bayesian reasoning can be carried out by local computations in a parallel network. However, the results to date seem to indicate that only very simple types of Bayesian reasoning can be handled efficiently by these kinds of networks.

A question one may ask is: Why should beliefs that concern often unrepeatable mental events be combined by the law that governs repeatable probabilistic events in the physical world? Pearl (1988) offers the following answer: "The fortunate match between human intuition and the law of proportion is not a coincidence. It came about because beliefs are formed not in a vacuum but rather as a distillation of sensory experiences. For reasons of storage economy and generality we forget the actual experiences and retain their mental impressions in the forms of averages, weights, or abstract qualitative relationships that help us determine future actions. The organization of knowledge and beliefs must strike a delicate balance between the computational resources these relationships consume and the frequency of their use." Although I agree with this argument in general, it does not by itself endorse the *precise* probabilistic laws to be used in descriptive modeling of reasoning; this is because there are many simplifications, heuristics, and rules of thumb involved due to time and space resource limitations, the need for an economic organization, and the need for generalization capabilities in commonsense reasoning (cf. Tversky and Kahneman 1983, Posner 1989, Cherniak 1986, etc.).

MYCIN, the early successful expert system, employs a special uncertainty calculus for propagating and combining beliefs (Buchanan and Shortliffe 1984). It is basically a set of heuristic methods. However, Heckerman (1985) shows that there is a probabilistic interpretation for the uncertainty calculus used in MYCIN for evidential combination, and thus such uncertain calculi are not at all a great departure from more traditional theories.

The *Dempster–Shafer calculus* (Shafer 1974) is another evidential reasoning scheme. It decomposes the world into sets of primitive events, assigns probability to these primitive events, and then combines them with various rules in ways consistent with the semantics of the decomposition (notably they are not limited to additive rules as in the weighted-sum scheme). In this way, a judgment is broken down into smaller pieces that can be dealt with easily and that can later be combined.

Nilsson's *probabilistic logic* (Nilsson 1986) represents a different approach in probabilistic reasoning. It makes precise the notion of the probability of a sentence through possible world semantics: it is the sum of the probability of all the possible worlds in which the sentence is true, and the logical entailment is thus reduced to matrix equations, and linear programming is used for solving these equations. The approach applies to any logical system for which the consistency of a theory can be established. Thus uncertainty is treated in a principled way in this framework. However, computational cost is tremendous with this approach, and the processes involved do not seem to be cognitively plausible.

One attempt at applying probabilistic approaches directly to analyzing human reasoning (which is termed *rational analysis*) is that of Anderson (1990). He proposes that human cognition should be analyzed at a more abstract level, from a purely phenomenological point of view, divorced from implementational considerations. (Implementation in a cognitive architecture should be performed at a later stage.) He analyzed a vast array of areas, proposing probabilistic formulations for these areas. He has had some success in accounting for experimental data. However, it seems clear that *not all* data can be dealt with in this way.

The arguments against probabilistic approaches can be summarized (from various previous discussions) as follows:

- These approaches seem too complex (computationally) to be used in human commonsense reasoning, and too complex to be implemented in "brainlike" network models directly. (Note that FEL can be viewed as a simplification of precise formal models of probability, under the assumption of independent evidence.)
- It is clear that human reasoning does not always conform to the assumptions and the laws of probability theory, in part because of the computational complexity of the formal models (Tversky and Kahneman 1983, Cherniak 1986).
- It is not always possible to obtain precise probability measures.

8.2.4 Fuzzy Logic

Fuzzy logic and its basis, the *fuzzy set* concept, have been around for almost thirty years, and have many important theoretical results and some significant applications. Specifically, the idea of *grades of membership* originates from Zadeh (1965), as does that of *linguistic variables* (Zadeh 1975). Later, the idea of *possibility* and *possibilistic logic* was discussed by Zadeh (1978). (Since there are many different versions of fuzzy logics, I can only cover the most common ones; for broader coverage, see Dubois and Prade 1988.)

In fuzzy logic, for each concept there is a set of objects satisfying that concept to a certain degree, which form a subset, namely *fuzzy subset*. This fuzzy subset contains as its elements pairs consisting of an object and its grade of membership, which represents the degree (i.e., the confidence) with which it satisfies the concept associated with the subset. As discussed before, one version of fuzzy logic is as follows:

$$\text{if } X \text{ is } B \text{ then } Y \text{ is } C$$

Given

$$X \text{ is } A$$

we can derive

$$Y \text{ is } \quad D = A \circ (\neg B \cdot C)$$

where X and Y are variables, A, B, C, and D are fuzzy sets, and the membership function for the result is

$$m_D(v) = \max_u \left(\min \left(m_A(u), \left(1 - m_B(u) + m_C(v) \right) \right) \right)$$

where u is used to denote the elements in the domain of the variable X, and thus *max* ranges over the domain of X; v is used to denote the elements in the domain of the variable Y, and m is the grade of membership for respective fuzzy sets.

If the condition of the rule consists of a conjunction, that is,

if X is A and Y is B and Z is C then W is D

and given

X is A' and Y is B' and Z is C'

where A, B, C, A', B', C', and D are fuzzy sets, the result D' (i.e., Y *is* D') can be deduced in the same way: let x, y, z, and w be elements of these subsets; then,

$$m_{D'}(w) = \max_{x,y,z} \min\big(\min(m_{A'}(x), m_{B'}(y), m_{C'}(z)),$$

$$\min\big(1, \big(1 - \min(m_A(x), m_B(y), m_C(z))\big) + m_D(w)\big)\big)$$

where m is the grade of membership of respective fuzzy sets.

FEL is inspired by and similar to fuzzy logic but is based on (and implemented in) connectionist networks. The difference between FEL and the aforementioned fuzzy logic is that FEL uses the weighted-sum computation of connectionist models for combining evidence cumulatively to reach a conclusion from a rule. With MAX/MIN, fuzzy logic as that of Zadeh (1988) does not accumulate evidence (only counting the evidence with the highest grade of membership), while such accumulation is important for common-sense reasoning. FEL provides a scheme for plausible reasoning, which accumulates evidence by using a weighted-sum computation, and it has a sound basis in logic in terms of reducing to classical logics when all values are zeros or ones. Unlike the fuzzy logic above, in FEL we do not have to know all the relevant grades of memberships in order to perform an inference step: if we have no information regarding the value of a fact, we simply assume it to be zero. In this way we can easily allow partial match with a rule, and draw tentative conclusions nonmonotonically. For example, we can have the following rules in FEL:

$$A \rightarrow C \quad (0.8)$$

$$AB \rightarrow D \quad (0.5, 0.5)$$

When only A is known (with confidence value 1), C is concluded. When A and B both are known (both with confidence value 1), D is concluded, because D is activated more strongly than C. This flexible handling results from the parallelism and the numerical weighting scheme of FEL.

Also, by using the weighted-sum computation and allowing the total weight of a rule to be less than 1, FEL rules can be uncertain (probabilistic) and are thus more expressive of complex real-world situations. From a different perspective, as mentioned in Section 8.2.3, FEL can be viewed as a way of reducing computational complexity of probabilistic approaches by simplifying the probabilistic formulas.

An issue here is that uncertainty (probability) and vagueness (fuzziness) are mixed together in FEL (as discussed in Chapter 5). *Vagueness* (or fuzziness) is the ill-definedness of concepts. It is usually handled with a linguistic variable (Zadeh 1975). For example, in the statement "John is tall" it is very difficult to know what "tall" means exactly: 6 ft, 6.5 ft, or 7 ft? A linguistic variable can be defined that draws its values from a fuzzy subset that defines "tall" with grades of membership (Zadeh 1988). On the other hand, *uncertainty* refers to the nondeterminism of an event, which has to be dealt with statistically. For example, "John might be home by 8 o'clock," which is a probabilistic statement. The foregoing method handles both the same way, and this mixing provides a uniform treatment of various types of inexactness, and therefore provides a computationally efficient way of dealing with these forms of inexactness. The overall measure serves as a unified device for measuring subjective confidence and for weighing different pieces of information in accordance with their relative importance in reaching the conclusion.

Summarizing the major differences of FEL as compared with the fuzzy logic (of Zadeh 1988):

- It uses addition and multiplication, which are natural for connectionist networks, instead of MAX and MIN.
- It allows partial matching and accumulation of evidence.
- It distributes weights to different pieces of evidence, and thus can emphasize certain information and disregard others as appropriate.
- It treats not only linguistic vagueness but also other kinds of inexactness in a uniform framework.

8.2.5 Representation and Reasoning with Rules

I want to comment briefly below on knowledge representation in general with rule-based approaches and their variants. Knowledge representation has been a central issue in traditional AI, and many different forms of representation have been explored, especially rule(logic)-based representation. Early knowledge representation research emphasized static representation, concerned mainly with the *form* of static representation (such as frames, semantic networks, and scripts), with little exploration of how useful conclusions can be drawn from them in a principled way. Representational frameworks were demonstrated by a few examples, often captivating but superficial; little theoretical analysis and fundamental work was done (cf. Woods 1975, Brachman 1985). Later, when the pitfalls of this direction became clear, the emphasis has been shifted to *inference* that can be performed, instead of how pieces of knowledge is actually organized and stored. In trying to delineate inferential processes, many questions have to be asked: For example, what are the types of inferences that are allowed in a particular representational framework? What are the types of inferences that are not allowed in a particular representational framework? What are the types of inference that are most readily made? And most important, why are they what they are?

Some progress has been made that leads to better understanding of inferential processes by the means of traditional and nontraditional logics, such as default logic, nonmonotonic logic, and autoepistemic logic (cf. Reiter 1980, McDermott 1982, Moore 1985, Shoham 1987, etc.). But as far as I can see, there is little principled understanding of what is underlying such inferential processes. In other words, the emphasis is on *surface features* of inferential processes rather than underlying causes or *first principles*. To see this, it suffices to mention the fact that inferential processes are characterized statically by mere enumeration of a set of axioms, instead of being characterized by deep explanations. Similarly, inferential processes are described in purely syntactic terms instead of involving semantics and/or implementational considerations. Last but not least, inferential processes are completely separated from knowledge represented in a given framework; that is, inference rules (and mechanisms that use these inference rules to draw conclusions) form a separate component, independent of knowledge bases.

The question of what kinds of inferences to make depends, to various degrees, on a large number of factors. Among them are purposes of making inferences, requirements regarding speed, accuracy, and generality (in a particular situation), and after all, underlying physical machinery (because substrata do constrain phenomena). Studying substrata can help to answer questions such as how certain inferences are facilitated and how certain inferences are prohibited. In other words, a (substratum-based) structural explanation for reasoning functions can be obtained. Moreover, at the same time, a functional (or teleological) explanation for (substratal) structures can also be obtained. Utilizing the parallel between structures and functions, the task of carving out the inferential processes in commonsense reasoning can be less underconstrained; various design choices can be explored; mappings from functions to structures and back can be made out, in the interest of building cognitively plausible intelligent systems. There are sufficient reasons to believe that inferential processes are inseparable from substratal structures (which therefore should also be taken into account in connectionist knowledge representation).

In considering substratal issues, one important constraint is the notion of *computation in place*, as introduced in Chapter 3. To be more concrete, pieces of knowledge can be distributed in a vast network linked up by inferential connections between them—inferential processes can be embodied in substratal structures. Computations necessary for such a network are carried out locally, within nodes and along links, without global control, monitoring, or storage. Considering the above two points (substratal structures and local computation) together, instead of separating knowledge to be represented and inferences that can be drawn from it into two distinct components as customarily done in traditional knowledge representation, we should integrate the two and view them as the two aspects of the same process (especially in connectionist knowledge representation, e.g., CONSYDERR; more on this later).

8.3 CASE-BASED REASONING

Now I shall take a detailed look at case-based reasoning and the related issues, including similarity and analogy.

8.3.1 Case-Based Reasoning in General

The idea of case-based reasoning is proposed as a strong antithesis (in a Hegelian sense) to the more traditional rule-based reasoning. It is claimed that "case-based reasoning is the essence of how human reasoning works" (Riesbeck and Schank 1989), or in other words, case-based inference is believed to be the most basic element of commonsense reasoning. Although it is said that "in a broad sense, everything is a case," it does not seem appropriate to call abstract rules cases, which is usually used to refer to concrete scenarios and episodes. So it is appropriate to evaluate the ideas of case-based reasoning with the usual meaning of the word *case* in mind. As explained in Chapter 1, Riesbeck and Schank (1989) characterize case-based reasoning as performing a sequence of steps: input, index, retrieve, adapt, and test–repair–store.

In general, I have the following reservations about the current approach in case-based reasoning (some details will be discussed later):

- Rules (encoding abstract knowledge) are the most important cognitive mechanisms, although no doubt there are other kinds of knowledge. Only when there is no rule directly applicable will cases (or analogous knowledge in general) be used. For example, suppose that a rule is: *if* a place is warm, flat, and with enough freshwater supply, *then* it can be a rice-growing area. When there is such a rule available, we apply the rule in deciding if an area is a rice-growing area; only when there is no such rule, or the conclusion of the rule is indecisive, may we apply analogous knowledge (or cases). (Of course, such rules may not be context-free and may not work in isolation.)
- There ought to be, therefore, both rules and cases (similarity matching of analogous knowledge) in a reasoner, and rules should take precedence.

- Similarity matching should be done at a lower level; that is, matching should be an intuitive, holistic process. In human reasoning, it seems that nonexplicit, subconceptual, and intuitive modes prevail, especially in similarity-based reasoning. Only when unexpected events occur and usually successful routines are interrupted, then explicit conceptual reasoning takes over in order to reason from rules and first principles to find a solution to the unusual situations (Agre 1988, Dreyfus and Dreyfus 1987, Heidegger 1927). Therefore, the question is: How can case-based reasoning model nonexplicit subconceptual reasoning, along with explicit conceptual reasoning?

- Similarity matching should be done in a massively parallel fashion and spontaneously, without incurring huge computational overhead, in order to be cognitively plausible. This is also argued by Waltz (1989) and Thagard and Holyoak (1989). Simpler algorithms are thus preferred.

In sum, although case-based inference (or the use of analogous knowledge in general) is very important for commonsense reasoning, it is supplementary to abstract knowledge encoded in rules. In other words, rules are primary, and concrete analogous knowledge is secondary. They should be integrated into a unified framework (as, e.g., CONSYDERR). Note that in case-based reasoning there are a variety of opinions not represented by Riesbeck and Schank (1989); it is beyond the scope of this book to review them all.

8.3.2 Similarity

Related to case-based reasoning (and often serving as its justification) is the study of similarity and analogy (analogical reasoning), which has been of long-standing interest to cognitive scientists and artificial intelligence researchers (see, e.g., Evans 1968, Tversky 1977). Lately there has been a new wave of interest in exploring various aspects of similarity and analogical reasoning from various perspectives (e.g., Vosniadou and Ortony 1989, Helman 1988, Way 1991, Indurkhya 1992).

One main issue (see Sun 1993d) is the role of similarity in representation and in some cognitive tasks that builds up or utilizes representation, such as categorization and classification decision making (which are essential in case-based reasoning). Rips (1989) presents a case for the dissociation between similarity and categorization. A number of experiments show that although there are some correlations between similarity and categorization in the experimental settings, the correlation is very weak, and something beside similarity judgments is needed to explain categorization. Rips' work casts doubt on the well-known theory of categorization by family resemblance, as it proves that at least in those circumstances demonstrated by the experiments, resemblances (or similarity) cannot fully account for the way categorization is done in human cognition. Rips proposes *explanation* as the other important factor that affects categorization: one typically uses the underlying nature of the objects and their interrelations as a guide. Conceptual theories can be the sources of explanations generated and categorization then amounts to inference to the best explanation. This shows the importance of rules in case-based reasoning, which relies on categorization.

Smith and Osherson (1989) provide a detailed model of how similarity figures into the classification decision-making process. Based on the similarity measure of Tversky (1977), they explain a number of phenomena in human decision making, such as the *conjunction fallacy*, the *base rate effect*, and *causal effects of base rate*. Their model is based on computing the overall similarity between the properties of the concept representation and the properties of the observed objects, utilizing the frame representation. This work represents a step toward a detailed cognitive model of similarity and its role in commonsense reasoning (as opposed to formal reasoning) and decision making.

Some researchers have been arguing for a holistic representation of similarity. Dreyfus and Dreyfus (1987) suggest that holistic, "holographic" similarity plays a large role in human intuition, and due to the distributed nature, connectionist models might be able to model intuition which traditional "symbolic" systems so far have failed to capture. Smolensky (1988) and Hinton (1990) also posit similar hypotheses. According to our earlier arguments, while rule application can be modeled at the conceptual level by a symbolic system, which represents explicit conceptual knowledge, fine-grained similarity matching can be modeled at the subconceptual level by an informal, holistic, structureless process, which embodies intuition. (Naturally, we will have to consider ways, such as that in CONSYDERR, to combine the two radically different aspects of cognition into one integrated architecture in order to utilize their synergy.)

8.3.3 Analogy

Analogy and analogical reasoning also figure prominently in case-based reasoning. There are many questions regarding them: What are they? How can they be carried out computationally? How can they be implemented? and so on.

Gentner (1989) studies mechanisms of analogy and how similarities are differentiated in constructing analogy. She claims that "an analogy is a way of focusing on relational commonalities independently of the objects in which those relations are embedded" and "people prefer to map connected systems of relations governed by higher-order relations with inferential import, rather than isolated predicates" (i.e., the *principle of systematicity*). Gentner proposes a classification of different similarities: *literal similarity*, in which both relational predicates and object attributes are mapped, *analogy*, in which only relational predicates are mapped, and *mere-appearance matches*, in which chiefly object attributes are mapped. In analogical mapping processes, relations must match identically, objects must correspond, and attributes must be ignored. One problem is that a perfect match of relations (especially high-order ones) is required, which, according to Gentner, avoids difficult decisions such as how much the tolerance for ambiguity should be, how much role the current context should play, and how the quality of match should be measured, but at the price of creating some unnecessary rigidity (e.g., there is no way one can perform a partial or approximate match). There is also the question of how it is related to other mechanisms and considerations. Some "implementation"-level constraints might be of help here.

Holyoak and Thagard (1989) present a computational model for analogical reasoning. Their mechanism for accomplishing this process is unified with rule-based representation and bidirectional search inference method. Thus their system deals with both the use of analogical knowledge and the direct application of rules. When directly applying rules fails to solve a problem, a number of factors lead to the activation of an analogous problem that has a stored solution. After establishing correspondence between the two problems, performing analogous action in the target problem is enabled, and a new solution is thus formed and proposed. A question is whether this particular rule-based architecture can be scaled up to problems of a realistic complexity. The system mixes rule-based reasoning with similarity-based (or case-based) reasoning, but they are carried out in very explicit fashions. A general problem with such explicit representation and reasoning is, as mentioned before, that it does not capture the subconceptual, holistic process that seems most likely to be underlying similar human reasoning. As a result, such models can be rigid (brittle) and unwieldy (of high computational complexity). A massively parallel connectionist model can be better off in avoiding being bogged down by combinatorial explosion.

8.4 CONNECTIONISM

Connectionism is a relatively new approach toward modeling intelligence and cognition. It started with network models inspired by biological nervous systems for solving reasoning-related problems (such as McCulloch and Pitts 1943), and throughout its ups and downs, it always has as one of its goals the modeling of reasoning, cognition, and intelligence. It utilizes the interaction of a network of simple nodes, and the properties emergent from this interaction. Although connectionism provides a very promising alternative for accounting for complex commonsense reasoning and for avoiding brittleness, there is relatively little effort utilizing the connectionist paradigm *directly* for the study of commonsense reasoning. Toward this end, the development of more sophisticated representation in connectionist models, the high-level connectionist models as they have come to be called, is necessary in view of the *inadequacy of simple connectionism thesis*. In this section I look into some efforts at developing high-level connectionist models and at understanding rules, cases, and commonsense reasoning within the connectionist framework. I discuss how such models fare as remedies to the brittleness problem.

8.4.1 High-Level Connectionist Models

Let us consider connectionist models of high-level cognitive processes in general, to see how these models can help to alleviate the brittleness problem. There are a large number of high-level connectionist models around. For example, Rumelhart et al. (1986) present many such models, ranging from sentence understanding to schemata processing. Because of the sheer number, it is impossible to have a thorough review and comparison—only a few of them can be examined.

In the work of Kosko (1986), causal inferences based on fuzzy logic are combined with connectionist models to enable fuzzy/inexact information to be used in reasoning. Each node in the system represents a fixed concept and has continuous activation values. However, there is no variable in the system and there is no mechanism for variable binding; this limits the capability of the system in representing causal relations. The way in which causal inferences are carried out in the system is not fully justified by either theoretical considerations or empirical means.

Derthick (1988) presents a connectionist knowledge representation system. Inferences in this system are carried out by constraint satisfaction through minimizing energy (which is proportional to the outstanding constraints). By constructing the energy function in a way that captures the underlying relations between logical formulas, energy minimization can produce an optimal (or near optimal) interpretation of the inputs. The process of energy minimization is performed by the *Boltzmann machine* settling procedure. Some minor problems with this approach include that the Boltzmann machine is extremely slow, and that it may not produce the best result. A serious limitation, however, is that not all the logical relationships and not all the inference modes can be captured in energy functions. As a matter of fact, most of the commonsense reasoning cannot be accomplished by this energy minimization procedure in any obvious way (Sun 1991a, 1992a).

Hendler (1989) presents a hybrid system of marker passing and connectionist networks, to augment symbolic planning systems in their ability to pick out right actions, by priming relevant concepts through connectionist activation propagation. The role of the connectionist network in this hybrid system is that of association, and thus there are no rules and no variable binding capabilities. Although this method works well in this particular type of applications, for more complicated tasks it is necessary to go beyond pure associations and to utilize more elaborate mechanisms for more systematic reasoning in the connectionist framework.

8.4.2 Connectionism and Rules

One important issue in modeling high-level cognitive capabilities by connectionist models is how to deal with rule-following behaviors and how to carry out rule-based reasoning. Because it is such an important issue by itself, I will discuss it separately in this subsection.

As mentioned before, connectionism has made some claims about rule-based behavior and reasoning. One point of view is that rulelike behavior is the result of complex interaction of network components, in deterministic or statistical ways, and therefore there is no fundamental difference between rules and nonrules. Another viewpoint advocates implementing rules directly in connectionist networks. The need for explicit rule-based reasoning is argued by, for example, Hadley (1990), Smith et al. (1992), and others. Among the works that implement rules directly in connectionist networks are those of Touretzky and Hinton (1985), Touretzky (1986), Barnden (1988), and Dolan and Smolensky (1989). Two systems developed more recently are those of Ajjanagadde and Shastri (1989) and Lange and Dyer (1989).

Now let us take a more detailed look at some early work (introduced in Chapter 1) designed specifically for reasoning in the connectionist framework: Touretzky and Hinton (1985) and Barnden (1988). These are all important pioneering efforts in this area; nevertheless, they each suffer from a number of problems from the standpoint of accounting for commonsense reasoning. In each of the two systems, parallelism is lost in some way, either because of the matching process of hardwired rules or because of a centralized working memory. As a result, the parallel and spontaneous nature of commonsense reasoning is not adequately accounted for, which in turn results in brittleness. For example, the work by Touretzky and Hinton (1985), the first to implement rule-based reasoning in connectionist networks, fits the description above. Their system emulates the structure of a symbolic rule-based (production) system, with separate modules for working memory, rules, and facts; an elaborate pull-out network is designed to match working memory data against rules and to decide which matching rule is to fire. Competition and winner-take-all processes are used for the matching purpose. There is no mechanism for backtracking, and there is no room for approximate reasoning. The mechanism does one match at a time and thus slows down reasoning. The resulting system is the equivalent of a simple sequential symbolic rule-based system. Barnden (1988) represents another early attack on the same problem. In his system, data reside in gridlike networks (called configuration matrices), coded with the help of adjacency relations and highlighting techniques; rules are hardwired with circuitry for detecting the presence of data that match a particular rule, and a conclusion module associated with each rule is used to add a new data structure to the network. The problem here is the symbolic manipulation necessary to match rules against data, which is a slow and complicated process in a connectionist network; as a result the intrinsic parallelism and spontaneity of commonsense reasoning are not fully captured. Although there is some parallelism in the model, the system is basically a sequential rule-based system, carrying out symbolic syllogistic reasoning.

I shall now turn to two pieces of more recent work on connectionist models of rule-based reasoning. Comparing Ajjanagadde and Shastri (1989) (and also Shastri and Ajjanagadde 1990) with the CL part of CONSYDERR, both models have connectionist networks that perform logical reasoning and handle variable binding, and both use local representation. Ajjanagadde and Shastri explore the temporal dimension of activation patterns for representing variables and bindings, while CONSYDERR utilizes the continuous activation values passed between nodes to handle variable binding. Ajjanagadde and Shastri's system performs backward-chaining reasoning, while CONSYDERR performs forward chaining. While both systems can employ classical logics, by introducing a fuzzy evidential logic, CONSYDERR is capable of approximate reasoning and it can accommodate partial information and inconsistency. CONSYDERR is based on the foundation of the DN formalism, which is the force integrating the whole architecture. Lange and Dyer (1989) present another connectionist rule-based reasoning system. This system is very close to the CL part of CONSYDERR. In their system, rules are used for selecting and activating frames. Activated frames help in deciding meanings of words in text, as the system is applied to the task of word sense disambiguation. Distinct values, which they call *signatures*, are used to represent particular bindings for variables.

In addition, Ballard (1986), Pinkas (1992), and Holldobler (1990) all implement first-order predicate calculus in connectionist models using complex network structures. Such work is concerned with the computational issues, not cognitive issues (including modeling commonsense reasoning).

As a historical footnote, Grossberg's work (e.g., as summarized in Grossberg 1987) is, to a large extent, for modeling some basic rulelike behavior: classical conditioning, but as in CONSYDERR, it also takes into consideration things that are internal, inexact, and holistic in nature, not just rulelike regularity. Rulelike regularity is embodied in network connections, each of which can be interpreted as a rule, but together they form a complex process. It can be viewed as one of the precursory work in combining rules with connectionist approaches.

Let us examine how these systems handle the important issues in implementing rules and variable binding that were discussed in Chapters 5 and 7:

- Touretzky and Hinton (1985) do not take into account *graded and fuzzy concepts* in reasoning. The other solutions cited above allow more general forms of rules and thus can potentially accommodate such concepts, but they do not provide any treatment.

- In the system of Touretzky and Hinton (1985), the issue of *binding generation* is taken care of automatically because of the way they encode rules, predicates (i.e., triples in their terminology), and arguments, in a distributed fashion. Shastri and Ajjanagadde (1990) deal with this issue explicitly, by gating activation flow with the firing pattern of a constant and by not providing any temporal firing patterns synchronized with an unbound variable. Others do not deal with the issue.

- When there are *multiple rules* applicable, Touretzky and Hinton (1985)'s system picks one arbitrarily, and thus the result is unpredictable. This is unsatisfactory if we want to make sure that all the relevant knowledge is brought to bear on a problem. Lange and Dyer (1989) use MAX for combining activations of rules but do not handle conflicting bindings. It is not clear how others deal with the problem.

- Shastri and Ajjanagadde (1990) perform limited *consistency checking* and *unification* in their systems with means different from CON-SYDERR. Touretzky and Hinton (1985) have built-in *unification* because of the distributed representation, but one drawback is that they only allow rules of a very restricted form. Lange and Dyer (1989) do not deal with this issue.

- As for *functional terms*, Ajjanagadde (1990) explores it briefly in a phase-based system. To my best knowledge, the other models do not deal with this problem.

However, some of these models do have some apparent advantages. I will look into the following issues:

- Touretzky and Hinton (1985) are capable of reusing the same rules many times so that infinitely long chains of reasoning are possible. This can be handled in CONSYDERR by feeding the current output back into the network to start the next cycle.

- By using distributed representation, Touretzky and Hinton (1985) exhibit many interesting characteristics of the distributed approach, such as approximate pattern matching, generalization, and graceful degradation. In contrast, the network in CL is localist, which in general does not have the foregoing characteristics. However, by implementing DN nodes in distributed networks (as explained in the Appendix of Chapter 7), similar characteristics can be obtained in CL.

- Shastri and Ajjanagadde (1990) are capable of dynamically assigning different phases to different variables and objects at different times, and therefore are able to fully utilize the limited range available. I should note that this on-the-fly assignment of phases or frequencies is not an intrinsic part of the reasoner and is carried out by mechanisms external to the network performing inferences. Similar mechanisms can be added

	Parallelism for Rules	Numbers of Variables	Time Complexity	Space Complexity	Inference Directions
CONSYDERR	Yes	No Limit	Low	Low	Forward
A & S	Yes	No Limit	Low	Low	Forward and Limited Backward
L & D	Yes	No limit	Low	Low	Forward
T & H	No	One	Very High	High	Forward
Barnden	No	No Limit	High	High	Forward

Figure 8.1. *Comparisons regarding performance.*

to CONSYDERR to fully utilize the available value range (which usually has only limited resolution) by dynamically mapping all relevant objects onto a set of values within the range. The value range in CONSYDERR is at least as wide as the phase or frequency range, especially if one believes that activation values represent neuron firing phases or frequencies.

- Lange and Dyer (1989) incorporate mechanisms for inhibitions and gating. CONSYDERR can certainly accommodate some mechanisms for inhibitions and gating, in addition to activation propagations, because of the generality of the DN formalism. However, unlike the activation propagation, which can be characterized by FEL, the logical characteristics of such mechanisms are unclear.

All of these aforementioned connectionist rule–based systems share much commonality with CONSYDERR in its CL part (there is no fundamental difference there), but they do not deal with similarity matching as in the CD part of CONSYDERR, and consequently they are unable to utilize the synergy between the two types of representation (which is essential to CONSYDERR). Therefore, they are unable to do more than what a traditional rule-based system is capable of, besides massive parallelism, and they do not deal with reasoning as complex processes. See Figures 8.1 and 8.2 for a complete summary comparison.

8.4.3 Connectionism and Cases

Connectionist models are inherently similarity-based: responses to input are determined by the similarity of the input to the prototypical cases in the previous training data. Some have described connectionist models as doing data clustering, while others have described them as performing statistical inferences (see Anderson and Rosenfeld 1988). Hinton et al. (1986) present an analysis of how similarity-based generalization can occur naturally in networks with distributed representation, which helps to deal with the

	Activation Values	Temporal Patterns	Symbolic or Subsymbolic	Approximate Reasoning
CONSYDERR	Numerical	No	Both	Yes
A & S	Numerical	Yes	Symbolic	No
L & D	Non-numerical	No	Symbolic	Limited
T & H	Numerical	No	Symbolic	No
Barnden	Non-numerical	No	Symbolic	No

Figure 8.2. *Comparisons regarding mechanisms.*

brittleness problem as discussed before. While these kinds of similarity tend to be unstructured and fine-grained, more structured types of similarity (and analogy) have been explored by other researchers.

Barnden and Srinivas (1990) describe an attempt at utilizing case-based reasoning in connectionist networks, for the purpose of combating the rigidity (i.e., brittleness) that is undermining both purely symbolic rule-based reasoning systems and some connectionist rule-based systems such as Barnden's (1988) (which is exactly the same idea as what motivates the CONSYDERR architecture). The system is adopted from their original rule-based connectionist system discussed before; it has multiple configuration matrices (CMs), each of which contains a case for short-term processing; a relatively small set of gateway CMs provides the interface between short-term processing and long-term memory, which encodes cases in connection weights; cases in nongateway CMs compete to have their contents copied into gateway CMs, where it can cause cases similar to it retrieved from long-term memory, and some symbol substitutions take place after the retrieval to adapt the cases to the current situation. Comparing CONSYDERR with this system, I notice the following: (1) CONSYDERR is more massively parallel: there are no gateways and complex copying and substitution processes that may hamper parallelism, and (2) matching in CONSYDERR is more automatic (spontaneous): there is no special matching mechanism. (This potentially limits the matching capability.)

Lange and Wharton (1992) propose a way of performing analogical retrieval through spreading activation, based on input cues. It uses a structured localist connectionist network for evidential propagation and combination. One problem with this system is the complexity of connections necessary to explicitly encode all knowledge regarding similarities (e.g., by implementing a semantic network), since the system utilizes only explicit conceptual-level representation.

Rumelhart (1989) proposes some ideas about similarity and analogy in the connectionist framework. Reasoning by similarity can be viewed as a continuum involving at one end simple remembering and at the other end analogical reasoning, while in between lie *generalization*, *reminding*, and *reasoning by examples.* Thus connectionist models, due to its similarity-based nature, offer ideal mechanisms for realizing similarity-based reasoning. In such connectionist networks, features are used to represent functions, properties, and abstract relations, and a particular situation is represented by a cluster of activated features. Memory accesses in connectionist models are determined by the similarities between the cue clamped to a network and the previously stored memory patterns in the network. Rumelhart indicates that by gradually weakening retrieval cues, releasing the most concrete ones first and progressively releasing more abstract features, a system will be able to recall previous patterns similar to the cue in more and more abstract ways. Analogical reasoning is thus achieved in such systems by keeping mainly the abstract relational features. In fact, there is another possibility (not discussed by Rumelhart) for achieving mapping of abstract relations, that is, using massively parallel feature comparisons as in CONSYDERR, which is more efficient computationally. By dividing representation into two levels, a distributed feature level and a localist concept level, when a concept node is activated, we can activate all the corresponding feature nodes and due to feature overlapping, all the concept nodes sharing some of these features will be activated to various degrees. In this way, analogies can be achieved without a search or a settling process; moreover, along with analogy, other similarity-based reasoning (such as *literal similarity* and *mere appearance match*) can also be achieved.

8.4.4 Integrating Rules and Similarities: Four Criteria

Now the question is: How should we integrate rule-based and similarity (case)-based reasoning in one architecture, so that we can have the best of both worlds, in a cognitively plausible way? Connectionist models are the natural choice for an integrated architecture, because they offer a vehicle that can carry out both processes as the foregoing discussion shows (see also Sun 1991b, 1993c). To help to choose the most plausible connectionist architecture that can integrate rule-based and similarity-based reasoning, four criteria can be hypothesized, based on all the discussions and arguments so far:

- *Direct Accessibility of Concepts.* To model conceptual-level reasoning and especially explicit rule-based reasoning, concepts (and reasoning processes) should be directly accessible and linguistically expressible; that is, they should be accessed without any intermediate steps and matching/extraction devices (involving extra network modules). This criterion basically rules out distributed representation, for a concept represented by a distributed pattern is not *directly* accessible. It thus leaves us with two options for representing concepts: purely symbolic representation and localist connectionist representation.

- *Direct Inaccessibility of Similarity Matching*. As argued before, at least certain types of similarity matching is done subconceptually, in a holistic way. The actual matching process may not be accessible conceptually. This is important, because holistic operations entertain a host of properties that other types of operations lack (e.g., context sensitivity and massive parallelism). According to this criterion, a distributed representation seems to be the only viable way for the similarity-matching purpose.

- *Linkages from Concepts to Features*. Once a concept is activated, its essential features should also be activated, either activated explicitly (conceptually) or primed somehow subconceptually. This (explicit or implicit) activation of features is important in subsequent similarity matching and other uses of information associated with features (cf. Barsalou 1989).

- *Linkages from Features to Concepts*. Once a certain portion of the features of a concept is activated (implicitly or explicitly), the concept itself should be activated to "cover" these features (i.e., the categorization process; cf. Smith and Medin 1981).

In light of the foregoing criteria we can examine some existing connectionist models that integrate rules and similarities. For instance, Barnden and Srinivas (1990) do not satisfy the second criterion, because they use explicit forms of similarity matching; on the other hand, Touretzky and Hinton (1985) do not satisfy the first criterion, because the rule application process is not directly accessible. CONSYDERR is an architecture that satisfies the four criteria: a two-level architecture that contains both localist and distributed representations with extensive cross-level connections. The localist network performs rule-based reasoning explicitly with directly accessible conceptual representation, and the distributed network encodes similarities implicitly with feature-based representation. Similarity matching is accomplished through a top-down/bottom-up cycle that directs the information flow in a circular way. Thus the similarity-matching process is not directly accessible conceptually. Such an architecture juxtaposes both types of reasoning and utilizes their interaction. The four criteria above thus collectively support the *dual-representation hypothesis* which I put forth in Chapter 3.

Compared with the other models discussed above, CONSYDERR has the following advantages: the overall architecture of dual representation is a principled way (based on the dichotomy of conceptual and subconceptual processing; Smolensky 1988) of integrating rule-based reasoning and connectionism, or rule-based components and similarity-based components. On the one hand, this integration adds continuity (embodied in similarity-based connectionist networks) to a discretized rule-based system, so that it can better model continuous thought processes; on the other hand, it adds structures (i.e., rules, as well as variables and bindings) to a structureless, associationistic network, giving it the rigor, precision, and directedness that it needs to model a wide range of cognitive tasks. One important point is that the architecture provides a unified framework (in a connectionist fashion) for both conceptual-level reasoning and subconceptual-level reasoning (in a limited way though), so that their synergy can be utilized, and brittleness, caused by one-sided overly explicit way of reasoning, can be alleviated while certain necessary precision and rigor can still be maintained. Another important point regarding CONSYDERR is that the very structure of a network is used to direct inferences in accordance with FEL rules. Thus inferential processes are captured right in representation. In other words, inferences are cast in a network fashion in CONSYDERR, so that the representational structure and the inferential process are unified, as argued for in the earlier discussion.

8.5 SUMMARY

In this chapter I bring together several paradigms of artificial intelligence and examine some representative models in each of them. The characteristics of each of these paradigms are identified and/or critically analyzed.

I advocate the integration of rule-based reasoning and similarity-based reasoning (as embodied in both case-based reasoning and connectionist models). Various existing paradigms have proven their relative advantages and usefulness, despite various shortcomings associated with each of them. It is argued that they have complementary characteristics and can work together synergistically.

Four criteria are hypothesized regarding the integration of rule-based and similarity-based reasoning processes: direct accessibility of concepts, direct inaccessibility of similarity matching, linkages from concepts to features, and linkages from features to concepts. These four criteria together determine a certain range of possibilities in terms of architectures for integrated representation. These four criteria lead naturally to a two-level dual-representation architecture, with one level for explicit, conceptual representation and reasoning and the other level for implicit, subconceptual processes. Judging from the investigations in the previous chapters, such a two-level architecture not only captures the distinction between conceptual and subconceptual processes, so that models of commonsense reasoning can be cognitively more plausible, but it also enables utilization of the synergy resulting from the interaction of the two levels, so that such models can alleviate the brittleness problem found in traditional rule-based systems (as shown in Chapter 4).

Conclusions

When we have done our utmost to arrive at a reasonable conclusion, we ... must close our minds for the moment with a snap and act edogmatically with our conclusion.
—George Bernard Shaw, ANDROCLES AND THE LION

9.1 OVERVIEW

The resurgence of connectionist models results directly from the dissatisfaction with explicit symbolic models in artificial intelligence, which have had successes but suffer from a variety of problems. The explicit symbolic models emphasize deliberative and analytical mode of reasoning (the conceptual-level reasoning) while discounting some other important and/or essential characteristics of human reasoning: the intuitive, holistic, and implicit mode in commonsense reasoning (the subconceptual-level reasoning). Earlier connectionist models complemented such models and succeeded in many tasks that traditional AI models fail to address. However, to claim that connectionist models provide a more feasible approach toward modeling cognitive processes, the complementary strength of traditional symbol processing models has to be taken into account, too. We need ways of incorporating symbolic processing into connectionist models and are thus in need of new kinds of connectionist models that go beyond mere pattern matching. This work tries to address such needs and attempts to develop symbolic processing capabilities in connectionist models. Such an attempt is clearly far from a regression back into the "good old-fashioned AI" (Dreyfus and Dreyfus 1987), namely, the traditional symbolic approach, but represents a synthesis (an integration) of the two sides: conceptual-level reasoning and subconceptual-level reasoning. The questions now are: What have we accomplished so far? How good is the integrated model? And what lesson can we draw that may have some generic and lasting values?

9.2   SOME ACCOMPLISHMENTS

So, after all is said and done, what has been achieved thus far? Or asking the question another way: How well have I succeeded in the tasks that I set out to do at the beginning of this book? Let us examine these questions by looking into the theory, the architecture, and the systems that have been developed.

A connectionist architecture CONSYDERR is developed that integrates rule-based reasoning into connectionist networks and couples localist representation with similarity-based distributed representation. It turns isolated, context-free, and all-or-nothing type rules into an interacting process enmeshed in a network with graded links and activations, which combines pieces of evidence and produces plausible conclusions based on given input regarding particular situations.

Collins' protocols and other data are accounted for by systems built with the CONSYDERR architecture. All the data enumerated in Chapter 2, including those that involve rules, those that involve mixed rules and similarities, and those that involve inheritance, are dealt with uniformly with the same simple architecture. The patterns that underlie the data come out naturally as a result of the working of a two-level structure with a weighted-sum computation.

A model of causality is developed to account for commonsense causal reasoning and can be carried out naturally by weighted-sum connectionist models in general and by CONSYDERR in particular. The fortuitous but extremely fortunate match between connectionist models and models of causal reasoning results in an efficacious analytical and computational tool, namely, the CONSYDERR architecture, that captures a range of commonsense causal reasoning.

CONSYDERR is developed with the aim of being an *integrated* model that can deal effectively and efficiently with a (seemingly disparate) set of important problems in commonsense reasoning (the basic elements of commonsense reasoning): rule application, evidential combination, similarity matching, inheritance (in both ways), and so on. The point to emphasize here is that these problems are handled together in a single unified framework that has no special mechanism for any single one of these problems. Through data and conceptual analyses, these problems are reduced into a simple framework: rule application plus similarity matching (or, more elaborately, a connectionist rule encoding scheme FEL plus a two-level structure that includes feature representation for similarity matching). This set of different problems turns out to be the different manifestations of the same problem. And this problem is handled by CONSYDERR, which thus serves as a unifying model for commonsense reasoning.

9.3 LESSONS LEARNED

One main lesson that can be drawn from this work concerns an explanation of the capabilities of CONSYDERR—how can we achieve the power as demonstrated above in a simple architecture? The answer is, simply put, that the power of CONSYDERR derives from:

1. The capability of the weighted-sum computation for representing and utilizing commonsense knowledge
2. The intensional approach, that is, combining the intensional (feature-based) representation with the extensional representation to utilize their synergy

Another important lesson that can be drawn concerns the relationship between rules, connectionist models, and causal reasoning. Through a logical formalism that connects a modal logic and the weighted-sum computation of typical connectionist models, rules and connectionist models are shown to be comparable in representation and reasoning power. Moreover, the logic formalism is meant to capture causality in commonsense reasoning; thus connectionist models are also capable of capturing commonsense causal reasoning.

9.4 EXISTING LIMITATIONS

There are undeniably shortcomings and limitations in CONSYDERR. Below I discuss some of them briefly.

One of the potential limitations is the simplicity of the feature representation adopted. Although this simple representation is justified in some ways and works well for the task at hand, it will have to be extended to more complex representations for more complex reasoning, for example, natural language processing, text understanding, and planning, judging from related research in AI.

Another limitation is in analogy-making, which is a natural extension of similarity matching used in this work. Viewed from the perspective of modeling analogy and analogical reasoning, the way in which similarity is found and the way in which the adaptation is made in CONSYDERR are admittedly not very sophisticated, and the architecture deals only with the most rudimentary forms of analogical reasoning. Thus the applicability of

CONSYDERR is potentially limited, and extensions have to be developed for more complex situations.

Beside the above, there could also be more complex interaction between the two levels, so that more sophisticated reasoning patterns can emerge into existence, and more levels with different granularities, so that finer and finer distinctions can be made.

There are some other shortcomings that limit the capability of CONSY-DERR in its present form. These shortcomings include the lack of treatments for the following aspects:

- The temporal aspect of Shoham's logic, which is ignored in this work for some reason (see Chapter 5 for some discussions).
- Temporal reasoning in general, which is a broad and difficult problem that is not dealt with here (see Chapters 4 and 5 for some suggestions).
- Backward chaining and other inference algorithms (except forward chaining), which might be needed in some commonsense reasoning tasks and are nice to have for the sake of completeness in terms of common-sense reasoning methods.
- Nonhierarchical rule sets, or recursive structures, in CONSYDERR, which constitute an unresolved problem and a limitation of CONSY-DERR with respect to its logical capabilities (see Chapters 5 and 7). This issue may interact with the temporal reasoning issue.
- Higher-order predicates beyond first-order ones, in FEL and in CON-SYDERR. This is a further extension of the variable binding problem.
- A complete analysis of interaction/generativity in CONSYDERR, especially a clear characterization of its scope. (Chapter 6 contains only some preliminary discussions of it.)

9.5 FUTURE DIRECTIONS

To make CONSYDERR more complete, more accurate, and more computationally efficient, it will be useful to look into the possibility of further developing the ideas embodied in the CONSYDERR architecture, I will look into a number of aspects that might help the most in further improving the architecture and in applying it to a wider range of domains.

One of these aspects, as mentioned in earlier chapters, is how **temporality** and **sequences** can be represented in CONSYDERR, so that it can be applied readily to many other domains, for example, planning, hierarchical decision making, and some aspects of natural language processing. As hinted in Chapter 4, temporal simulation can be used to handle temporality. In so doing, some sort of feedback connections may be needed in one level or the other in order to update the current state of the reasoner, to set the stage for the next step, to keep track of sequences, and also to assert choices, preferences, and constraints.

Another aspect that is of importance for the further development of CONSYDERR is **automatically developing distributed representation**, through grounding high-level processes into low-level processes (i.e., symbol grounding; Harnad 1990) and/or through mapping syntactic representation into semantic representation by learning algorithms (Dyer 1990). Hopefully, features developed this way (which may be uninterpretable) may better capture the similarities between concepts involved in given situations and may lead to more accurate models of commonsense reasoning.

An important aspect to be pursued is **learning**, which includes learning of rules in CL, incorporation of rules into CD, and rule interaction in learning. This is difficult, especially when the architecture is applied to problems of realistic sizes (i.e., not toy problems). The study of learning can intermix with the study of representation, and together, a better understanding of connectionist models of commonsense reasoning can be achieved (cf. Levine 1991).

In addition, it is important to study in greater detail the interaction between distributed feature representation and explicit localist representation, especially in relation to the exploration of the synergy that interaction generates. For one thing, a concept, especially when developed in the ways described above, can have **weighted features** with weights indicating their relative importance or salience in relation to a given concept, so that the mutual influence between the concept and a particular feature is proportional to the weight the feature has to the concept (relative to other features). In this way, a minor, less salient feature of a concept, if activated, will be less likely to fire up the concept, and the concept, if activated, will in turn activate the feature to a lesser degree, so that other concepts that share this feature will be activated to a correspondingly lesser extent—all proportional to their correlational strengths. In other words, a feature connected to a concept with a higher weight is more contingent to the concept, and a feature with a lower weight is less contingent to the concept (Leonard 1967).

Note that the similarity-matching measure used in this work, which is implemented with feature representation, can easily be extended by adding nonlinear activation functions and/or thresholds to interlevel links and/or nodes involved at either level; this extension can be useful for complex situations that require complex similarity matching (e.g., nonlinear combinations of features). An intermediate level of "hidden" nodes can also be added between CL and CD to provide more complex nonlinear mapping capabilities.

I believe the issue of **interaction and generativity** is important and should be studied further. In Chapter 6 we touch on this issue, taking a cursory look at how interaction and generativity work in CONSYDERR to fill in knowledge gaps and to produce new concepts dynamically. Further explorations may reveal additional properties. Related problems that are worth pursuing include what the requisite minimal built-in structure is, how consistency can be maintained, and how the recruitment learning algorithm can be used to select CL nodes for newly generated concepts.

Yet another aspect is the development of more complete and more sophisticated mechanisms for taking **contexts** into consideration. This includes learning of context rules, hierarchical structuring of contexts, and more elaborate interaction of contexts and reasoning.

Let us broaden our perspective and look beyond the present work. Overall, research in connectionist models has passed its infancy and is now fully grown and ready to take on hard problems encountered in traditional AI. When more and more difficult problems are addressed by connectionist models, the development of new representational techniques and new network constructs becomes necessary.

While connectionist models are getting increasingly more complex, modular, and heterogeneous, it is important to keep in sight the original goal of the connectionist paradigm and to retain the original appeal of connectionist models in their uniformity and simplicity. It is undeniably hard to maintain the balance between the two conflicting goals: to develop sophisticated representation and to develop simple, uniform, and mathematically analyzable representation. In trying to deal with this problem, alternatives in representation should be explored, and trade-offs between them should be understood; the biological connection of connectionist models can be very useful: biological constraints can be used as part of the design constraints for intelligent systems modeling cognitive processes, and special-purpose biological neural network circuits can be employed in constructing connectionist architectures.

The convergence of connectionist AI and traditional "symbolic" AI is also in sight. These two approaches represent two different philosophical backgrounds and emphasize two different aspects of cognition. However, more and more connectionist researchers start to tackle problems in traditional AI, such as reasoning, belief representation, and text understanding, while more and more AI researchers start to adopt connectionist models in dealing with problems difficult for traditional methods, such as rule learning, symbol grounding, and concept formation. It seems very promising that a consolidated field for the study of intelligence and cognition utilizing a wide range of techniques will emerge and will make great progress in producing powerful models and in understanding fundamental issues in the field, by combining the complementary strengths of both approaches.

Such convergence may well lead to the development of brand new types of massively parallel intelligent systems that are not mere parallelizations of serial reasoning systems but represent a completely different kind of processes—interacting, complex processes, grounded semantically, reasoning systematically, capable of producing results that are not explicitly stored in them, and having a range of properties not seen in either purely rule-based reasoners or simple connectionist models.

To advance our understanding of human reasoning and cognition further and to produce truly intelligent systems, it is necessary to explore the relationship between different types (modes) of thinking and the different types of models that can capture them, for example, purely symbolic models, localist connectionist models, distributed connectionist models, and other models employing distributed representation and/or numerical representation. Future models need to relate not only to deliberative, analytical reasoning but also to intuitive, automatic reasoning. Further explorations in this direction can be expected to produce new insights into the working of, and the interaction between, various reasoning capacities in cognition.

9.6 SUMMARY

It is the end that crowns us, not the fight.
—Herrick, HESPERIDES

In short, a connectionist architecture for robust commonsense reasoning, CONSYDERR, is proposed to account for some common patterns in commonsense reasoning and to remedy to a certain extent the brittleness problem found in traditional "symbolic" systems (although, of course, it cannot completely eliminate the brittleness problem). Different from other existing connectionist models, a dual-representation scheme is devised, which has extensional objects (i.e., localist representation) as well as intensional objects (i.e., distributed representation with features). By using feature-based distributed representation in addition to localist representation, I explore the synergy resulting from the interaction between them and from the interaction between rule-based reasoning and similarity-based reasoning. This synergy helps to deal with problems such as partial information, lack of applicable rules, property inheritance, representational interaction, and others. In addition, a logic is developed for capturing and utilizing commonsense causal knowledge, which is equivalent to a weighted-sum connectionist model. Therefore, combining the two aspects, the CONSYDERR architecture is capable of accounting for many difficult patterns in reasoning. This architecture demonstrates that connectionist models equipped with symbolic processing capabilities are effective tools for modeling commonsense reasoning capacities and suggests that they may also be useful for constructing efficient practical systems. This work thus shows that connectionist models of reasoning are not mere implementations of their traditional "symbolic" counterparts.

References

Agre, P. (1988). The dynamic structure of everyday life, *Technical Report*, MIT AI Laboratory, Cambridge, MA.

Ajjanagadde, V. (1990). Reasoning with function symbols in a connectionist system, *Proc. 12th Cognitive Science Conference*, Lawrence Erlbaum Associates, Hillsdale, NJ.

Ajjanagadde, V., and L. Shastri (1989). Efficient inference with multi-place predicates and variables in a connectionist system, *Proc. 11th Cognitive Science Cociety Conference*, Lawrence Erlbaum Associates, Hillsdale, NJ, pp. 396–403.

Aleksander, I. (1989). The logic of connectionist systems; In: I. Aleksander, ed., *Neural Computing Architectures*, MIT Press, Cambridge, MA.

Anderson, J. R. (1983). *The Architecture of Cognition*, Harvard University Press, Cambridge, MA.

Anderson, J. R. (1985). *Cognitive Psychology and Its Implications*, W. H. Freeman, New York.

Anderson, J. R. (1990). *The Adaptive Character of Thoughts*, Lawrence Erlbaum Associates, Hillsdale, NJ.

Anderson, J., and E. Rosenfeld, eds., (1988). *Neurocomputing*, MIT Press, Cambridge, MA.

Anderson, J., and R. Thompson (1989). Use of analogy in a production system. In: S. Vosniadou and A. Ortony, eds., *Similarity and Analogical Reasoning*, Cambridge University Press, New York.

Ballard, D. (1986). Parallel logical inference and energy minimization, Technical Report 142, Department of Computer Science, University of Rochester, Rochester, NY.

Barndens, J. (1988). The right of free association: relative-position encoding for connectionist data structures, *Proc. 10th Conference of Cognitive Science Society*, Lawrence Erlbaum Associates, Hillsdale, NJ, pp. 503–509.

Barnden, J., and K. Srinivas (1990). Overcoming rule-based rigidity and connectionist limitations through massively parallel case-based reasoning, Technical Report, New Mexico State University, Las Cruces, NM.

Barsalou, L. (1989). Intraconcept similarity and its complications. In: S. Vosniadou and A. Ortony, eds., *Similarity and Analogical Reasoning*, Cambridge University Press, New York.

Besnard, P. (1989). *An Introduction to Default Logic*, Springer-Verlag, New York.

Blelloch, G. (1986). AFL-1: a programming language for massively parallel computers, Master's thesis, MIT AI Laboratory, Cambridge, MA.

Bookman, L. (1989). A connectionist scheme for modeling context. In: D. Touretzky et al., eds., *Proc. 1988 Connectionist Summer School*, Morgan Kaufmann, San Mateo, CA, pp. 281–290.

Brachman, R. (1985). I lied about the trees, *Artificial Intelligence Magazine*, Fall, pp. 80–93.

Buchanan, B., and E. Shortliffe, eds. (1984). *Rule-Based Reasoning: The MYCIN Experiment*, Addison-Wesley, Reading, MA.

Bunge, M. (1963). *Causality*, Meridian Books, Cleveland, OH.

Chang, C., and R. C. Lee (1973). *Symbolic Logic and Mechanical Theorem Proving*, Academic Press, New York.

Charniak, E. (1983). Passing markers: a theory of contextual influence in language comprehension, *Cognitive Science*, 7(3), pp. 171–190.

Cherniak, E. (1986). *Minimal Rationality*, Academic Press, San Diego, CA.

Chomsky, J. (1980). Rules and representation, *Behavioral and Brain Sciences*, pp. 1–16.

Collins, A. (1978). Fragments of a theory of human plausible reasoning: In: D. Waltz, ed. *Theoretical Issues in Natural Language Processing II*, Ablex, Norwood, NJ, pp. 194–201.

Collins, A, and J. Loftus (1975). Spreading activation theory fo semantic processing, *Psychological Review*, Vol. 82, pp. 407–428.

Collins, A., and R. Michalski (1989). The logic of plausible reasoning: a core theory, *Cognitive Science*, Vol. 13, No. 1, pp. 1–49.

Creswell, M. J., and G. E. Hughes (1968). *An Introduction to Modal Logic*, Routledge & Kegan Paul, Boston, MA.

Davidson, J., and R. Davidson (1980). *The Psychology of Consciousness*, Plenum Press, New York.

Davis, E. (1990). *Representations of Commonsense Knowledge*, Morgan Kaufmann, San Mateo, CA.

de Kleer, J., and J. Brown (1986). Theories of causal ordering, *Artificial Intelligence*, Vol. 29, pp. 33–61.

Dennett, D. (1983). Cognitive wheels: the frame problem of AI, Technical Report, Tufts University, Medford, MA.

Derthick, M. (1988). Mundane reasoning by parallel constraint satisfaction, Technical Report CMU-CS-88-182, Carnegie-Mellon University, Pittsburgh, PA.

Dolan, C., and P. Smolensky (1989). Implementing a connectionist production system using tensor products. In: D. Touretzky et al., eds., *Proc. 1988 Connectionist Summer School*, San Mateo, CA, Morgan Kaufmann, pp. 265–272.

Dreyfus, H. (1972). *What Computers Can't Do*, Harper & Row, New York.

Dreyfus, H., and S. Dreyfus (1987). *Mind over Machine*, The Free Press, New York.

Dubois, D., and H. Prade (1988). An introduction to probabilistic and fuzzy logics. In: P. Smets et al., eds., *Non-standard Logics for Automated Reasoning*, Academic Press, San Deigo, CA.

Duval, B., and Y. Kodratoff (1986). Automated deduction in an uncertain and inconsistent data basis, *Proc. European Conference on Artificial Intelligence*.

Dyer, M. (1990). Distributed symbol formation and processing in connectionist networks, *Journal of Experimental and Theoretical Artificial Intelligence*, Vol. 2, pp. 215–239.

Edelman, G. (1987). *Neural Darwinism*, Basic Books, New York.

Evans, T. (1968). A program for the solution of geometric analogy intelligence test questions. In: M. Minsky, eds., *Semantic Information Processing*, MIT Press, Cambridge, MA.

Fanty, M. (1988). Learning in structured connectionist networks, Technical Report 252, Department of Computer Science, University of Rochester, Rochester, NY.

Feldman, J. (1986). Neural representation of conceptual knowledge, *Technical Report 189*, Department of Computer Science, University of Rochester, Rochester, NY.

Feldman, J., and D. Ballard (1982). Connectionist models and their properties, *Cognitive Science*, July, pp. 205–254.

Fodor, J., and Z. Pylyshyn (1988). Connectionism and cognitive architecture: a critical analysis. In: S. Pinker and J. Mehler, eds., *Connections and Symbols*, MIT Press, Cambridge, MA.

Forbus, K. (1985). Qualitative process theory. In: D. Bobrow, ed., *Qualitative Reasoning About Physical Systems*, MIT Press, Cambridge, MA.

Gallant, S., (1988). Connectionist expert systems, *Communications of the ACM*, Vol. 31, No. 2, pp. 152–169.

Gelfand, J., D. Handelman, and S. Lane (1989). Integrating knowledge-based systems and neural networks for robotic skill acquisition, *Proc. IJCAI*, Morgan Kaufmann, San Mateo, CA, pp. 193–198.

Gentner, D. (1989). The mechanism of analogical learning: In: S. Vosniadou and A. Ortony, eds., *Similarity and Analogical Reasoning*, Cambridge University Press, New York.

Girotto, V., and P. Legrenzi (1990). New European contributions to the psychology of reasoning, *GOLEM*, Vol. 1, pp. 103–118.

Grossberg, S. (1987). *The Adaptive Brain*, North-Holland, New York.

Grossberg, S., and G. Carpenter (1987). A massively parallel architecture for self-organizing neural pattern recognition machine, *Computer Vision, Graphics, and Image Processing*, Vol. 37, pp. 54–115.

Guha, R. V., and D. Lenat (1990). CYC: a midterm report, *Artificial Intelligence Magazine*, Vol. 11, No. 3, pp. 32–59.

Hadley, R. (1990). Connectionism, rule following, and symbolic manipulation. *Proc. AAAI-90*, Vol. 2, pp. 579–586, MIT Press, Cambridge, MA.

Hammond, K. (1989). *Case-Based Planning*, Academic Press, San Diego, CA.

Hanson, S., and D. Barr (1990). What does the connectionist model learn: learning and representation in connectionist models, *Behavior and Brain Sciences*, Vol. 13, No. 3, pp. 1–54.

Harnad, S. (1990). The symbol grounding problem, *Physica D.*, Vol. 42, No. 1–3, pp. 335–346.

Hayes, P. J. (1977). In defence of logic, *Proc. 5th IJCAI*, Morgan Kaufmann, San Mateo, CA, pp. 559–565.

Hayes, P. J. (1978). The naive physics manifesto. In: D. Michie, ed., *Expert Systems in the Microelectronics Age*, Edinburgh University Press, Edinburgh, Scotland.

Hayes, P. J. (1979). Naive physics I. Manuscript.

Hayes-Roth, F., D. A. Waterman, and D. B. Lenat, eds. (1983). *Building Expert Systems*, Addison-Wesley, Reading, MA.

Heckerman, D. (1985). Probabilistic interpretation of MYCIN's certainty factors. In: L. N. Kanal and J. F. Lemmer, eds., *Uncertainty in Artificial Intelligence*, Elsevier, New York, pp. 167–196.

Heckerman, D. (1987). Modularity of rule-based system, *Proc. AAAI*, Morgan Kaufmann, San Mateo, CA.

Heidegger, M. (1927). *Being and Time*, Harper & Row, New York.

Helman, D. ed. (1988). *Analogical Reasoning*, Kluwer, Dordrecht, The Netherlands.

Hempel, C. (1965). *Aspects of Scientific Explanation*, The Free Press, New York.

Hendler, J. (1989). Marker-passing over microfeatures: towards a hybrid symbolic/connectionist model, *Cognitive Science*, Vol. 13, pp. 79–106.

Hink, R., and D. Woods (1987). How humans process uncertain knowledge, *Artificial Intelligence Magazine*, No. 8, pp. 41–53.

Hinton, G. (1990). Mapping part–whole hierarchies into connectionist networks, *Artificial Intelligence*, Vol. 46, pp. 47–76.

Hinton, G., J. McClelland, and D. Rumelhart (1986). Distributed representations. In: D. Rumelhart et al., eds., *Parallel Distributed Processing*, MIT Press, Cambridge, MA.

Hofstadter, D. (1985). *Metamagical Themas*, Basic Books, New York.

Holland, J. (1986). Escaping brittleness. In: R. Michalski, J. Carbonell, and T. Mitchell, eds., *Machine Learning*, Vol. 2, Morgan Kaufmann, San Mateo, CA, pp. 593–625.

Holland, J., N. Nisbitt, T. Thagard, and J. Holyoak (1986). *Induction: A Theory of Learning and Development*, MIT Press, Cambridge, MA.

Holldobler, S. (1990). On high-level inferencing and the variable binding problem. In: G. Dorffner, ed., *OEGAI-90*, Springer-Verlag, Berlin, pp. 180–185.

Holyoak, K., and P. Thagard (1989). A computational model of analogical problem solving. In: S. Vosniadou and A. Ortony, eds., *Similarity and Analogical Reasoning*, Cambridge University Press, New York.

Hopcroft, J., and J. Ullman (1979). *Introduction to Automata, Language and Computation*, Addison-Wesley, Reading, MA.

Hopfield, J. (1982). Neural networks and physical systems with emergent collective computational abilities, *Proc. National Academy of Science*, Vol. 79.

Hornik, K., M. Stinchcombe, and H. White (1989). Multilayer feedforward networks are universal approximators, *Neural Networks*, Vol. 2, pp. 359–366.

Horty, J., R. Thomason, and D. Touretzky (1987). A skeptical theory of inheritance in nonmonotonic semantic networks, *Proc. AAAI*, Morgan Kaufmann, San Mateo, CA, pp. 358–363.

Horty, J., R. Thomason, and D. Touretzky (1990). A skeptical theory of inheritance in nonmonotonic semantic networks, *Artificial Intelligence*, Vol. 42, pp. 311–348.

Hume, D. (1740). *A Treatise of Human Nature*.

Indurkhya, B. (1992). *Metaphore and Cognition*, Kluwer, Dordrecht, The Netherlands.

Isreal, D. (1987). What's wrong with non-monotonic logic? In: M Ginsberg, ed., *Readings in Nonmonotonic Reasoning*, Morgan Kaufmann, San Mateo, CA, pp. 53–55.

Iwasaki, Y., and H. Simon (1986). Causality in device behavior, *Artificial Intelligence*, Vol. 29, pp. 3–32.

Johannessen, K. S. (1990). Rule-following and intransitive understanding. In: *Artificial Intelligence, Culture and Language*, Springer-Verlag, Berlin.

Johnson-Laird, P., and P. Wason, eds. (1977). *Thinking*, Cambridge University Press, New York.

Kant, I. (1953). *A Critique of Pure Reason*, Macmillan, New York.

Keil, F. (1989). *Concepts, Kinds, and Cognitive Development*, MIT Press, Cambridge, MA.

Klahr, J., P. Langley, and R. Neches (1989). *Production System Models of Learning and Development*, MIT Press, Cambridge, MA.

Kosko, B. (1986). Fuzzy cognitive maps, *International Journal of Man–Machine Studies*, Vol. 24, pp. 65–75.

Lakoff, G. (1986). *Women, Fire and Dangerous Things*, MIT Press, Cambridge, MA.

Lange, T., and M. Dyer (1989). Frame selection in a connectionist model, *Proc. 11th Cognitive Science Conference*, Lawrence Erlbaum Associates, Hillsdale, NJ, pp. 706–713.

Lange, T., and C. Wharton (1992). REMIND: retrieval from episodic memory. In: J. Barnden and K. Holyoak, eds., *Advances in Connectionist and Neural Computation Theory II: Analogical Connections*, Ablex, Norwood, NJ.

Leonard, H. (1967). *Principle of Reasoning*, Dover, New York.

Levine, D. (1991). *Introduction to Neural and Cognitive Modeling*, Lawrence Erlbaum Associates, Hillsdale, NJ.

Lewis, D. (1975). Causation. In: E. Sosa, ed., *Cause and Conditionals*, Oxford, University Press, Oxford, England.

Mackie, J. (1975). Causes and conditions. In: E. Sosa, ed., *Cause and Conditionals*, Oxford University Press, Oxford, England.

Marcus, S., ed. (1989). Special issue on knowledge acquisition, *Machine Learning*, Vol. 3.

Marr, D. (1980). *Vision*, MIT Press, Cambridge, MA.

McCarthy, J. (1968). Programs with common sense. In: M. Minsky, ed., *Semantic Information Processing*, MIT Press, Cambridge, MA.

McCarthy, J. (1980). Circumscription: a form of non-monotonic reasoning, *Artificial Intelligence*, Vol. 13, pp. 27–39.

McCulloch, W., and W. Pitts (1943). A logical calculus of the ideas immanent in nervous activity, *Bulletin of Mathematical Biophysics*, Vol. 5, pp. 115–133.

McDermott, D. (1982). Non-monotonic logic II: nonmonotonic modal theories, *Journal of the ACM*, Vol. 29, No. 1, pp. 33–57.

McDermott, D., and J. Doyle (1980). Non-monotonic logic I, *Artificial Intelligence*, Vol. 13, No. 1–2, pp. 41–72.

Michalski, R. (1989). Two-tiered concept meaning. In: S. Vosniadou and A. Ortony, eds., *Similarity and Analogical Reasoning*, Cambridge University Press, New York.

Michalski, R., and P. Winston (1986). Variable precision logic, *Artificial Intelligence*, Vol. 29, pp. 121–146.

Mili, H., and R. Rada (1990). Inheritance generalized to fuzzy regularity, *IEEE Transactions on Systems, Man and Cybernetics*, Vol. 20, No. 5, pp. 1184–1197.

Minsky, M. (1985). *The Society of Mind*, Simon and Schuster, New York.

Moore, R. C. (1985). Semantical considerations on nonmonotonic logic, *Artificial Intelligence*, Vol. 25, pp. 75–94.

Neal, R. (1990). Learning stochastic feedforward networks, *Technical Report CRG-TR-90-7*, University of Toronto, Toronto, Ontario, Canada.

Newell, A., and H. Simon (1972). *Human Problem Solving*, Prentice-Hall, Englewood Cliffs, NJ.

Nilsson, N. (1980). *Principle of Artificial Intelligence*, Tioga, Palo Alto, CA.

Nilsson, N. (1986). Probabilistic logic, *Artificial Intelligence*, Vol. 28, pp. 71–87.

Norman, L. (1977). *Human Information Processing*, Academic Press, San Diego, CA.

Nosofsky, R. (1986). Attention, similarity and the identification–categorization relationship, *Journal of Experimental Psychology: General*, Vol. 115, No. 1, pp. 39–57.

Oden, G. C., and R. Jenison (1990). Fuzzy implication formation in distributed cognitive modeling, *Proc. Cognitive Science Society Conference*, Lawrence Erlbaum Associates, Hillsdale, NJ, pp. 860–867.

Osherson, D., E. Smith, and E. Shafir (1987). Some origins of belief. *Cognition*, 1987. (Also, *Technical Report 3*, Cognitive Science and Machine Intelligence Laboratory, University of Michigan, Ann Arbor, MI.

Osherson, D., O. Wilkie, E. Smith, and A. Lopez (1990). Category-based induction, *Psychological Review*, Vol. 97, No. 2, pp. 185–200.

Osherson, D., J. Stern, O. Wilkie, M. Stob, and E. Smith (1991). Default probability, *Cognitive Science*, Vol. 15, pp. 251–269.

Pearl, J. (1988). *Probabilistic Reasoning in Intelligent Systems*, Morgan Kaufmann, San Mateo, CA..

Perlis, D. (1986). On the consistency of commonsense reasoning, *Computational Intelligence*, Vol. 2, pp. 180–190.

Pinkas, G. (1992). Representing unstructured first order logic in connectionist networks. In: R. Sun et al., eds., *Working Notes of AAAI Workshop on Integrating*

Neural and Symbolic Processes, American Association for Artificial Intelligence, Menlo Park, CA.

Pinker, S., and A. Prince (1988). On language and connectionism. In: S. Pinker and J. Mehler, eds., *Connections and Symbols*, MIT Press, Cambridge, MA.

Pollack, J. (1988). Recursive auto-associative memory, *Proc. Cognitive Science Conference*, Lawrence Erlbaum Associates, Hillsdale, NJ, pp. 33–39.

Posner, M., ed. (1989). *Foundations of Cognitive Science*, MIT Press, Cambridge, MA.

Pustejovsky, J. (1993). *Generative Lexicon*, MIT Press, Cambridge, MA.

Putnam, H. (1992). Is the causal structure of the physical itself something physical? In: H. Putnam, *Philosophy with a Human Face*, Macmillan, New York.

Reiter, R. (1980). A logic for default reasoning, *Artificial Intelligence*, Vol. 13, pp. 81–132.

Riesbeck, C., and R. Schank (1989). *Inside Case-Based Reasoning*, Lawrence Erlbaum Associates, Hillsdale, NJ.

Rips, L. (1989). similarity, typicality, and categorization. In: S. Vosniadou and A. Ortony, eds., *Similarity and Analogical Reasoning*, Cambridge University Press, New York.

Rumelhart, D. (1989). Towards a microfeatural account of human reasoning. In: S. Vosniadou and A. Ortony, eds., *Similarity and Analogical Reasoning*, Cambridge University Press, New York.

Rumelhart, D., J. McClelland, and the PDP Research Group (1986). *Parallel Distributed Processing: Explorations in the Microstructures of Cognition*, MIT Press, Cambridge, MA.

Salmon, W. (1984). *Scientific Explanation and Causal Structure of the World*, Princeton University Press, Princeton, NJ.

Schoppers, M. (1989). In defense of reaction plans as caches, *Artificial Intelligence Magazine*, Vol. 10, No. 4, pp. 51–60.

Schultz, T. (1982). *Rules of Casual Attribution*, University of Chicago Press, Chicago, IL.

Shafer, G. (1974). *A Mathematical Theory of Evidence*, Princeton University Press, Princeton, NJ.

Shastri, L. (1988). A connectionist approach to knowledge representation and limited inference, *Cognitive Science*, Vol. 12, pp. 331–392.

Shastri, L., and V. Ajjanagadde (1990). From simple association to systematic reasoning, *Technical Report MS-CIS-90-05*, University of Pennsylvania, Philadelphia.

Shastri, L., and J. Feldman (1987). Evidential reasoning in semantic networks, *Proc. 9th IJCAI*.

Shoham, Y. (1987). Reasoning about change: time and causation from the standpoint of artificial intelligence, Ph.D. dissertation, Computer Science Department, Yale University, New Haven, CT.

Shoham, Y. (1990). Non-monotonic reasoning and causation, *Cognitive Science*, Vol. 14, pp. 213–252.

Shoham, Y., and T. Dean (1985). Temporal notation and causal terminology, *Proc. 9th Cognitive Science Conference*, Lawrence Erlbaum Associates, Hillsdale, NJ, pp. 90–99.

Shultz, T., et al. (1989). Managing uncertainty in rule-based reasoning, *Proc. 11th Cognitive Science Conference*, Lawrence Erlbaum Associates, Hillsdale, NJ, pp. 227–234.

Simon, H. (1965). Causal ordering and identifiability, In: D. Lerner, ed., *Cause and Effect*, The Free Press, New York.

Sloman, S. (1992). Feature-based induction, *Cognitive Psychology*, in press.

Smith, E., and D. Medin (1981). *Categories and Concepts*, Harvard University Press, Cambridge, MA.

Smith, E., and D. Osherson (1989). Similarity and decision making. In: S. Vosniadou and A. Ortony, eds., *Similarity and Analogical Reasoning*, Cambridge University Press, New York.

Smith, E., C. Langston, and R. Nisbet (1992). The case for rules in reasoning, *Cognitive Science*, Vol. 16, pp. 1–40.

Smolensky, P. (1987). On variable binding and representation of symbolic structure, *Technical Report*, University of Colorado, Boulder, CO.

Smolensky, P. (1988). On the proper treatment of connectionism, *Behavioral and Brain Sciences*, Vol. 11, pp. 1–43.

Sosa, E. (1975). *Cause and Conditionals*, Oxford University Press, Oxford, England.

Sowa, J. (1982). *Conceptual Structure*, Addison-Wesley, Reading, MA.

Stein, L. (1990). Skeptical inheritance, *Proc. AAAI*, MIT Press, Cambridge, MA, pp. 1153–1158.

Sun, R. (1989). A discrete neural network model for conceptual representation and reasoning, *Proc. 11th Cognitive Science Society Conference*, Lawrence Erlbaum Associates, Hillsdale, NJ, pp. 916–923.

Sun, R. (1990a). Rules and connectionism, *Proc. INNC–Paris*, Kluwer, The Netherlands, p. 545.

Sun, R. (1990b). Reasoning at conceptual and subconceptual level: a connectionist model, *Technical Report CS-90-136*, Computer Science Department, Brandeis University, Waltham, MA.

Sun, R. (1991a). Integrating rules and connectionism for robust reasoning: a connectionist model with dual representation, Ph.D. dissertation, Brandeis University, Waltham, MA.

Sun, R. (1991b). Connectionist models of rule-based reasoning, *Proc. 13th Annual Conference of Cognitive Science Society*, Lawrence Erlbaum Associates, Hillsdale, NJ, pp. 437–442.

Sun, R. (1991c). Chunking and connectionism, *Neural Network Review*, Vol. 4, No. 2, pp. 76–78.

Sun, R. (1991d). The discrete neuronal models and the probabilistic discrete neuronal models. In: B. Soucek, ed., *Neural and Intelligent System Integration*, Wiley, New York.

Sun, R. (1992a). A connectionist model for commonsense reasoning incorporating rules and similarities, *Knowledge Acquisition*, Vol. 4, pp. 293–321.

Sun, R. (1992b). Fuzzy evidential logic: a model of causality for commonsense reasoning, *Proc. 14th Cognitive Science Society Conference*, Lawrence Erlbaum Associates, Hillsdale, NJ, pp. 1134–1139.

Sun, R. (1992c). On variable binding in connectionist networks, *Connection Science*, Vol. 4, No. 2, pp. 93–124.

Sun, R. (1992d). Connectionist models of rule-based reasoning, *AISB Quarterly*, special issue on hybrid systems, No. 79, pp. 21–24.

Sun, R. (1993a). An efficient feature-based connectionist inheritance scheme, *IEEE Transactions on Systems, Man and Cybernetics*, Vol. 23, No. 2, pp. 1–12.

Sun, R. (1993b). Beyond associative memories: logics and variables in connectionist networks, *Information Sciences*, special issue on AI and neural networks, Vol. 70, No. 1–2, pp. 49–74.

Sun, R. (1993c). Connectionist models of reasoning, In: O. Omidvar, ed., *Progress in Neural Networks*, Vol. 5, Ablex, Norwood, NJ.

Sun, R. (1993d). Similarity in cognition, *Artificial Intelligence Magazine*, in press.

Sun, R. (1993e). A neural network model of causality, *IEEE Transactions on Neural Networks*, in press.

Sun, R. and E. Schalit (1989). Is the tag necessary? *Brain and Behavior Sciences*, Vol. 12, No. 3, p. 145.

Sun, R., and D. Waltz (1990). Neural networks and human intelligence, *Journal of Mathematical Psychology*, Vol. 34, No. 4, pp. 483–488.

Sun, R. and D. Waltz (1991). Neurally inspired massively parallel model of the rule-based reasoning. In: B. Soucek, ed., *Neural and Intelligent System Integration*, Wiley, New York, pp. 341–381.

Sun, R., L. Bookman, and S. Shekhar, eds. (1992). *Working Notes of the AAAI Workshop on Integrating Neural and Symbolic Processes*, American Association for Artificial Intelligence, Menlo Park, CA.

Suppes, P. (1970). *A Probabilistic Theory of Causation*, North-Holland, Amsterdam.

Thagard, P. (1989). Explanatory coherence, *Behavioral and Brain Sciences*, Vol. 12, pp. 435–502.

Thagard, P., and K. Holyoak (1989). How to compute semantic similarity, *Proc. DARPA Case-Based Reasoning Workshop*, Morgan Kaufmann, San Mateo, CA, pp. 85–88.

Thomason, R. (1990). Fahlman's NETL and inheritance theory, manuscript.

Touretzky, D. (1985). *The Mathematics of Inheritance*, Morgan Kaufmann, San Mateo, CA..

Touretzky, D. (1986). Representing and transforming recursive objects in a neural network, *Proc. IEEE Neural Network Conference*, IEEE Press, New York, pp. 12–16.

Touretzky, D., and G. Hinton (1985). Symbols among neurons, *Proc. 9th IJCAI*, Morgan Kaufmann, San Mateo, CA, pp. 238–243.

Towell, G., J. Shavlik, and M. Noordewier (1990). Refinement of approximate domain theories by knowledge-based neural networks, *Proc. 8th National Conference on Artificial Intelligence*, Morgan Kaufmann, San Mateo, CA, pp. 861–866.

Turing, A. M. (1950). Computing machinery and intelligence, *Mind*, Vol. LIX, No. 236.

Tversky, A. (1977). Features of similarity, *Psychological Review*, Vol. 84, No. 4, pp. 327–352.

Tversky, A., and D. Kahneman (1983). Extensional versus intuitive reasoning: the conjunction fallacy in probability judgement, *Psychological Review*, pp. 439–450.

Vosniadou, S., and A. Ortony, eds. (1989). *Similarity and Analogical Reasoning*, Cambridge University Press, New York.

Waltz, D. (1988). Connectionist models: not just a notational variant, not a panacea. In: D. Waltz, ed., *Theoretical Issues in Natural Language Processing III*, Ablex, Norwood, NJ, pp. 1–8.

Waltz, D. (1989). Is indexing used for retrieval? *Proc. DARPA Case-Based Reasoning Workshop*, Morgan Kaufmann, San Mateo, CA, pp. 41–45.

Waltz, D., and J. Feldman (1986). Connectionist models and their implications. In: D. Waltz and J. Feldman, eds., *Connectionist Models and Their Implications*, Ablex, Norwood, NJ, pp. 1–7.

Waltz, D., and J. Pollack (1985). Massive parallel parsing, *Cognitive Science*, Vol. 9, pp. 51–74.

Waterman, M. (1985). *An Introduction to Expert Systems*, Addison-Wesley, Reading, MA.

Way, E. (1991). *Knowledge Representation and Metaphor*, Kluwer, The Netherlands.

Wilkins, D., and K. Tan (1989). Knowledge base refinement as improving an incorrect, inconsistent and incomplete domain theory, *Proc. 6th Workshop on Machine Learning*, Morgan Kaufmann, San Mateo, CA, pp. 332–337.

Woods, W. (1975). What is in a link? In: D. Bobrow and A. Collins, eds., *Representation and Understanding*, Academic Press, San Diego, CA.

Yager, R. (1989). Inheritance and possibility, *IEEE Transactions on Systems, Man and Cybernetics*, pp. 248–252.

Zadeh, L. (1965). Fuzzy sets, *Information and Control*, Vol. 8, pp. 338–353.

Zadeh, L. (1975). The concept of a linguistic variable and its application to approximate reasoning, *Information Science*, Vol. 8, No. 3, pp. 199–249; Vol. 8, No. 4, pp. 301–357; Vol. 9, No. 1, pp. 43–80.

Zadeh, L. (1978). Fuzzy sets as a basis for a theory of possibility, *Fuzzy Sets and Systems*, Vol. 1, pp. 3–28.

Zadeh, L. (1983). Commonsense knowledge representation based on fuzzy logic, *Computer*, Vol. 16, No. 10, pp. 61–66.

Zadeh, L. (1988). Fuzzy Logic, *Computer*, Vol. 21, No. 4, pp. 83–93.

INDEX